WITNESS IN THE DESERT

Witness
in the Desert

THE LIFE OF CHARLES DE FOUCAULD

BY JEAN-FRANÇOIS SIX

Translated by LUCIE NOEL

THE MACMILLAN COMPANY

NEW YORK

First Printing
The Macmillan Company, New York
Collier-Macmillan Canada, Ltd., Toronto, Ontario
Library of Congress catalog card number: 65–15571
Printed in the United States of America

This book was originally published in France under the title *Vie de Charles de Foucauld* by Editions de Seuil, 1962.

Nihil obstat, John A. Goodwine, J.C.D., *Censor Librorum*
Imprimatur, ✠ Francis Cardinal Spellman, Archbishop of New York

November 24, 1964
The nihil obstat and imprimatur are official declarations that a book or pamphlet is free of doctrinal or moral error. No implication is contained therein that those who have granted the nihil obstat and imprimatur agree with the contents, opinions or statements expressed.

Contents

III. AT THE HEART OF THE WORLD (*Continued*)

WITNESS IN THE DESERT

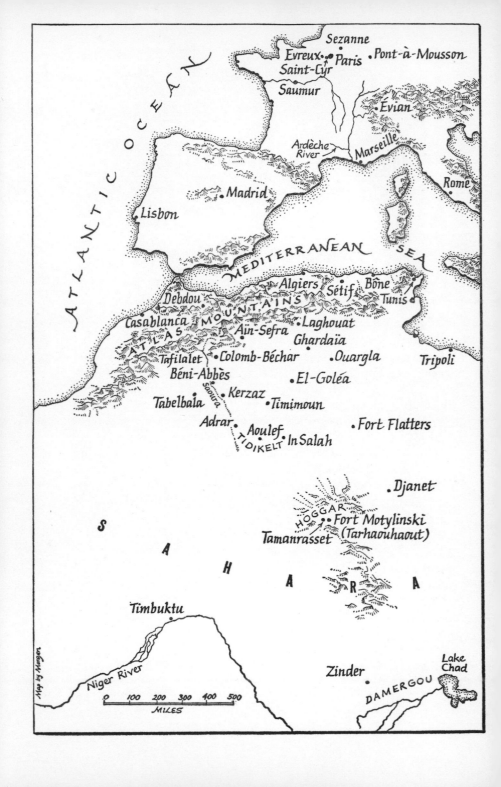

❦I.

THE YOUNG PRODIGY, 1858-1866

Oᴄᴛᴏʙᴇʀ, 1878. A room in France's famous Saumur Cavalry School. A young viscount, Charles de Foucauld, is comfortably installed. Having just turned twenty, he has come into his inheritance, which amounts to a sizable fortune. As soon as he arrived at Saumur, young Charles made provision for an ample supply of good food and fine wine.

"The man who has never seen Foucauld in his room, wearing frog-fastened white flannel pajamas, comfortably resting on a chaise lounge or in a fine armchair, enjoying a delicious *pâté de fois gras* and washing it down with choice champagne, doesn't know how much a man can enjoy life." Thus wrote one of his friends, the future General d'Urbal, about Charles de Foucauld at Saumur.

This twenty-year-old youth has always been a heavy eater. He adores lengthy, rich meals. He has become fat and heavy. He is of no more than average height, and he had nearly been refused admittance to Saint-Cyr because of his weight. All told, his looks are not in his favor. Still, he has great elegance. His barber is the best in town, and, to spare himself the tiresome trip, Charles has him come to his rooms. He spends a fortune at the local tailors and bootmakers. He entertains on a grand scale, gambles only for high

1

stakes, never bothers with change from a waiter, and does not pick up his army pay.

Soon the extravagant young Viscount de Foucauld is a celebrity in the school and in the town. His escapades are common gossip. Once, when he was refused a pass to go to a dance at the nearby town of Tours, he dressed in civilian clothes, put on a false beard, slipped out of the school, and took a train to Tours against the regulations. Unhappily, poor Charles's beard became unglued in spots. He was taken for a bandit, arrested in the station at Tours, and hauled off to jail. Eventually he was able to prove his identity, and was freed. Discarding his beard, he raced off to the dance. But luck was not with Charles. The first person he met at the party was the commanding officer of the school. The next fifteen days Charles spent in a cell.

To summarize Charles's stay at Saumur, the official report had this to say:

"He has a certain distinction. He is well brought up. But he is not serious and is interested only in amusing himself."

To all outward appearances, Charles is a man who is happy to be alive, who thinks only of amusement, clothes, masquerade, and pleasure. But—and no one has suspected it—Charles has a mysterious side to his character.

For example, one night at Saumur, Charles suddenly disappeared. Mystified and worried, his best friend, the Marquis de Morès, went to the police and discreetly asked for their help. On the day before Charles would have been classified as a deserter, he was found in a tiny lost village in the Maine-et-Loire region. Disguised once again, but this time as a tramp, he had been roaming the countryside, begging for something to eat.

In the face of such adventures a question arises: Who is Charles de Foucauld? What thoughts really lead him? Beneath his stout exterior, behind the extraordinary reserve that no one has been able to pierce, what really motivates him?

1.

A Child Alone

A glance back into his childhood will help one begin to understand. The childhood of Charles de Foucauld was not a happy one. He was born in Strasbourg on September 15, 1858. Three years later, his sister, Marie, was born. His carefree years, if he had them at all, were few. When he was five his father contracted tuberculosis and was obliged to give up his job as an inspector of Water and Forests. Sick and irritable, the father soon went to Paris to live with his sister, Inès, a beautiful woman who had been painted by Ingres and who had married a man named Moitessier. At the same time, Elizabeth de Foucauld, Charles's mother, took her two children to live with her father, Colonel de Morlet.

A few months later, on March 13, 1864, Elizabeth de Foucauld had a miscarriage, and died. Five months later, far away in Paris, Charles's father died.

Charles was an orphan at the age of five. All his life he was to remember the times when his mother was alive and had guided him toward God.

Charles and Marie were put in the custody of their grandfather. The grandfather proved to be perhaps too lenient with the children, particularly with Charles, who reminded him very much of his daughter.

When he was ten, Charles entered the sixth grade in the school at Strasbourg. His teacher there later said, "He was intelligent and studious, but he displayed nothing of the passionate and impulsive nature that he was eventually to show."

As a child, Charles was sleepy rather than wild. He hated noise and sought solitude. He was self-absorbed and extremely sensitive. The death of his parents had dealt him a strong blow, leaving him vulnerable and exposed, aggressive and impatient.

Then Charles discovered a new door open to him. His Aunt Inès

3

invited him to her country house near Évreux. It was there that
Charles was to spend many happy vacations. Most important, it was
there that he first met the girl who would be a second mother to
him, Marie Moitessier. Nine years his senior, she was a quiet, simple
girl, deeply religious and profoundly good. She understood Charles.
Showing great patience, she helped him through his long years of
mistakes as well as in his religious life.

But the hours of happiness were all too few. In 1870, when Charles
was twelve, the Franco-Prussian War broke out.

In the face of the enemy, Charles's grandfather, Colonel de Morlet,
took the children and fled Strasbourg. The disaster of Sedan, the
siege of Paris, famine, defeat, civil war—Charles missed none of it.
The events left a heavy mark on the spirit of a child who had a profound feeling for the misfortunes of his country. At the end of the
war, Strasbourg having been yielded to Germany, Charles's grandfather moved the family to Nancy. On October 1, 1871, Charles
entered school there in the tenth grade.

On April 28, 1872, Charles took his first Communion, an event
which made a lasting impression on him. Twenty-five years later
he described it: "A first Communion surrounded by grace and the
encouragement of a Christian family, witnessed by those whom I
cherished most in the world." Marie Moitessier was there, having
come from Paris for the occasion. As a gift she brought him a book
by Bossuet—a book that was to help in restoring his faith a few
years later.

Although his first Communion was pious and took place only
after long and careful preparation, Charles's religious fervor soon
faded. A few months later, in October, 1872, Charles, now in the
eleventh grade, began to read all sorts of books. At fourteen, an
introverted boy, he read everything he could. The result was that
while he learned a great deal, his faith began to be shaken. He
began to doubt everything. His teachers were absolutely neutral
on the subject of faith; they offered him no guidance. The spirit of
the times was one of disbelief and skepticism.

What Charles needed, as he himself said, was help from one of
those "men who knew enough about religion to explain the reasons
for their beliefs." But Charles met no religious teacher. His grand-

father had faith, but he was an aesthetic man who loved literature and archaeology and could not begin to reply to his grandson's questions on religion.

Little by little, Charles de Foucauld drew away from religion and religious practices. A complete loss of faith followed. He did not become an atheist. He didn't deny the existence of God; for him God was simply the unknowable. His studies helped confirm his doubts; he began to seek out writers who were masters of skepticism, Montaigne, for example, and Voltaire. "Some of Voltaire's works have a certain spice," he wrote to one of his friends, "that I shouldn't like to have to do without."

Later he described how he felt when he was fifteen. "There was not sufficient proof of anything for me. The complete faith people had in such *different* religions seemed to me to condemn all religions."

Still, he remained respectful to the Catholic religion and clergy. But he doubted his own capacity to find the truth. "I lived twelve years denying nothing and believing nothing," he once wrote, "despairing of truth and not believing in God. No proof seemed evident enough."

Perhaps Marie Moitessier could have helped Charles during this period, but on April 11, 1874, Marie became the Viscountess Olivier de Bondy. With Marie married, Charles found himself more alone than ever. The girl he had thought of as his second mother was taken from him. It seemed to him that the strongest tie to his past —human and religious—was broken.

The same year, having been given a special "age dispension," since he was only fifteen, Charles passed his baccalaureat examination. He had long ago decided to prepare for a military career. His grandfather would have liked Charles to attend the École Polytechnique where he had gone, but Charles preferred Saint-Cyr because it was easier to be admitted to Saint-Cyr. Charles was lazy.

To prepare for Saint-Cyr, Charles was sent to Paris for classes at the school of Sainte-Geneviève, where the work was difficult and the discipline strict. Charles could barely stand the atmosphere, and he worked very little. Still, he succeeded in passing the second part of the baccalaureate.

In October, 1875, he went back to Sainte-Geneviève for his second year. He was just seventeen, and it was a terrible year for him. "I was never in a worse mental state," he wrote of that year. "In some ways I have done worse things at other times, but there was a little good along with the bad. At seventeen, I was impious, a complete egoist; I preferred evil to good—I was like a madman."

The way circumstances evolved shows that it was not moral errors or sin that caused Charles de Foucauld to lose his faith. First, there were doubts. Then his faith began to leave him, and when his faith was gone he adopted an undisciplined attitude toward morality.

"I lived as one can live when the last spark of faith has been extinguished," he said.

He had a will to reject all belief and all rules. He was so completely consumed with his attitude that it appeared to him to be the only *natural* attitude to have. "When I was at my worst," he said, "I believed that my life was in order and that it was perfect."

Even at that time, Charles was not a young man who was frantically looking for the "roads to freedom," nor was he looking for ways to be evil. He was completely self-absorbed; he was immoral and lazy, an indolent adolescent with no taste for work or action. At times he was explosive, as, for example, when he wrote a forty-page letter to his grandfather begging him for permission to return to Nancy, and given to temper tantrums.

In March, only three months before the Saint-Cyr exams, he was sent home from Sainte-Geneviève because of his laziness and misconduct. His grandfather quickly found a tutor, and, his entrance having been made a point of honor, Charles was admitted to Saint-Cyr, the eighty-second student out of the 412 accepted.

On October 27th he left Nancy and entered Saint-Cyr. He was just eighteen. At Saint-Cyr the young officers were smitten with ambition and dreamed of glory; they wanted to erase the defect of 1870. In Foucauld's class, there were many men who were to become famous: Driant, Sarrail, Pétain. But there was not much of the spirited soldier about Charles. He was known in the school only for being overweight and for the fact that the quartermaster had no uniform large enough to fit him.

2.
High Life

Charles spent two indolent years at Saint-Cyr. He rarely worked. Life for him was not, however, one big party. On the contrary, he had a rather solitary existence and life moved at a slow pace. He was bored. He was aware that he was lonely and depressed and that nothing interested him. He seems to have been indifferent about life. He took no more interest in his work during the second year than he had taken the first. On February 1, 1878, he was called to Nancy. His grandfather was gravely ill, and two days later he died.

Charles's love and respect for his grandfather had kept him from living a life of worse debauchery. With the death of his grandfather, the last check on his behavior was gone.

This blow threw Charles into a state of depression, a state of apathy and indifference. His punishments during this period were not for disobedience, but for poor grooming: "dirty trousers," "needs a haircut"—all signs that he had lost interest in living. He never studied. In April he lost his stripes. On August 19th he graduated 333rd out of 386, a big drop over the preceding year.

With Saint-Cyr behind him Charles entered the cavalry school at Saumur in November. When he graduated in October, 1879, he was eighty-seventh out of a class of eighty-seven.

With the rank of second lieutenant, Charles found himself with the 4th Regiment of Hussars at Sézanne, a small town on the Marne. Bored, he asked to be removed, and was assigned to Pont-à-Mousson, which he found more agreeable, especially since it was near Nancy. He rented a bachelor's apartment at Pont-à-Mousson and another apartment in Paris on the rue La Boétie for his leaves.

What did the people around Charles think of him? His superior officers found him lacking in intensity and too soft in character. They felt that he did not measure up to his responsibilities. His

7

friends and fellow officers—what did they think? The Duke of Fitz-
James, Charles's great friend, wrote:

He was fat and jolly and we quickly struck up a friendship that
was ended only by his death. How could one not love and respect
such a good friend? With great tact and delicacy, Foucauld made
it possible for us to enjoy his fortune with him. Often, when we
gambled for drinks, if he was winning too much, I have seen him
expertly and deliberately play to lose. A great gourmet, he loved
to entertain us, first one then the other of us in small groups.
Sometimes we were invited to his small, comfortable apartment
to eat sandwiches of *foie gras* followed by an excellent cherry
brandy. He had a manservant, an English carriage, and a horse.
He usually invited a friend to ride with him in his carriage, but
it was rarely the same friend. He never showed his carriage in his
neighborhood. He never tried to impress you with his luxuries.

The life of pleasure and amusement he had led at Saumur continued, only more so. Everyone in the small Lorraine village, the
military and the clergy, talked about the strange ways of Lieutenant
de Foucauld and of his scandalous behavior. Charles gaily spent his
fortune. His expenses, difficult to estimate, were certainly enormous,
and his annual income amounted to several million francs. He gave
sumptuous parties as well as intimate dinners. On occasion an express train from Paris delivered parties of fancy, perfumed young
ladies of easy virtue. At that time, Charles de Foucauld was having
an affair with a certain Mimi, a *demi-mondaine* who was as witty
as she was flighty.

Always distinguished and also reserved and cool, Charles continued to have wild parties, but he had become more and more
mournful and melancholy. He appeared to be a *bon vivant*, making
a game out of life, passing from one pleasure to the next, always
hoping to find something even giddier.

But what he felt in his heart, he told no one: "A painful emptiness, a sadness that I had never experienced before would return
to me every night when I was alone in my apartment. It left me
speechless and crushed during so-called parties. I organized them,
but when the moment came I would be overcome by silence, disgust

and infinite boredom. This disquiet, a wave of bad conscience, showed that my conscience might be asleep but it was not altogether dead. Since that time, I have never felt that sadness, that sickness, that unrest."

Nevertheless, Charles spent the entire year of 1880, his twenty-second year, going from party to party. Suddenly, in December, the monotonous life of the barracks was interrupted. The 4th Regiment of Hussars was suddenly assigned to become the 4th Regiment of African Chasseurs. Their headquarters were to be at Sétif and Bône. For Foucauld, this merely meant one more adventure. He would leave Pont-à-Mousson, but he would not change his manner of living. In Sétif, it was again the army life—and idle life for Charles, and he was soon bored.

He was not alone. Mimi was with him, a rather lighthearted and irresponsible decision of Charles's. She had traveled with him on the boat, and landed in Africa under the name of Viscountess de Foucauld. Charles took no pains to dispel the ambiguous relationship. On the contrary, he advertised the liaison.

Advice, remonstrances, and finally orders from his superior officers —Foucauld listened to nothing. He wished to live his life exactly as he pleased. Even if Mimi was not a significant person in his life, even if they had nothing in common, even if she didn't keep him from being lonely—Charles's pride would permit no interference in his private life. He was ready to face society and to run his life as he saw fit. Rather than submit to orders to be more discreet with Mimi, Charles preferred to leave the army. He was put on inactive duty "for insubordination and conduct unbecoming an officer."

On March 20, 1881, he returned to France with Mimi, and they set up housekeeping in Évian.

3.
Africa

Charles de Foucauld had left Africa, but France in the year 1881 was taking a long look south, toward Africa. This was the year that the French Protectorate was established in Tunis. It was also the year that the government was sending expeditions across the Sahara to survey the possibilities of building a railroad. Colonel Flatters, massacred by the Tuareg tribe, led one such mission. The Madrid Conference on Morocco had taken place the year before: Moulay-Hassan had been obliged to make a commercial agreement with the European nations. Brazza had explored the Gabon in 1875, and the International African Association was founded in Brussels the following year. France intervened in Madagascar in 1883.

At the same time, things were happening at home in France. In 1880 a Republican majority took power. The Catholics were mainly monarchists, and they established a veritable cult around the Royal Pretender. In Lille, in 1880, the commanding officer of a Legitimist Battalion was discovered distributing "soldiers' manuals" that were published by a Catholic house. The first ninety-five pages were devoted to explaining "one's duties toward God."

Louis Veuillot, director of the newspaper *l'Univers,* and spiritual guide of most of the French clergy for the preceding thirty years, was more papist than the pope and more royalist than the king. The "Republican" priests were a very weak minority.

On March 15, 1879, Jules Ferry presented two projects for educational reform, one of which contained a provision, Article 7, by which certain religious groups were forbidden to teach. A year later the government issued two decrees on "nonauthorized congregations." Nine thousand priests and one hundred thousand nuns were forbidden to continue their work. Catholic indignation resulted in every kind of campaign. Abbé Félix Klein wrote in his memoirs that while he was in the eleventh grade at the Meaux Seminary, he composed a call to the people that ended with these words: "To arms, sons of the crusaders! Long live Liberty and long live Religion. Long live the King and long live Christ! Death to the fleecers! Kill the Republicans! To arms! To arms!"

The other side published pamphlets such as *The Crimes of the Cloth* and *The Love Affairs of a Jesuit*. During the entire year of 1889, priests particularly Jesuits, were expelled. Another law, on July 12, 1880, suppressed Sunday as a day of rest.

Leo XIII was made pope in 1878 and was a less absolute ruler than his predecessor, Pius IX. He tried to be tactful and he was careful not to be harsh.

Meanwhile the social season was in full swing in Évian, and Charles de Foucauld, with Mimi, was right in the middle of it. The whirl in Évian was one way to avenge oneself against life and its humiliations. Foucauld looked for new pleasures in which to immerse himself, but, unhappier than ever and seized by disgust, he sank to utter hopelessness. One day he cried, "I am a finished man."

The mediocrity of his life was very dangerous: the great dreamer that Charles de Foucauld was, the man who in his childhood was profoundly grieved by the death of his parents and who apparently never adjusted to life, seemed doomed to eternal, banal, and useless adolescence.

Three months later, in June, Foucauld opened a newspaper and this headline caught his eye: "Uprising in South Oran." Then, "4th Regiment of Chasseurs Are in Battle." He couldn't take his eyes from the page.

His comrades were fighting! With his characteristic impetuousness, he left the Évian countryside and the happy, easy life and went straight to Paris, where he obtained an audience with the Minister of War and demanded to be reinstated into the army. He offered to accept any conditions that would be imposed. (He even offered to resign his commission and to enlist as an ordinary soldier in the Spahis.) However, his rank was restored, and he rejoined his regiment in South Oran. The army pulled him out of the mire into which he was sinking.

How would he be able to adapt to this new life in the desert of Africa—this lazy, greedy, sensual man, this proud and independent officer? On the verge of battle and faced with hardship, Foucauld did more than "adapt." Laperrine described his deportment: "In the middle of the dangers and the privations of the expeditionary forces, this learned merrymaker revealed himself to be a soldier and a leader; supporting cheerfully the hardest of personal trials, concerning himself with the devotion of his men, Foucauld was admired by the most experienced men of the regiment, the soldiers who had fought in Mexico."

The commanding officers were reassured. Veterans of the Mexican War, they were amazed by this daring second lieutenant who was also agreeable, frank, helpful, and gay. The fact was that Lieutenant de Foucauld became relaxed and happy when he ceased being a merrymaker. However, he remained facetious and skeptical.

General d'Amade, who had lived with him at Sétif, told the story about the day Foucauld's horse fell while racing. The veterinary decided to shoot the horse. Foucauld agreed under one condition. He wanted to speak at the horse's burial. Here is what he said: "You were a good horse, an excellent horse. You are among the horses that go straight to heaven. I regret this because this means that you and I will never meet again."

Could Charles's departure for Africa, then, be considered as the beginning of his conversion? There was in this action a desire to participate in a work for humanity. And in this, his object was, perhaps, if not to grow up, to forget. It is possible to escape from life through actions as well as through dreams—an escape perhaps more dangerous because it is more subtle. Anyway, his departure, governed above all by self-examination, was to have unpredictable consequences that would form a real step toward conversion.

What, then, were the effects of this first plunge into Africa? At the beginning of the expedition in South Oran, Charles de Foucauld discarded the solitude with which he had surrounded himself. He entered into contact with other people.

First of all, he was rehabilitated in the eyes of his family. He had suffered in realizing that, for example, his aunt, Madame Moitessier, considered him cowardly and spineless. Charles, however, had a true admiration for his aunt. She was, for him, his family. Madame Moitessier, who was intelligent, understood at once that it had taken courage for Charles to leave Évian. She heard of her nephew's good work in the African fighting. Charles felt that he was reunited— and as an adult—with the relative whom he considered representative of his whole family tradition.

Lieutenant de Foucauld made a second discovery—that of the army and of the fraternity of fellow soldiers. In South Oran he was no longer a prisoner of lonely pleasures. He was mixing with men whose lives he shared. He was a commanding officer—and he loved being in command—of troops who would do anything he asked because they knew that he loved them. Testimony from the men who served him is extremely moving. It shows a Foucauld who never thought of himself but who was at the service of the men he led, particularly of the ordinary soldiers.

There was also a third bond created during the South Oran expedition. In the midst of battle, Foucauld met not only with the men in his army, but with his enemies; he confronted them. And it was there that, little by little, in the contact that war affords, Foucauld began to appreciate his enemy and even want to know it.

After the South Oran expedition, Foucauld was sent to a garrison at Mascara. But, as he later admitted, "The Arabs had made a profound impression on me." And soon, at Mascara, he began to learn Arabic. There was no doubt that he had been taken with the South, with the desert. He was always to retain a nostalgia for Africa, the great continent that Lyautey spoke of in his diary (Lyautey was himself discovering Africa in those same years of 1881–1882): "Africa—what is it that I have loved if not the intoxication of two years . . . oblivion . . . a pure drunkenness, an intoxication from the sun, the light . . . artistic plenitude in the full meaning of the word."

Foucauld had glimpsed, on his marches to the south, the immense spaces that unlocked immense dreams, something indefinite that attracted and conquered him. He experienced something that would satisfy his thirst for boundless freedom. And if, for him, infinity was purely terrestrial, we can but think that he had the same impressions as Psichari: "Because I know great things are coming from Africa, I can exact everything from Africa, and I can, by Africa, exact things from myself. Because Africa is the expression of eternity, I

exact from her the true, the good, the beautiful, and nothing less.
. . . Sidia came to me moved and transfigured, and making a grand
gesture toward the horizon, said: God is great."

4.

Liberation

In January of 1882, Foucauld asked his commanding officer for
leave to make a trip to the Orient. His request was refused, and at
the end of the month he resigned. His resignation was accepted in
March, and he then went to Algiers to work on his Arabic and
to learn whatever he thought necessary for a new exploration project.
He had decided to explore, not the Orient, but Morocco, those areas
where no one had yet been.

This young twenty-three-year-old man had a compelling need to
make himself grow in importance in his own eyes as well as in the
eyes of others. There were many ways to achieve that goal. In the
mind of Foucauld, one of the best ways would be to explore a country that had the reputation of being mysterious and dangerous. In
order to exalt himself, actual combat—a collective effort—seemed
less effective than exploring, which would be a solitary adventure
where heroism depended on the initiative and courage of the individual. And what joy to think that he would penetrate the *bled es
siba,* country that was completely unsubdued, and that he would be
the first to do so.

On June 30, 1883, he left Algiers determined to succeed come what
may. On the way, he wrote to his sister, who had become very un-
easy about him. He promised to "do everything possible to return
as soon as possible after carrying out the itinerary *to the end.*"

He again wrote to her, "When one leaves saying that one is going to do something, one cannot return without having done it." On his return, after a terrible year-long journey across Morocco, he met his friend, the Duke of Fitz-James, and told him, "It was hard but very interesting, and I succeeded." In two words he defined his tenacity and his will to succeed.

In reading the account of his voyage, notes taken day by day, one can see that the young explorer felt an enormous inner joy and that he seemed victorious, even in the middle of great difficulties. He walked with the step of a young god.

When Monsieur Duveyrier presented a report on Foucauld's voyage, and announced that the young explorer was being awarded the first gold medal from the Société de Géographie, he said, "One doesn't know which to admire the most—the beautiful and useful results or the devotion, courage and the ascetic abnegation by which this young officer obtained them." He added that the explorer had "sacrificed things other than comfort, having made and held until the end more than vows of poverty and misery." Later, Charles de Foucauld said that it had been for his own pleasure that he endured such privations and suffered such scorn.

Foucauld had wished to accomplish his goal all alone. He succeeded. Practically overnight, he had become a celebrated young explorer. Hostesses vied for his presence, a turn of events that was very flattering to Madame Moitessier's family pride.

But during his Moroccan explorations—and this he himself didn't see at the time—Charles had made discoveries that were much more important than his geographical discoveries. He had learned a great deal more; he had received more from his trip than he thought. The world he had explored had penetrated him thoroughly. He had come to conquer, but he had been conquered.

First by the Moslems. Several times on his voyage, Foucauld had been effectively protected by Moroccans who had saved his life. They knew who he was. Without hesitating, they had come to his rescue. Without them, Foucauld would have been assassinated, not in 1916, but in 1894. Without really comprehending, Foucauld discovered the greatness of the Moslem world, where one respected one's enemy, even if the enemy were from another nation and another religion. He had discovered a Moslem world where brotherhood and hospitality were truly practiced.

He discovered more in this Moslem world. He met men for whom God counted above all else. He had seen Arabs, completely prostrate, recognize the control of God over them. He had studied Arabic from the Koran; he had read the teachings of the Prophet: "God is one; to Him, all is subjected; nothing escapes Him. He has the right to be worshiped." And he saw men live by the teachings of the Koran.

Through contact with these men of faith, he began to realize that God alone is important and the life of men is very simple. It must consist of complete devotion to the Almighty; existence is unified only by the unconditional surrender to God.

What he learned from the Moslems burned him like a red-hot iron and woke him from his numbness. His whole being was seized with a trembling at the prospects of an Almighty God from whom the life of a man attains its meaning.

Several days after his ordination, dreaming of a return to Morocco, he wrote to his cousin Henry de Castries on July 8, 1901: "Yes, you are right. Islam produced a complete upheaval in me. The sight of this faith, of those men living in the continual presence of God, made me see something far greater and truer than mundane occupations. . . . I studied Islam, then the Bible, and thanks to the grace of God, my childhood faith was reaffirmed and renewed."

A week later, he wrote again to Henry de Castries, "Mohammedanism is extremely captivating; it has captured me completely." This seduction was not a simple romantic seduction, an attraction toward Arabic customs. It was a religious seduction, "The simplicity of Mohammedanism pleases me—simplicity of dogmas, hierarchy, morals."

Charles de Foucauld wanted to leave the complicated uneasiness of his youth. It was for that reason that the simplicity of Islam was just right to capture his spirit and his heart. Even after his conversion, it was moving to watch Foucauld continue to pray with passages from the Koran. When he once again found God, he gave brotherly recognition to those who had their own way of acknowledging Him: the Moslems of Morocco.

In addition to the Moslems, Foucauld owed a great deal to the Jews whom he had met on his voyage to Morocco.

Talking of Foucauld at this period, Laperrine wrote, "Living for a year in the middle of believers put a final end to Foucauld's skepticism. He admired the force with which the Moroccans followed their faith—fanatic and fatalistic Moslems—and the Jews as well . . . Jews whose attachment to their religion was unshakable despite centuries of persecution."

To make his exploration, Foucauld had discarded European clothes and worn those of a Jew. For one year he wore a red skull-cap and a black silk turban. For that year he was Rabbi Joseph Aleman, born in Russia and expelled from Russia by the most recent pogroms. (He was supposed to have come from Jerusalem and to be making various pilgrimages.) During that year Foucauld mixed with the Jewish communities! He tried hard to put himself in the skin of a Jew, a race that was despised. The Moslems regarded any member of the Jewish race with great contempt.

Foucauld wrote that on a certain Moroccan road no Moslem passed him without greeting him with this insult: "May God consume with eternal fire the father who begot you, Jew!"

Before he entered Morocco, Foucauld had realized the conditions under which the Jews lived. At Tlemcen, wearing his Jewish costume, he was sitting on the ground in a public square, eating bread and olives, when a group of officers—the African Chasseurs—passed. Foucauld knew almost all of them. "The men passed either without noticing or with glances showing contempt. One of them sniggered and said to his comrades that the little Jew squatting there and eating olives looked like a monkey. Not one of them recognized me." And it is certain that Foucauld had encountered violent anti-Semitism at Saint-Cyr and Saumur. From his voyage he learned what it was really like to belong to the race in which Jesus Christ was born. He shared the shame and the lowly state that the Jews were obliged to suffer.

The Jews saved his life on several occasions during his trip. In 1912, several years before his death, Foucauld sent a message to David Morciano, a Jew from Debdon, to thank him for having saved him from death and for having treated him like a son.

Several days before the end of his exploration, Foucauld learned what hospitality, as practiced by the men of Israel, means. In a small room that he shared with a Jew, Charles began to wash his beard. His companion was shocked—a true Jew never washes his beard. Foucauld remembered the custom too late. But those who were in the room promised not to betray him, and no one ever did. The rules of hospitality were never broken.

Foucauld encountered faithful Jews continually. He himself posed as a rabbi. His companion, Mardochée, took him to the synagogue. Later, in telling of his trip, Foucauld recounted how he attended a service:

> The synagogue presents the image of all of the Jewish temples that I was to see in Morocco. It was a rectangular room with a sort of desk in the center, and on the wall there was a cupboard. The desk served to support the Book of Law at public readings, held twice a week. In wealthy communities there is a platform, sometimes with a dais; in the poor villages, it is made of one piece of wood supported by two posts. The cupboard contained one or more examples of the Law, written on parchment and rolled on wooden cylinders (like Roman works, except that they were rolled on two cylinders instead of one); the double rolls were about two feet high and were covered by three or four layers of rich fabrics. Such is the synagogue: a bench, fastened to the wall, runs completely around the room. After dinner, one after another, thirty or forty men gather here. They sit on the benches and talk in low voices; they are the local Jews who congregate to say their evening prayers together. At a signal, everybody rises, faces East, and begins his prayers in a hushed voice. Embarrassed, I watch them to learn how to behave.

In this way Foucauld entered into the Jewish world of prayer, and even though it might have been to keep his true identity from being revealed, he did imitate the Jews in their attitudes of prayer.

To penetrate Morocco, Foucauld was surrounded by two human brotherhoods—the Moslem and the Jewish. His explorations led him to discover men who had a fraternal attitude toward him, an attitude that touched him so that he wanted to become a brother to them all, Moslems and Jews alike.

This was how Charles de Foucauld, the unbeliever, in a quest to explore parts of the world, met men for whom the world of God was all-important. Their attitude of adoration penetrated his spirit and made him search with passion for the Almighty God whose presence he had felt in their midst.

This double transformation didn't happen instantly. On his return from Morocco, he was caught up again in a brutal lust to live. After so many dangers and tensions, Foucauld wanted to know the rewards of victory. His exploits had hardened him.

His explorations scarcely over, he threw himself anew into a life of debauchery. "On my return from Morocco, I was no better than I had been several years before, and my first days in Algiers were filled with wrongdoing."

It was the kindness of his cousin that saved him from his downfall. Contact with her goodness caused Foucauld's unyielding personality to become unexpectedly malleable.

5.

A Solitary Existence

Foucauld arrived in Paris on June 17, 1884. Having gone to Madame Moitessier's château near Bordeaux, he saw, once again, Madame de Bondy. She was extremely kind to him, so kind that he felt himself "begin to see and respect goodness forgotten for ten years." His cousin was most attentive. Charles de Foucauld reveled in the comfort of this atmosphere. "I arrived in the country this morning; I enjoy this place a thousand times more than Paris," he wrote. "Solitude in the company of those whom I love most in the world, a beautiful countryside, all water, all green—it is more than enough to make me completely happy."

"Completely happy"—it had been a long time since Charles de Foucauld had talked of happiness, but what was behind this happiness? It was a mixture of silence and friendship. Foucauld was at that moment, and would always be, a man who loved solitude, but a solitude that included the quiet presence of those he loved.

What a difference there was between Foucauld the empty-headed young officer and Foucauld the reflective and deliberate man. He searched for peace and for stability. He even thought of getting married. In Algiers he had met an officer's daughter, a young girl of twenty-three who had been born a Protestant but had just been converted to Catholicism.

Many years after their meeting, Mademoiselle Titre said she had felt that Foucauld had complete mastery of himself. She had found him serious and as sure of himself as if he had been a man of forty-five: "He was an excellent conversationalist—wise, serious, tender —always self-possessed without being overly involved, and deeply reflective. With all that, he was unaffected and his behavior was perfect. He was well groomed—with an air of the military about him, although he was a civilian at the time."

But Madame de Bondy, hearing of his plan and fearing that it might be a hasty decision, counseled him against the marriage. Later Foucauld understood that she had been right.

Charles de Foucauld then spent more than a year writing about his trip. For the sake of accuracy, and prodded by an admirable professional conscience, he decided to make another trip, this time in the south of Algeria and Tunisia. He wanted to be able to see and to note the resemblances these places might have with the south of Morocco.

In February, 1886, he was in Paris, having rented an apartment at 50 rue de Miromesnil. He wished to close himself up in a life of work and preparation for his other explorations. In his apartment he lived like an Arab. He had no bed but, instead, slept on the floor in a burnoose. He wore a *gandourah* to work in. He lived only six hundred feet from the church of Saint Augustine and very near Madame Moitessier and Marie de Bondy, who had a house on the rue d'Anjou.

On the outside, the atmosphere was troubled. General Boulanger was the Minister of War. Franco-German relations were strained; people talked of war by summer. Everyone marveled at the Daimler automobile that could go twelve miles an hour. The International Exposition was drawing near, and the Eiffel Tower—which some Catholics violently objected to because it seemed like a new tower of Babel—was being constructed. In New York, Bartholdi's Statue of Liberty was inaugurated, and Ferdinand de Lesseps headed the French delegation.

He lived on in silence: "A life of serious study, an obscure life, a solitary existence."

II.

GOD ALONE, 1886-1901

"By her silence, her gentleness, her goodness . . ."

Wнат was Charles's state of mind in February, 1886, when he went to live in the solitude of his apartment on the rue de Miromesnil?

Looking back some years later, he wrote in a prayer to God:

> My heart and my spirit were still far away from You, but I was no longer living in so tainted an atmosphere; it was not an atmosphere of goodness and light, I admit, but neither was it any longer one of deep degradation or odious evil. . . . Little by little, the way was clearing . . . the waters of the flood still covered the earth, but they were receding and the rain had stopped. . . . You had shattered obstacles, softened the soul, prepared the soil by burning brush and thorns.

Since he was working on a report of his explorations, he thought back over all his encounters in Morocco. Was he tempted at this point to become a Moslem?

Charles de Foucauld did not think Islam the true religion because he did not find it sufficiently logical; it did not incorporate that morsel of truth that was already within him and to which he was bound. "I saw clearly," he told Henry de Castries, "that it [Islam] had no divine base and that the truth was not to be found there."

Why? Because "the basis of love and adoration is to lose oneself, to immerse oneself in that which one loves and to consider all the rest as nothing. Islam has not enough contempt for living creatures to instill a love of God that is worthy of God. Without chastity and poverty, love and adoration remain imperfect, for when one loves passionately one separates oneself from everything and refuses to be distracted even momentarily from the loved one—one throws oneself upon Him and loses oneself totally in Him."

God continued to prepare him. Speaking of February, 1886, Charles later confided, "Chastity became pleasant, a heartfelt necessity," and he added: "it was necessary in order to prepare my heart for the truth: the demon has too much control of an unchaste heart to allow the truth to enter it."

This yearning toward chastity seems to have been helped by the fact that Foucauld was in close contact with his family—Madame Moitessier, who lived a few hundred yards away in a townhouse on the rue d'Anjou with her daughters Madame de Bondy and Madame de Flavigny.

Highly intelligent, with a bearing that can be admired in the portrait by Ingres, Madame Moitessier had the stubborn will of the Foucauld family. She had managed with great success to organize the political salon of Louis Buffet, her husband's nephew who became a government minister at the age of thirty.

She had reconciled herself with Charles de Foucauld, and if his glory and success in exploring Morocco played no small part in bringing about the reconciliation, still Madame Moitessier felt real affection for Charles—an affection that was rather harsh but was nevertheless profound.

As Charles's conversion proceeded, he considered the restoration of his "old admiration" for his aunt and cousin to be a gift from God. The way his family received him was also, he thought, a divine gift:

You inspired them to receive me as the prodigal son without their ever making me feel that I had left the paternal roof. You gave them the same kindness toward me that I might have expected had I never failed. . . . I drew closer and closer to this beloved family. I lived in such an atmosphere of vitue that life returned to me, visibly. It was like spring giving life to the earth after winter. A desire for good ripened in this gentle sunlight—revulsion from evil, the impossibility of backsliding into certain errors, the search for virtue.

His pursuits were still entirely humanist during the spring of 1886; he had "tastes of virtue—pagan virtue." He read the pagan philosophers but was deeply disappointed: "I found only emptiness and disgust."

It was then that he came across Bossuet's *Elévations sur les Mystères* (*Praise to God Through the Sacraments*), the book that his cousin had given him for his first communion. If he felt the "warmth and beauty" of the book, he was still far from truth. "It gave me an inkling that perhaps the Christian religion was true," he explained.

He even used the book in a way that took him still further from the truth, hoping to find in Bossuet aspects of the stoic ideal.

"If I could not find the truth (I did not think men could ever find it), I expected at least some lessons in virtue," he wrote, and he set himself to "seek lessons of pagan virtue from Christian books. . . ." Clearly, he was still at the purely ethical level. He did not resolve the core of his problem; he did not feel at that time that he could find truth and discover at last that there is one true religion.

This research opened the way for the decisive influence—that influence which is felt not only through the will but also through the heart and mind.

Marie de Bondy's goodness had already attracted Charles toward greater moral courage. It was now the beauty of her soul that drew him toward "the truth."

"Her soul is so intelligent," he reasoned, "that the religion in which she so firmly believes couldn't be as foolish as I thought." Similarly, he told Henry de Castries that, confronted by a person so intelligent and so devout, he had said to himself, "Perhaps this religion isn't so absurd."

Thus Marie de Bondy was God's first instrument in the conversion of Charles de Foucauld.

"If you hadn't converted me, brought me back to Jesus, taught me little by little and word by word all that is pious and good, where would I be today?" he wrote to her later.

Actually, to teach him Christ's love "word by word" she had literally not uttered a syllable. Recalling God's mercy during the last months before his conversion, Charles wrote in November, 1897, that Marie de Bondy had helped him on his way by working with God, "by her silence, her gentleness, her goodness, her perfection; she was good and seemed imbued with a delicious essence, but she did not act." Her silence, then, was Marie de Bondy's chief course of "action."

In using this "method," Madame de Bondy was following the usual advice of her spiritual guide, Abbé Huvelin, who since 1875 had been curate of the Moitessiers' parish of Saint Augustine. Marie de Bondy had entered his confessional box "by chance" one day in 1876 and was struck by his great spiritual insight. Having chosen him to guide her, she introduced him to her relatives and he then became the family's counselor.

Abbé Huvelin's own life was one of self-effacement and seeming ineffectiveness. His mission consisted in expressing—with kindness and patience—deep friendship to the souls he met. As he often said, "When you want to convert a soul, you shouldn't preach to it: the best way is not to sermonize but to show love."

Charles de Foucauld was deeply struck to see such a "method" followed by an intelligent woman capable of debate and argument, and by a priest who—since he possessed an advanced degree in history and was a skilled orator—could have brought his immense talents of persuasion to bear. Later he was to follow this method and ask his followers to save their brothers by their presence and by being silent witnesses of Christ's love.

1.

"Lord, If You Exist . . ."

During October, 1886, Foucauld felt a craving for God and a deep
need to turn toward Him. Entering churches for hours at a time,
he wearily repeated again and again his strange prayer. "Lord, if
You exist, make Yourself known to me."

Henceforth, God was no longer a truth to be discovered, but a
personage whom Foucauld wanted to meet and to know—someone
who he hoped would introduce Himself.

Foucauld did not await God's answer passively. Seeking initiation,
he wanted to question "a master of religion," a man who would
have an acquaintanceship with God. His cousin mentioned Abbé
Huvelin, and one morning late in October, Foucauld entered the
Church of Saint-Augustine.

Finding that Abbé Huvelin was in his confessional as usual,
Foucauld told him that he had come not to confess, but to seek
enlightenment on God and religion. Abbé Huvelin answered
quietly, "Kneel and make your confession." Immediately after, he
sent him to Communion.

It may seem astonishing that Abbé Huvelin had so quickly and
vigorously told a man to confess who had said he had no faith.
But it is nearly certain that the abbé was aware of Foucauld's crises
in the last days of October. After all, he had seen him spend long
hours in the church, and Madame de Bondy had undoubtedly repeated the questions her cousin had asked her.

Above all, Abbé Huvelin had, his contemporaries had often remarked, great intuition, and he sensed that Charles had fought his
last battle and that he now wished not to debate but to belong.
Furthermore, Foucauld's personality was strong enough for him
to have refused to confess had it truly been against his will.

The conversion was total and unconditional. Foucauld believed.

The Lord had granted him faith, and with all of his being Foucauld wanted to answer Yes to God who had given Himself to him.

A few months before, Charles had written to his childhood friend, Gabriel Tourdes, "Definitive—you know what meaning to give that word. You and I are too philosophical to think that anything in the world could be definitive." Now he had yielded to God the absolute gift of his own life. It was a radical transformation. "As soon as I believed that there was a God, I realized that I could do nothing else but live for Him alone."

Hoping to find out what God wanted of him, Charles de Foucauld asked himself again and again how he could express his conversion in his daily life, how he could give himself to God, and, above all, how God wanted Charles de Foucauld to give himself to Him. The "hard battle of vocation, hard as death itself," had begun.

In Rome in December, 1896, ten years later, he wrote in a meditation, "In the ten years since You brought me back to the fold and converted me—and even more during the last eight years—the question keeps returning to my lips: 'What is it that you ask of me?' "

For twenty-five years of his long search he was helped by the priest who had told him to confess. Abbé Huvelin was like a friend and a father to the young convert, and these two words may help trace his exact influence during Charles de Foucauld's spiritual journey. Foucauld's temperament and his desire to give all that he could made him want to follow a straight line and to obey in every detail, but Abbé Huvelin did not respond to his pupil's desires. Instead, his correspondence shows that often he simply made his pupil aware of the demands of his vocation without giving him precise answers. When the abbé acted, it was in order to wear down signs of Foucauld's old wish to dominate.

What Abbé Huvelin wanted was to instill a simple and burning love for Jesus Christ. And when Charles de Foucauld tried to define what his director had given him, he spoke of the sprig of love that had so patiently been grafted on his heart, "the love of Our Lord that you put into my heart as best you could and with so much care."

In the months immediately following the conversion, Abbé Huvelin's role consisted above all in helping Charles de Foucauld understand his chaotic condition after twelve undisciplined years.

First, he had to restore the elements of faith and to remove elements that were foreign to the revelation of Jesus Christ.

"At first," Foucauld wrote, "there were many obstacles for faith to overcome. Having doubted for so long, I took more than one day to believe everything." There were two main difficulties. "The miracles of the Gospel seemed incredible and I kept wanting to interpolate parts of the Koran into my prayers." These difficulties do not seem to have lasted long. "The clouds lifted through the grace of God and through the counsel of my confessor."

There was also the problem of finding a religious order, for Charles wanted to give himself entirely to God by becoming a priest in an austere order. Rather than study the history and rules of religious orders, Abbé Huvelin suggested that he read the Gospel. "I did not know what order to choose: the Gospel taught me that the first commandment is to love God with all one's heart and that this love should be all-embracing."

From then on, Foucauld wanted to imitate Jesus and to love Him beyond measure. Having met his fellowmen, it was a great discovery to contemplate Jesus, to love Him, and to wish to live in complete communion with Him. In the Gospel he began to search passionately for His words and His acts so that he might follow them as closely as possible. Despite sidetracking, contradictions, obstacles, failures, and backsliding, the rest of his life was to be dedicated to a single-minded search for Jesus.

The search for a life according to the Gospel, for an exact imitation of Jesus Christ in day-to-day existence, is a terrible battle. According to his friends, Charles de Foucauld was tense and sorrowful at this time. He was alone in the night, looking for the way in which he could imitate Jesus.

2.

In the Light of Events

During 1888, his thirtieth year, God gave him the light on his vocation that he had wanted so ardently. Three events explained more precisely to Charles de Foucauld the meaning of a true imitation of Jesus Christ.

The first of these events was a phrase from a sermon of Abbé Huvelin: "You deliberately took the last place and no one wanted to take it from you." Charles de Foucauld, until then, had always looked for the first place. Suddenly he discovered that Jesus Christ had taken the last place, had become everyone's servant, had conquered nothing by force, and that Jesus had presented Himself as a pauper, the last of the paupers.

The second event was a visit, with Marie de Bondy, to the Trappist abbey of Fontgombault. The buildings were extremely poor; the monks lived miserably. There Charles de Foucauld met a brother who had just been converted. He was dressed as a true pauper. For Charles it was a new revelation of Jesus. "There was a brother in a dirty and threadbare habit and that poverty fascinated him," Madame de Bondy related.

But by this chance visit to the abbey, Charles had seen a living example that made him know how he could imitate the extreme poverty of Jesus. The brother at Fontgombault was a concrete model during his search for the last place.

The third event was a pilgrimage to the Holy Land, which he made between the end of November, 1888, and the beginning of February, 1889. It was Abbé Huvelin who asked him to make the pilgrimage. Although he was not eager, Foucauld obeyed. He started off simply, a solitary pilgrim. The plan was to spend two weeks in and around Jerusalem, two weeks in Galilee, and another two weeks in Judea. One can follow his itinerary by the flowers, the blades of grass, and the pebbles that this pilgrim piously collected in the different places where Christ had passed. This was still another proof of the careful tenderness that fits his character so well.

Some weeks after his ordination he spoke of those weeks in the Holy Land: "You know the good that my pilgrimage to the Holy Land did me was infinite, incomparable. It was twelve years ago, but what a benign influence it has had on my life!"

Charles de Foucauld felt much more than fervent emotion when he was in the places that Christ had known; in the Holy Land he discovered the concrete countenance of Jesus.

First of all, there was the Infant Jesus of Bethlehem, the poor child of the Manger. It was a great joy for Charles to be in Bethlehem, for it was Christmas. He prayed in the Grotto of the Nativity, and his heart was at one with Mary and Joseph in the adoration of the Infant God. But the joy of Christmas was soon replaced by suffering. The pilgrim who had traveled through Jerusalem suddenly discovered on his return to Bethlehem, during the last days of December, the Mystery of the Cross:

> Having spent Christmas of 1888 in Bethlehem, having attended Midnight Mass, and having received Holy Communion in the Grotto, in two or three days I returned to Jerusalem. The gentleness I felt praying in that Grotto which had resounded with the voices of Jesus, of Mary and of Joseph and where I was so near to them was indescribable. But, alas, after an hour's walk, the dome of the Holy Sepulcher, Calvary, the Mount of Olives appeared before me. It was necessary, whether one wanted to or not, to change one's thoughts and to find oneself at the foot of the Cross.

In developing this understanding of the Cross, a few days later, on January 10, in the same town of Nazareth, Charles de Foucauld began to be aware of ordinary elements in Jesus' daily life, a life even and commonplace.

The humility of Jesus, which had so impressed him on Calvary, was a part of the daily life in Nazareth. Thenceforth, Charles wanted his personal life to be a life that was deprived, a life of poverty. "I had a thirst to pursue, finally, the life I had been looking for for seven years," he wrote in 1896. "It is the life that I saw and divined while walking—following the steps of the poor artisan, Our Lord, in the streets of Nazareth."

The prilgrimage to the Holy Land was important. From January, 1889, Charles de Foucauld knew better how he would imitate Jesus —in poverty, a simple life, the life of Nazareth. And he began to practice it. Little by little, he began to experience it and to discover that this life was quite different from that which he had glimpsed in 1889. Little by little, in living it, he came to know Jesus himself: "Jesus said—it is his first word to the Apostles—his first word to everyone who had a thirst to know, 'Come and see'; begin with 'coming'—'following me and imitating me and practicing my teachings—and after you will *see;* you will rejoice in the light in the same measure as you will have practiced. . . . Come and see.' I have seen, completely, through my own experience, the truth of these words."

Because of his tender and absolute love toward Jesus, every day he felt an irresistible drive to imitate the "poor artisan" of Nazareth as completely as possible. Upon his return from the Holy Land, Abbé Huvelin persuaded him to make a retreat at Solesmes. Charles agreed, and he took a letter of introduction from Abbé Huvelin:

> My Very Reverend Father: Viscount Charles de Foucauld, who will give you this, is a former officer, a fearless explorer of Morocco, a fervent pilgrim to the Holy Land, a perfect gentleman, a good Christian who makes a love of religion. For some time, I have noticed that his preferences are taking him toward a monastic life. He needs the life; he has been training for it for months. . . . I have advised him to live that life several days at Solesmes, and I beg of you, Reverend Father, to let him see this life by living among you. I have known Monsieur de Foucauld for years. He is absolutely *sure,* and his vocation seems to me to be serious, if not for Solesmes, then at least for some monastic family. I rather prefer Solesmes.

In retreat, Foucauld heard words that were engraved on his heart —he was moved by the words Dom Delatte, prior of the abbey, said to him when he left, "During hours of sadness, always remember two things: that God loves me *and* that life on earth is not eternal."

At Solesmes he was told that he would be better fitted to become a Trappist monk. He went, then, to Soligny. The life of a Trappist appealed to him. He felt it to be a life that better approached the life of Jesus of Nazareth. Abbé Huvelin had a close friend at the Aiguebelle Trappist Monastery, Dom Chautard. Aiguebelle had founded, in the Ardèche, a small abbey, Our Lady of the Snows. It was the highest monastery in France, in barren country where winter lasted six months of the year. It was a very poor monastery. Abbé Huvelin knew all this, and he was answering Charles's desires by suggesting Our Lady of the Snows. There was even more to it than that.

Our Lady of the Snows possessed a promise of greater poverty: the decrees of expulsion of March 29, 1879, had struck the abbey and to provide against the eventuality of exile, Our Lady of the Snows had founded at Cheikhlé, near Akbès in Syria, a small, extremely poor priory, Our Lady of the Sacred Heart. This priory, since April, 1882, had been under the direction of Dom Polycarpe, former abbé of Our Lady of the Snows. Abbé Huvelin knew of this. Akbès corresponded exactly to the wishes of Charles de Foucauld: to leave his family forever and to go far away, to embrace the greatest possible poverty, to imitate as closely as possible the poverty of Jesus. On October 20th he went to Our Lady of the Snows. There he spent ten days testing his calling against the existence led by the monks of the abbey.

Upon returning, he seems to have had agonizing, last-minute doubts. Madame de Bondy, always attentive, understood this ultimate anxiety, as she had in October, 1886. She suggested that he make a retreat at the Villa Manrèse, at Clamart, near Paris. That retreat, made under the direction of a Jesuit father, was decisive. At the beginning of December, he wrote to his sister:

I returned yesterday from Clamart and I have finally taken, in great security and great peace, following the formal counsel, which was complete and without reservation, of the Father who directed me, the resolution I have been thinking about for so long: to become a Trappist. It is definite at last. I have thought of it for a long time. I have been in four monasteries and in all four I was told that God was calling me and that He was calling me to be a Trappist. My soul calls me toward this and my director is of the same mind. It is decided and, as such, I tell you about it. I will enter the monastery of Our Lady of the Snows, where I was a short time ago. When? The date is not yet fixed. I have several things I must take care of. Above all, to come to tell you good-bye.

On the 11th of December, he went to Dijon, stopping at the house of Madame de Blic. He went to Nancy on the 18th of December, and returned to Paris. He gave his sister everything that had come to him through his inheritance.

In the last months of 1889, the desire, born at his conversion, to give all reached its fullest. He had searched for a way to make the greatest possible sacrifice to God, and at last he had found it: "Thirsty to make the greatest sacrifice it is possible for me to make for You, leaving forever my family who have given me all of my happiness, and going far from them to live and to die."

3.

Trappist's Desert

It was on January 15th that he made the complete offering of himself.

The night after he arrived at Our Lady of the Snows, he wrote a heart-rending letter to his cousin that shows his extreme sensibilities. He had wanted the sacrifices with all his heart, but he suffered.

"My eyes will never again see your eyes. We were apart so little in the past, how can we be so completely apart in the future? This, however, is the truth. I know it. I wish it, and I cannot believe it." The sentences express the remarkable awakening that connected him, not to the Stoics, but to St. Paul, who, glorying in his weaknesses, found hope in his misery. "To gain strength from my weakness, to serve God from this same weakness, thank Him for this unhappiness and offer it to Him."

It is necessary to remember "gain strength from my weakness." It was the first principle of the spiritual life that was increasingly important to him. At his conversion, Charles de Foucauld had recognized the greatness of God. As he began to know Jesus better, he understood that the only possible answer was to give oneself to God the Father as completely as had His son, Jesus, the poor, the unknown, the despised, the crucified.

His act of January 15, 1890, was a continuation of his search for Jesus. The man who entered Our Lady of the Snows did so in order to return God's love with love, imitating Jesus as closely as possible.

His great spiritual discovery of September, 1889, "Our Lord permits us to suffer his pain," had been accepted by God in the act of January 15, 1890, and in this sacrifice one could say that Charles de Foucauld saw the face of Jesus. And the new Trappist monk could then say that his spirit entered into union with the crucified Christ. This spiritual marriage gave him great happiness. He invited Madame de Bondy to share in his rejoicing.

To unite oneself with Christ was to wish, with Him, to save mankind, to teach mankind to love. For Charles de Foucauld, these were not hollow words. He was determined to make this wish a reality of his life:

I love our Lord Jesus with a heart that wishes to love more and better. I love Him and I could not stand to follow any life other than His. I could not stand a life of ease and comfort when His had been the most difficult and the most despised that ever existed. I do not wish to cross through life in first class while He whom I love crossed in the last class.

This constant intimacy with Jesus, following the sacrifice of January 15th, brought his soul an extraordinary peace. "In 1890 when I received this marvelous peace, it was a peace that He chose to maintain for me without interruption."

This peace spread and stayed alive, despite his hard trials, between the time he entered a Trappist monastery and his ordination. On August 14, 1901, he confided to his friend De Castries, "This infinite peace, this radiant light, this unalterable happiness I have been enjoying for twelve years. . . ."

What does this peace consist of and where does it come from? It was born of the union with Jesus. On January 19th, three days after his arrival at the Trappist monastery, he noted: "The Good Lord has made me find—through solitude and silence—a consolation that I hadn't counted on. I am absolutely and constantly with Him and with those whom I love."

From then on, with great simplicity of heart, he began to become more and more "patient" with God, captured by Love, a captive of Love. This state did not express itself in ecstasies, but in ordinary daily life.

The life of a Trappist monk is extremely harsh. Silence reigns. Food is sparse. There are long prayers in the middle of the night. And Our Lady of the Snows, where Charles de Foucauld arrived on the 16th of January (in the coldest of winter) was not only the highest monastery in France, it was also the coldest.

The days passed in simplicity: "Of myself I have little to tell. No outside sound reaches us. There are solitude and silence with the Good Lord. The time is spent in prayer and in reading books that bring us closer to God, and in manual work in imitation of Him and in communion with Him. That fills all the days except Sundays and holidays, when work ceases. I could live like this a long time without talking much about myself," he wrote to his sister on February 18th, one month after his arrival.

He was given manual work to do with the recommendation that he "take his time so that he could meditate," because he was always impatient and eager to finish quickly any enterprise he undertook. He learned to pray while working. He felt at one with Jesus, who had been a laborer in Nazareth. Neither cold nor hunger affected him. He endured fasting and manual labor with apparent ease. "The material things in my life did not cost me a shadow of a sacrifice," he said.

He faced up well to the terrible existence of the monastery, but was it truly easy for him to do so?

Charles de Foucauld found the separation from his family extremely painful. To be sure, God had given him peace and serenity, but "they had not succeeded in filling the gap. . . . God knows that it will be a welcome day when this exile is ended, for there is more strength in my words than in my heart."

The separation from his family soon became even more of a separation. In June, after six months at Our Lady of the Snows, Brother Marie-Albéric (for that was the name Charles chose) was sent, in answer to his own request, to another Trappist monastery, that of Our Lady of the Sacred Heart, in Syria.

On the eve of his sailing, he wrote from Marseille: "I see myself on the ship that will take me away tomorrow. I will feel every wave that, one after the other, will separate us more. It seems to me that my only resources will be to think of each one of them as a step toward the end of my life."

One other thing made him suffer—the necessity to obey. He was naturally independent, and his personality, which was not used to restraint, suffered from the narrow, confining life of a monk. He who loved freedom was bound by a set of rigid rules. On the eve he entered into the community, he wrote this to his cousin:

"This is the last sealed letter you will receive." On Whitsun Monday, May 26, 1890, he wrote that the temptations he felt were "mainly temptations against spiritual obedience." On the eve of his departure from Marseille, he let slip an indication of his desire to be alone and free: "From Marseille to Alexandrette I shall be alone; the Brother who was to accompany me is staying behind. This solitude satisfies me. I shall be able to think *without constraint.*"

Charles de Foucauld had definitely left; he wanted to put thousands of miles between his family and himself, to separate himself totally from them. "And so I shall finish my days under different skies."

The skies were those of Asia. Brother Marie-Albéric debarked at

Alexandrette after a twelve-day crossing on July 9th. The heat was scorching. A Trappist father from Our Lady of the Sacred Heart awaited him, and together they left for the place where Brother Marie-Albéric wanted to bury himself forever. Since the country was far from safe, they were escorted by Turkish police and then by Kurdish warriors. Taking eighteen hours to travel the sixty-two miles that separated Alexandrette from the monastery of Akbès, they arrived Friday night, July 11th.

The monastery was in a wide valley 1,800 feet high and surrounded by savage peaks. "The mountains are entirely covered with tall parasol pines below which there are massive gray rocks pierced by an occasional cave. It is full of partridge and fallow deer; in winter numerous panthers, bears, and wild boar wander by." The silence was that of the desert. "We fully enjoy this silence that is so dear to us."

Compared to some of the larger monasteries, Our Lady of the Snows was poor, but the one at Akbès was poorer still. "The monastery, or rather the huts with thatched roofs and walls made from rushes that shelter us," was the way Charles de Foucauld described it.

The monastery had come into being as the result of a dramatic event. "Thirty years ago," Brother Marie-Albéric explained, "this place was inhabited and the region that is now empty was well populated. After several insurrections, the Turks made a desert of it, never thinking they were preparing it for us." The Trappists of Our Lady of the Snows had arrived in that devastated valley eight years earlier.

They cleared the ground, aided by a few Kurds who were half brigands and half laborers, and slowly a group of buildings rose, mostly farm buildings, stables, and barns. The monastery of the Sacred Heart looked like a miserable farm in the middle of an abandoned region.

For Charles de Foucauld, this life was like that of Jesus of Nazareth. A year after his arrival, he wrote to his sister:

You asked for news of what we do in the monastery. There are about twenty of us Trappists, including novices. As you can see from the photographs, we are living in fairly large huts. We have all the cattle necessary for farming—oxen, goats, kids, donkeys. Under our huts live about fifteen to twenty Catholic orphans, aged between five and twenty; we give shelter to ten or fifteen lay workers, and the number of our guests varies. Monks, you know, are hospitable. If you read Montalembert's *The Western Monks,* you will have a fair idea of our life—with one difference. The monks he describes study more than we do, copying manuscripts, for example. Our chief occupation is to work in the field, that is the difference between the older monks and the order of St. Bernard, to which we belong. Our work is to gather the grapes and keep the fields in order; in winter we saw wood; in spring we tend the vines; in summer we harvest and bring in the hay. It is a peasant's work, infinitely good for the soul. While the body labors, the soul is free to pray and meditate; furthermore, this work, which is much harder than one thinks, gives one compassion toward the poor and charity toward workmen and laborers! One really feels the price of bread when one knows at what cost it is produced, and one feels pity toward those who work when one shares their labor.

Continuing, he described one of his days to his sister:

You wanted me to describe one of our days; at two o'clock in the morning we get up and run to the church where we recite psalms aloud for two hours in the choir, then we are free for an hour or an hour and a half, during which we read and pray and the priests say their Mass. Toward five-thirty we return to the choir to recite psalms again; it is time for Prime and we attend community Mass; from there we go to the chapter where we pray, the Superior discusses a passage from the rules, and if we have erred we accuse ourselves then, in public, and we are punished. (The punishments are not usually severe—on the contrary.) Then we have more free time for three-quarters of an hour, during which we read and pray; then we have the short Terce service, and our work begins toward seven. The Superior gives each person his job as he leaves the Terce, and we work at it until eleven o'clock when Sext is said; then we go to the refectory at eleven-thirty. After lunch (known as "dinner" in monastic parlance), we go to the dormitory and sleep until one-thirty, when we attend None. We have three-quarters of an hour interval for private prayer and reading, then Vespers at two-thirty. After Vespers, work until five forty-five, supper, a little free time, then at seven-fifteen reading for all the community in the chapter, then Compline, singing of the Salve, and bedtime. We go to bed at eight.

At Akbès, Brother Marie-Albéric continued his novitiate, having started it at Our Lady of the Snows, under the direction of one of the most spiritual of Trappists—Dom Polycarpe. Formerly an abbé of Our Lady of the Snows, Dom Polycarpe, whose great love was for little children and for the very poor, wanted to end his days in the silence and oblivion of Akbès. He chose the humblest of occupations. After his death, Brother Marie-Albéric was asked to write his obituary. He wrote:

He was well educated and loved to study, yet he plunged into humble manual labor with great delight! When he no longer had the strength to till the soil, he washed clothes; then he had to be content with mending. It was an uplifting experience to go into his cell during the work period and see him, needle in hand, darning stockings.

Brother Marie-Albéric spoke of him to Abbé Huvelin: "It is good for me to be under his direction, which is strong and clear. He is delicate and kind in the extreme."

At the same time he was being influenced by Dom Polycarpe, Brother Marie-Albéric was also being influenced by St. Teresa of Ávila, whose works he read during reading periods. St. Teresa, with her ardent soul, had resolved to brave everything necessary to accomplish her aims, to fulfill the vocation she had received from God.

Charles de Foucauld saw in her a kindred spirit. The Foucauld family motto, "Never turn back," could easily have been the motto of Teresa of Ávila. Their characters bore the same mark. Both overcame obstacles by sheer will. Both characters grew when things were difficult, and they found joy in danger. Both had an unquenchable thirst for the absolute. Both had an extraordinary dynamism that carried them forward. Both their lives were based on the highest possible aim, for each possessed a great awareness of God and of His honor.

During their early years neither had turned toward God. There had been crises of conscience for Teresa between her pious childhood and the time when, inspired by something she read, she felt ready for martyrdom; and Charles de Foucauld, too, had had crises between his fervently experienced first Communion and the time he was ready to give himself to God. The death of her mother left in Teresa's heart a sore need for affection. Charles de Foucauld had known the same trial. Both had impetuous characters that made their desires limitless. Teresa had made a subtle art of attracting suitors. Foucauld had had a life of parties and pleasure. Teresa had been envious of her brothers who sailed to the newly discovered continent of America. Charles de Foucauld had looked for danger in an exploration of Morocco.

But one day these proud explorers were blessed with the grace of recognizing the splendor of God. Their inclination to conquer everything was transformed by this new call. From then on there was but one way of life—to live for Him alone. Before Almighty God, these exceptional souls found themselves to be feeble and miserable. Yet they were assured of the graces they would receive from God, relying completely on the power of God, and recognizing that God could be served by their weaknesses. By their union with God, forgetting themselves, they led lives of immense love.

Charles de Foucauld headed each of the notebooks that were to form his diaries from 1908 until his death with a short poem of St. Teresa's that ended, "God alone suffices." This line expresses their entire lives.

Brother Marie-Albéric copied numerous passages from the life and writings of St. Teresa. It was the life of this older sister, whom he admired, that taught him to pray and live in union with the Lord Jesus. Like Teresa, he studied Jesus, what He did and what He said. Like Teresa, who had a simple love for Jesus and who told of her meeting with Him, Charles had a keen sense of the concrete.

These two, then, were not abstract personalities. They were people who experienced life. They were not intellectuals escaping from life; they were active people. Like St. Teresa, Brother Marie-Albéric wanted to respond concretely to the love of God who loves us above all else. Like Teresa, he wished to be progressively filled with the love of God. Like Teresa, he wanted to give to Him who loved him a daily response of love with never-ending fidelity.

Brother Marie-Albéric followed the daily life in the Trappist monastery with profound joy. He applied to himself words written by Teresa of Ávila: "When I found myself sweeping during a time I had customarily devoted to my pleasures and to my appearance, I reminded myself that I was finally free from all of those vanities; a new joy flooded my spirit. The joy surprised even me and I could not understand where it came from."

It was in this spirit of joy that he undid, little by little, the ties that bound him to the material world. On October 24, 1890, he sent a letter of resignation to the geographical society. On January 3, 1891, he gave everything he owned in the way of furniture and objects to his sister: "I write to you today to give to you everything that is in my apartment in Paris. From now on, it is yours to do with as you please—sell, give, have it brought to you, it is yours."

When one realizes that Foucauld had lived in his apartment on rue de Miromesnil for several years and that he had prepared his *Reconnaissance au Maroc* (*Understanding Morocco*) there and that it was there that he had found God, one can measure the importance of this gift.

On July 16th, he resigned his reserve officer's commission in the army and asked to be transferred to the territorial army as an enlisted man. "By January 15th, I was without possessions. There remained only the miserable encumbrances of my rank and of my small fortune. It gave me pleasure to throw them out of the window."

On February 2, 1892, Brother Marie-Albéric took his simple vows and received his tonsure. It was a reciprocal gift of love between God and Charles de Foucauld:

Since yesterday I belong completely to Our Lord. About seven o'clock, I pronounced my vows; toward eleven, they cut off a few locks of my hair in church, then my head was shaved, leaving only the crown. Now I no longer belong to myself. I am in a state unlike any I have ever known, unless it was after my return from Jerusalem. . . . I need thought and silence—to be at God's feet and to contemplate him in silence. One feels—and one wishes to continue to feel, indefinitely without saying it—that one belongs to God and that He belong to us. The words of St. Teresa, "Is it nothing to belong completely to God?" can serve as a prayer.

4.

"We Are Not Poor. . . ."

How could one not then be astonished to read the words he wrote on August 15, 1896, "I never found, even in the first days, my ideal at Our Lady of the Snows." Did he find the answer at the Trappist monastery of Akbès? Three months after his arrival, he wrote to Abbé Huvelin: "You hope that I have enough poverty? No. We are poor for the rich but not poor as was Our Lord and not poor as I was in Morocco and not poor as was St. Francis." What must he do to know poverty as he wanted to know it? He had a project to ask for leaves, later on, that would permit him to practice a life of poverty. However, one must think of what he was to write about Dom Polycarpe: "For years we saw him live in a hut of only a few square feet, with a thatched roof so low you could touch it with your hand; the only light was from a skylight that could not be closed except by a piece of cloth. It was the smallest and the poorest hut he could find, and that was his preference. He had truly married poverty, that inseparable companion of Our Lord Jesus Christ."

Would that not have sufficed for Charles de Foucauld? But there was something that made him fear that he would never be able to live the life of a pauper. There were those who dreamed of making him become a priest. To study for the priesthood would take him away from the last place, where he wanted to live. To become a priest, to him, meant to lead and to teach, and he wished to occupy no recognized position; he wished to be the last socially and to experience more and more the poverty of Jesus. As the months passed, his life changed. His hours of manual labor were shortened and he was made to study theology three hours a day and to give an algebra lesson once a week. Not only were his hours of labor shortened, but he was put in charge of workers. He was put in charge of the construction of a road, and he supervised the workers. It was contrary to the last place. Instead of being a servant, he was a master. It was an intolerable role for him.

What was he to do? Should he stay on at the monastery and try to effect a change in its inner workings? Was it possible to reform the monastery and to make it into something that would offer a life of poverty? Brother Marie-Albéric did not dare to dream of that. In Ocotber, 1892, the Trappists held their general chapter, and the decisions were not in the direction of the reforms he would have liked.

Brother Marie-Albéric saw a possible solution—he would found a new order where one could follow the life of Nazareth.

On September 22, 1893, he wrote to Abbé Huvelin. It was not pride that made him found a community of Nazareth. It was not his project, but the project of God. His hopes were based on his passionate desire to love Jesus and to be loved by Jesus and on his true poverty and his confidence in Jesus:

When I think of this, I find it perfect, it could only be excellent to follow the example and counsel of Our Lord. In addition, it is just what I am looking for; I only came to the monastery to find it; it is not a new vocation; you know that if a meeting of souls had existed several years ago, I would have run straight to it.

Since it doesn't exist and nothing approaching it exists and nothing that replaces it exists, isn't it necessary to try to establish it? . . . But when I look to the subject to whom this thought has come—and come so ardently—the subject, this weak and miserable sinner whom you know so well, I do not see in him the material God ordinarily uses to make good things. He uses good material to make good works. . . . Having begun, if the thought came from God, then He will give it its growth and He will send quickly the souls who are capable of being the foundation stones for the house—souls in front of whom I will remain a nonentity, my rightful position. . . . One other thing gives me courage to undertake a work so ill suited to a sinner and to his miseries: Our Lord has said that when one has sinned much, one must love much. . . .

How can one go about realizing a life that would be like that of Jesus of Nazareth? One follows the examples of Our Lord: He worked with his hands; He did not live from collections or from offerings, "nor from the work of foreign laborers whom he was content to supervise."

One listens to Our Lord's advice: "All of the advice comes from the Lord's mouth":

Dispossess yourself of all your property, goods and chattels.

Forego any lawsuit or claim.

Give all to charity; share everything; live from day to day, depriving yourself as much as possible.

5.

Nazareth

Following the example of Jesus of Nazareth, Brother Marie-Albéric's primary purpose was to engage in humble work. Jesus was not a rabbi who wanted to influence the great schools of Israel. Jesus was a common man, a man of the common people, a man who lived as a member of the community, a carpenter.

Unlike Jesus, Charles de Foucauld, until the age of twenty-eight, had been a nobleman of great pride. In the true tradition of his class and his time, manual labor to him meant forfeiting class privileges. Manual labor, for an aristocrat, was degrading. Jesus, as a worker in Nazareth, was proof to him that humility existed through love. He wanted to imitate the Son of God and to participate truly in the daily lives of people. The problem was to choose a humble work, a work that would put him close to God.

After his hard labor in the fields at Akbès, Brother Marie-Albéric was to know another kind of work. In November, 1892, he was found to have a high fever. The diagnosis was tuberculosis in its early stages, and he was ordered to rest; he was taught to mend and darn. On January 9, 1893, he wrote to his cousin: "My thoughts turn constantly to Our Lord and to the Holy Virgin, and I am happy in Their company. As I mend clothes for the poor orphans, I tell myself how happy I am to do work so usual in the House of Nazareth."

Above all, he wanted the new community that he wished to found to be a community of workers, following the spirit of Jesus, worker of Nazareth. The workers were to be the foundation for "the House of Jesus." The community would be made up of simple, uneducated people who would live their lives from day to day and who would be devoted to ordinary work. Everyone would work and everyone would be equal. He recalled the converted brother from Fontgombault, in his ragged habit, and he hoped that his monastery would have only men of that type. He did not want monks who had consecrated themselves to study living next to those who were manual laborers. Humble work was to be the heart of his monastery. Community life was to be centered upon work.

He did not want the artificial separation that had grown up between "workers" and "intellectuals." In a monastery that would revive the life of the Gospel, there should be no social distinctions.

The life of Nazareth was his "prototype." If he referred to the monastic foundations of St. Benedict, it was only in passing, and it was not because they were closer in spirit to the life in Nazareth than the Trappist monasteries. And if he criticized the Trappist monastery, where he himself was a monk, it was only because he cared more about the life of Nazareth, where Jesus had worked.

Foucauld, as we know, was a man who saw things through to their logical conclusions. When he saw how the true disciples of Jesus lived, he told himself that the manner of prayer must be made acceptable to the poor and easy for them. As he wanted to open up his community primarily to the poor, Foucauld rejected spiritual exercises and observances that required lengthy intellectual initiation. He did not want St. Benedict's complicated liturgy. He did not want the Mass of the Choir, an obstacle for foreigners. He did want many prayers, long sermons, Holy Masses. A series of extremely simple prayers, nothing but the simple, would be brought to the simple.

Who were they to be, these poor and ordinary people he wished to call to his community to live in complete daily brotherhood? He looked about him and saw the farmers and the young orphans. Many of them were Catholic; the others were Moslems. These were the people he wanted—if it was what they wanted—to live in his community. He wanted them to feel welcome and at home.

These people were workers, and it was for them that he looked for a simple liturgy and for them that he wanted to leave behind the question of language and of the monastic tradition of Latin. "Our liturgy closes the door of our monasteries to Arabs, Turks, Armenians, and others who are good Catholics but who do not know one word of our languages." He knew that in the East the languages of the country were used in the services. It made no sense to him that there at Akbès—where people spoke Arabic, Turkish, or

Armenian—the liturgy should be Latin, a language that was not understood by the workers and orphans who came into the Chapel. How could these youths and men ever become traditional Trappist monks? It would not be possible. Yet God had called on people from the East to serve Him. How could one help them lead a life consecrated to God? The Trappist monastery as it existed could not welcome them. Therefore, something different needed to be done.

But here it is necessary to try to understand the depth of his thoughts. He was a Trappist monk. He had gone to Akbès. Was he truly able to understand the spirit of the monastery? The Trappist monastery is a world all its own, a place where one prays to God for all mankind, but where one has no contact with other people of the world. Perhaps when Charles de Foucauld came to the monastery, he possessed another wish in addition to the wish to consecrate himself to God.

Three days after his arrival at Akbès, on July 14, 1890, he wrote to his cousin, "I hope that the good Lord will bless this monastery which can do much good in the midst of a population of Moslems, mixed with a number of Christian sects."

Thus from the start he regarded the monastery not only as a place for the silent worship of God but also as a place surrounded by human beings. He looked toward God in profound adoration and he also looked toward the poor of Akbès and wished to consecrate himself to them. From that time on, there were two streams he wished to follow: imitation of Jesus of Nazareth and penetration into the heart of the lives of the poor.

Because his monastery would be in the midst of men, Foucauld wanted it to be a living sign of Jesus for those who did not believe in Him. How could communities of simple men bear witness to the existence of the Artisan of Nazareth if they consisted of grand buildings with lots of land? Could one demonstrate the poverty of Jesus from a wealthy monastery? For the natives of the country even Akbès with its huts gave testimony to the contrary, because of the vast lands that surrounded the huts. The communities, then, should be restrained and should not be a showplace of power. "Many monasteries, almost out of necessity, have a material importance that is the enemy of abject humility," he wrote to Madame de Bondy on October 4, 1893. The communities could only be "of the country" if they were very small and also very poor. It was not only individual humility but a social condition of a man who possessed few resources and little support; a large monastery represented great assurance for each of the monks. What head of a family who lived a miserable life at Akbès knew the same security as even the poorest of the monks at Akbès? One can better understand the cry of Brother Marie-Albéric from an event that shows the condition of the lives of the people of Akbès at the beginning of April, 1894. "I was sent to pray for a poor native worker, a Catholic, who had died in a neighboring village. What a difference between that house and our lodgings! I long for Nazareth!"

He wanted, then, little communities that, as he wrote to Abbé Huvelin, renounced "absolutely all property, collective as well as individual," communities "where one did not live from charity," but "solely from the work of one's own hands."

It was his hope that such small communities would sprout up *everywhere*. But where did he want the first community to be established? "I so hope to see these little nests for fervent and laborious life, which would imitate the life of Our Lord, established near each of the missions of the isolated East and existing under the protection of Our Lord and of Joseph and Mary," he wrote to Abbé Huvelin. He had made the journey to Jerusalem. In Akbès he was close to the Holy Land. He had found in the small corner of Turkey the world of the Moslems he had known in Morocco. More than ever his heart was filled with a great desire: to give witness of Jesus to those who knew Him not. He wanted to show the presence of Jesus and the fraternity of Christ, in the midst of non-Christians rather than in the midst of Christians. That was the essence of his calling. In the same letter, dated September 22, 1893, he wrote, "Should we not try to form this community in the hope that it will spread to all of the infidel countries, Moslems and others?"

This man who had met with Jesus and who had given himself entirely to Him wished then to give himself to all those who were ignorant of Jesus, to those who were furthest from Him, and to all of those who, without knowing it, were at the last place. He was consumed with a passion to occupy the last place—the place of Jesus

—and to take everybody who was in the last place, the lost souls, along with him to join Jesus. For him, it was the same love—his love for Christ and his love for non-Christians. That was his vocation, the source of all his discoveries, of all the inventions of his heart: in one dynamic movement to unite Christ and the poor, the poor who had missed knowing Christ, the poor who had missed knowing love.

In explaining how he wished to live in the evangelical fraternity that Jesus had shown him, he shows us more than has ever been shown before of the heart of Christ: the aims of the community he wished to found, the ways in which he wished it to function are extraordinary manifestations of Jesus Christ.

In reading his letter to Abbé Huvelin, one sees how he wants to translate the Gospel for non-Christians, and one is aware of the inner presence of Christ—Christ who went first to the sick and not toward the well, who went first toward the lost sheep and not toward those who considered themselves saved, who went toward the poorest and not toward the rich neighbors. He wished to imitate Christ. Without losing time on words, he imitated Him. He wished to go among the poor, those furthest from God, the non-Christians—to be sent to them as Jesus was sent to them, as a poor man who would truly share his life with the poor, with those who had not found God and had no hope, with those who needed support. He wished, too, to share his life with anyone who wanted to live as Jesus had lived, in poverty, with no material possessions . . . with those who wanted to live by their hands alone and who wanted to live in complete equality with those around them.

6.

Waiting

His projects were indeed revolutionary. How was he going to make them a reality? He asked his spiritual father for advice.

Just as he had made Charles de Foucauld wait three years before he allowed him to enter a Trappist monastery, Abbé Huvelin again asked him to wait. The years 1894, 1895, and 1896—among the hardest of his life—Charles spent in painful waiting. Everything within him called out for Nazareth.

On February 19, 1896, he wrote to his cousin: "My spirit is always in the same state; my thirst grows day by day to search outside the monastery for the life of Nazareth. I am at peace, but I am impatient for the hour to strike and end my waiting and trial so that I can go where God calls me." A month later: "My thirst to trade my religious status for that of a life as a daily worker in a simple family monastery grows more and more intense . . . they are the same inspirations, but every day they are stronger."

In June of 1896, after turning it over and over in his mind, he finished an outline of rules for his projected foundation. He explained clearly the unique, twofold orientation the "little brothers of Jesus" would follow:

1. To reproduce as faithfully as possible the life of our Lord, Jesus Christ of Nazareth, because the greatest perfection and the greatest love of Our Lord is to be expressed in imitating Our Master, so well loved.

2. To follow this life in Christian countries, Moslem countries, or in other countries with love for Our Lord in the hope of giving our blood in His Name; to follow this life with a love for mankind in the hope that our presence and our prayers and, above all, that the Holy Sacraments will bring good to these unfortunate brothers.

We wish to reproduce the hidden life of Our Lord as St. Francis of Assisi reproduced His public life.

Our lives are divided between prayer and work, the former taking precedence over the latter.

We cannot dream of reciting the Holy Office in European languages to the children, the ignorant, the illiterate, or to foreigners. It will be replaced by the Adoration of the Holy Sacraments, prayers, the saying of the Holy Rosary. We will pray morning and night in front of the Holy Sacraments; the days will be consecrated to work.

The "Rule" contains the principal elements that Foucauld had written in a letter to Abbé Huvelin three years earlier. Some rules for the project are practical rules of life:

The conversion of men: each morning and each night there will be a half-hour prayer to ask God to save all men whom Our Lord had so ardently asked Him to save during His life.

One of the fundamental points of the Congregation is that, following the example of Our Lord of Nazareth, it must support itself by manual labor.

It is forbidden to receive any gift, big or small, for any reason whatsoever—not even for Masses or offerings for prayers or for distribution to the poor. Absolutely nothing must be accepted— not money, not provisions. We will live solely by the work of our hands. In order to be charitable and to help the poor, we will keep no money from one week to the next. On Saturday, when the weekly pay is received, all money that is left over from the week before will be given to the poor. The same applies to provisions. Nothing will be kept from one week until the next.

How will the work be done? We will follow the practices of the poorest people in the poorest country. [The work was to be] easy to do for everyone alike—the educated and ignorant, the strong and weak *alike* would be able to do it.

We will have nothing. . . . We will be like workers working for a proprietor.

Each "Nazareth" will be composed of ten to eighteen brothers.

. . . Men of letters, illiterates, old, young, priests and laymen will be received equally.

No distinctions will be made between the fathers and the brothers, or converts. Everyone will be equal and everyone will be called "Brother."

The superior will be called "Brother Servant"; he must be educated, but he need not receive Orders.

Following the example of Our Lord, we will be established in villages—in towns of heathen countries throughout—but where there are already missionaries, in villages such as Nazareth, we will be in the outskirts where the land is cheaper and where the poorer people live.

The house will be built like the poorest of the country, with rough stones or planks or twigs interlaced—like the poorest of the region. That is the only Rule.

Around the house, there will be a little garden. . . . Each house and its little enclosure will not be bought, but rented.

If one of the brothers is sent on a voyage, he will travel in the lowest class as the poorest of the poor. He will walk where the poorest walk. If he goes by public transportation—trains or boats—he will travel in the manner of the poor; he will always take the lowest class, the last place in the manner of Our Lord or of the Holy Virgin or St. Joseph.

The poor and the others will always pass in front of the brothers and the sick will pass before the healthy.

The last words of the "Rule" said, "All of our efforts will be dedicated to have within us and to show unto others charity, compassion, tenderness, and the infinite goodness of our divine Master."

In this "Rule" of 1896, the word "martyrdom" is mentioned several times. Brother Marie-Albéric wished, in going to the non-Christian countries, to bear witness to Jesus until his death. The desire was made even stronger by a terrible persecution that had just taken place: the Turks massacred, in 1895, nearly 140,000 Armenian Christians. In March, 1896, the persecutions reached Akbès. Foucauld himself might have faced death as a martyr. On

June 24, 1896, a few days after he had finished writing his "Rule," he wrote:

All around us, there were horrors . . . massacres, fires, and lootings. Many Christians were true martyrs who died voluntarily without defending themselves, preferring death to the renunciation of their faith. I write to you to ask for donations, not for us, praise God, for I can never be poor enough, but for the victims of the persecutions. . . . In Marrache, the closest village, 4,500 Christians were killed in two days. We in Akbès—and all of the Christians within two days' walking distance—should have been killed. I was not worthy. Pray for me that I will convert myself and that I will not be passed over another time, despite my misery, at the door of heaven, which was left ajar.

The Europeans are protected by the Turkish government and, in a way, we are safe: soldiers are posted at our door to stop anyone from doing us harm. It is painful to be on good terms with those who cut the throats of our brothers. It would be better to suffer with them than to be protected by their persecutors. . . . It is shameful of Europe—one word could have stopped these horrors, but it was not said. It is true that the world knows little of what has happened here. The Turkish government has bought the press, having given an enormous amount to certain newspapers to publish only government dispatches. Still, the governments know the truth from their embassies and consulates. . . . I ask your help in our effort to relieve, to stop the deaths from famine of several thousand Christians who escaped massacre and are now refugees in the mountains. They do not dare come out from hiding for fear of being massacred and they have no resources whatsoever.

Charles de Foucauld wanted to share the life of those who were persecuted, of those who knew the misery of the Exodus, of those who were being hunted down.

His life seemed too easy for him. It was not exactly the imitation of Jesus that he hoped for.

And so the persecution of the Armenians awakened in him a wish to be a martyr, and it also brought forth another thought: the desire to be a priest. "At the height of the Armenian persecutions, I wished that I were a priest who knew the language of the poor persecuted Christians and who could go from village to village and give them courage to die for their God."

It was during this persecution—with his great desire to share his life with the poor and the persecuted—that Charles de Foucauld first revealed that he was considering the priesthood. It would permit him, he said, truly to share the miseries and the sufferings of the people of the country. He wished to be a part of the country, to know the language, to participate in their persecutions, and to help them in their sufferings and in their deaths to bear witness to the crucified Christ who died for all. He wanted to be among Christians who, even in a non-Christian country, witnessed at their deaths the existence of Christ Risen.

The Abbé Huvelin, to whom he had sent his "Rule," replied: "Your rule is absolutely impractical. The Pope hesitated to give his approbation to the Franciscan rule, which he found too severe. But this rule! To tell you the truth, it frightens me! Live at the door of a community in the abjection you wish, but do not, I beg of you, make a rule."

7.

Rome

Though Abbé Huvelin wished to hear no more of the "Rule," he did not wish further to oppose Foucauld's leaving the Trappist monastery in order to live alone at the door of a monastery, and it was that that Foucauld seized upon from the letter. He wrote to Dom Polycarpe and to the Abbey of Our Lady of the Snows, both of whom wrote to Dom Sebastien, Abbot-General of the Trappists of

Rome. Dom Sebastien's reply arrived at Akbès on September 10, 1896. Brother Marie-Albéric was told to go to the Trappist monastery of Staouéli, near Algiers. There, on October 12th, Dom Louis de Gonzague met him and told him the decision: he was to study theology for two years in Rome. Without a word, he obeyed.

He arrived in Rome on October 30, 1896—ten years to the day after his conversion. Ten years and how many events! They included his departure for the poorest and the highest monastery in France; even greater, his removal to the skies of Asia, his nearness to the Holy Land, the huts of Akbès, the world of Moslems, of persecutions. After six years in Asia, he was sent back to Africa, the Africa he had left ten years ago. Suddenly, he was in another Trappist monastery at Staouéli, but it did not have the misery of Akbès. It was a large, rich, and prosperous agricultural colony. And then he was in Rome to study theology—a turn of events that he did not at all wish for!

However, Brother Marie-Albéric arrived there feeling confident and at peace. "You realize that my own desires have not changed," he wrote on October 2nd. "They are firmer than ever. But I obey with simplicity, with extreme gratitude, and with confidence that at the end of this long trial the will of God will manifest itself clearly."

If he searched more than ever, it was better to love and better to serve God. He wrote to a young Trappist at Staouéli, "I prayed for you with all my heart, and for myself as well, in the Basilica of St. Paul, praying to that apostle who loved Jesus so much, who worked for Him and who suffered so much for Him! May he lead us and help us to learn how to love!"

He told also of a visit to the Coliseum: "What flames of love rose from there to Heaven. What are we next to such spirits? But we have hearts just as they had and Our Lord loves us as He loved them, and we can, we must, love Him as much!"

At the age of thirty-eight, in the midst of young clerics, he went to the College of Rome. He had three classes in Latin a week. "I, who am so far from Latin! Old, ignorant, unused to Latin, it is painful for me to follow the courses," he wrote to his young Trappist friend. "We have not yet reached the age to work with St.

Joseph. We are still learning to read, with the Infant Jesus, but later, humble manual labor . . . will take its place, the grand place."

The months in Rome were very trying. It was in those moments that the authenticity of the love of Charles de Foucauld could be measured, he who loved freedom above all else, he who could revolt and refuse, had offered to God his freedom. He who could forcefully present his point of view and who could succeed in imposing it accepted the wishes of his superiors. During those months in Rome, a light shone from his face: he was a man who had given himself absolutely to God. And what hope he had!

In a notebook where he kept his meditations, he wrote in December:

> It was at the moment when Jacob was on the road, poor, alone, when he sank naked to the ground in the desert to rest after a long journey on foot, it was at the moment when he was in the painful situation of an isolated traveler in the middle of a long voyage in a strange and savage country, without shelter, that was the moment when he found, in his sad condition, that God had heaped incomparable favors upon him.

Jacob was truly Charles de Foucauld, who was disoriented, who waited to know what God wished of him, who was asking himself which road God wished him to take. Foucauld was searching with a great passion for the Will of God that night. To know what it would be, Foucauld had chosen simply to practice obedience. In December, he wrote about the sacrifice of Abraham, "Obedience is the consummation of love!" And again: "Good Shepherd, answer me. You know and love Your lambs. Turn Your eyes toward this one and tell him what he should do to give himself unto You in the most complete way."

At Staouéli he had been told that he would study theology for two years. At the beginning of December, they told him it would be three years. The time when he would be able to lead the life of Nazareth was set back.

Christmas, which had always been so important to him, was approaching. It had been slightly over ten years since he had found himself in churches crying from the bottom of his heart, "O Lord, if You exist, make Yourself known to me!" At that point he wanted to know God; now he wanted to love Him and to tell Him of his love. But he recognized his weakness. "My Lord, I am powerless, even to tell You that I love You."

On January 15, 1897, Brother Marie-Albéric reached an extremely important moment in his life: "The end of this month and the beginning of the next are crucial, for on February 2nd, it will be five years since I took my first vows. According to the *Constitutions* I must at that time either take final vows or leave the Order. . . ." On that Friday, January 15, 1897, seven years after he had left his family for a Trappist monastery, he felt that his mind was fixed. He was sure of his vocation and he was sure that it would be accepted.

Thus, simply and silently during that week from the 15th of January to the 23rd, Brother Marie-Albéric died to himself in an extraordinary act of love. On Sunday, January 24, 1897, he described this act of obedience and told what the preceding week had meant to him: "Before the Abbot-General took his decision I had promised the Good Lord to comply with anything that my Most Reverend Father might demand after examining my vocation, and also to do everything my confessor counseled. So that, had I been told, 'You shall be ordained,' I would have obeyed with joy, certain that I was fulfilling God's will . . . for since I sought God's will and since my superiors also sought it, it was not possible that God would not make His wishes known."

Thus he thought of the solemn vows and priesthood very positively, and even with joy, although he wanted them less than ever. And all week long he prayed, not that his superiors would understand about Nazareth and let him go, but simply that God's will would be known.

On the night of January 23rd, Dom Sebastien told him that it was God's will that he follow the attraction that was pulling him out of the monastery and toward Nazareth. Dom Sebastien had reached this decision without Charles asking it or even mentioning it. Instead of presenting his views and defending them, Charles de Foucauld had remained silent. The decision was announced when he least expected it:

The Good Lord granted what I had prayed for so hard and what I had not hoped to obtain for two and a half years. And He granted it as only He can, with a perfection that surpasses all human hope, and not on my own request but on the initiative of my superiors—not just any superior but the Most Reverend Abbot-General.

My Lord, how good You are!

Since you are my Father, my Lord, how much hope I can place in You!

And also, since You are so good to me, how good I must be to others!

Since You wish to be my Father, how deep must be my brotherly feelings toward all men, whoever they are, and no matter how wrong they might be!

Dom Sebastien suggested that Brother Marie-Albéric write to Abbé Huvelin, and he did so at once, expressing his wish to be a servant in an Eastern monastery. Abbé Huvelin agreed: "Yes, my dear child, like you, I think of the East. . . . I consider Akbès impossible. . . . I prefer Capernaum or Nazareth or a Franciscan monastery—not in the monastery itself but in its shadow, asking nothing but its spiritual resources and living in poverty . . . at its gates. . . ."

On February 14th, Brother Marie-Albéric received dispensation from his first vows and on the same day he took, before his confessor, two vows:

"1. A vow of perpetual chastity.

"2. A vow of perpetual poverty, by which I promise never to own or have about me more than would a simple worker."

"My new life which I am now beginning will be much more hidden and solitary than that which I am leaving." On Wednesday, February 17th, he left for the Holy Land from Brindisi. "All the doors are open for me to stop being a monk at heart and to descend to the rank of a domestic servant." On January 24th, he had written to his Trappist friend at Staouéli: "God leads us on such unexpected roads! Look at how I have been driven and shaken about these past six months—Staouéli, Rome, and now the unknown!"

He was to lead the life of Nazareth at Nazareth itself.

8.

The Servant

When he embarked for the Holy Land, Charles de Foucauld was guided by his vows of chastity and poverty that would enable him to lead a Christly life and also, because of the second life, make him share the poverty of workmen who were his contemporaries.

Foucauld had not made a vow of obedience—not because he did not wish to obey, but simply because in his new life he was not to have a superior. He was right to say that doors were opening, although they were doors that led him downward to the world of workers and servants and not upward to glory, riches, or social, personal, or religious advancement. He was alone on his road, and his road was Jesus of Nazareth. Like St. Francis of Assisi, who began by preaching the Gospel on the road, he had begun the great adventure of emulating the poverty of Jesus.

When he debarked at Jaffa on February 24th, Charles de Foucauld changed his Trappist habit for the clothing of a Palestine beggar— a long-hooded, blue-and-white-striped shirt and blue cotton pants. Around his white skullcap he wound a piece of cloth to make a turban and on his feet he wore sandals. His costume, resembling his old Moroccan beggar's outfit, was far from the uniform and evening dress he had once worn, and in it he retraced his pilgrimage of 1888 to Aïn el Kurum, Bethlehem, and Jerusalem.

After eight days in Jerusalem, Charles de Foucauld went on foot across Samaria to Galilee. Arriving at Nazareth on March 5th, he stayed at the Casa Nova and learned that the Poor Clares planned a mass for St. Colette's feast day the next day.

He arrived at dawn to pray before the Holy Sacrament, and when the bell rang for lunch at eleven o'clock he told the nun in attendance to leave for her meal as he intended to stay and pray. Not daring to refuse, the sister nonetheless kept an eye on him for fear that he might steal the Monstrance.

On the advice of the Franciscans of Nazareth, who had no work for him, he regretfully left Nazareth to see if the Franciscan fathers of Mount Tabor could offer something, and there on the mountain of the Transfiguration he confessed to a Franciscan and told him of his vocation and his wish to be a servant.

By an extraordinary chance—almost as if God had made him renounce Nazareth in order to lead him there Himself—the Franciscan was the chaplain of the Poor Clares in Nazareth, and he sent Foucauld back there after telling the abbess about him. She agreed to employ him as a servant, and he began work there the next day, March 10th.

He was offered the gardener's cottage but preferred the tool shed, which was furnished with a mattress, a small table, and a stool. "I serve Mass and the Holy Sacrament; I sleep, I run errands; in short I do whatever is asked. Work begins after Mass at eight in the morning and it finishes at the time of the blessing of the Holy Sacrament, which occurs, every other day at least, at five in the afternoon. On Sundays and holidays I have nothing to do and can pray all day."

He was no longer Brother Marie-Albéric, but simply Brother Charles, the Poor Clares' odd-job man. He was mason, carpenter, gardener, and sexton. His time was spent on the two aims of his life at Nazareth—prayer and labor. "I have everything I dreamed about for years," he wrote his sister, "and it seems as if this place was waiting for me; and indeed it was awaiting me, for nothing happens by chance and God has foreseen all: I am the servant and valet of a poor religious community."

And so his days passed in great joy, gentle and filled with a continuous sense of union with Jesus. The work he was doing was not painful to him: it was not the hardest place he had wanted, but the most humble. Abbé Huvelin was pleased to see Charles imitating Christ's life by being "humble, poor, obscure, as he wished to be, and unknown," and he considered this the first realization of Charles's vocation.

In Brother Charles's life, reading and written meditation assumed greater importance than they had at Akbès. He consulted the Bible constantly at a time when few Catholics did so. Abbé Huvelin had advised him to write his meditations because he was having trouble praying, and so every night Charles prayed before the Holy Sacrament by filling copybooks with humble commentaries on the Holy Scriptures.

These hundreds of pages of meditations are a patchwork of daily occurrences in the life of the Poor Clares, the crises, disappointments, and spiritual joys of a search for a greater love of Jesus, and the waiting for Jesus when He seems absent. By the unadorned simplicity of their expression these copybooks powerfully and truthfully express the Gospel and make it live again. This return to the original source of life, of all our poor lives, was what was remarkable in Charles de Foucauld; he showed the Risen Christ living once again the life of Nazareth.

The meditations show an intense and extreme abandon, an abandon that, like that of Jesus, was one of obedience, of placing oneself in the hands of God. Meditating on the last prayer of Jesus, he wrote:

"Unto Thy hands I commend my spirit": those were the last words of our Beloved Master. . . . May they also be our own . . . and may they be ours not only in our last moments but in every moment: Father, I commend myself unto Thy hands; Father I abandon myself to You, I give myself to You; Father, do with me as You wish; whatever You may do I shall thank You; I thank You for everything, and I am ready for everything; I accept everything; I thank You for everything; may Your will be done on all Your creatures and all Your children, on all whom Your heart loves. I desire nothing else, my Lord. Unto Thy hands I commend my spirit; I give it to You, my Lord, with all my heart because I love You and because my love demands that I give myself, that I put myself entirely in Your hands: I put myself in Your hands with infinite confidence, for You are my Father.

In his constant readings of the Gospel, Brother Charles sought to discover what Jesus had said and done in order that he might imitate Him. On November 11, 1897, he wrote:

My Lord Jesus: how quickly he who loves You with all his heart would make himself poor in order that he be not richer than his

Beloved. . . . My Lord, I do not know if it is possible for certain souls to see Your poverty and still remain willingly rich, to see themselves so much more exalted than their Beloved Master and not want to resemble You in everything as much as they can, especially in Your humility. I should like to think that they love You and yet I feel that their love lacks something. In any case I cannot conceive of love without a need—a great need—of sharing all the pains, difficulties, and hardships.

This intimacy with Jesus did not isolate him from others. In his cabin Brother Charles was not cloistered with the Poor Clares, but lived between the convent and the village of Nazareth, a neighbor of both. Wishing to bring his image of Jesus to all men, he affirmed the mission that Jesus had given him: "You shall spread the Gospel across the rooftops, not with your words but by your deeds."

One day, after he had been in Nazareth a year, Brother Charles was meditating on the passage in the Gospel where Mary, awaiting the birth of Jesus, goes to her cousin Elizabeth to help her. In the mystery of the Visitation, he saw that Jesus was the Saviour before he was born and that He inspired His mother to work with Him to help others. When Jesus gave Himself to someone, it was so that that person would in turn give himself to others.

He imagined Jesus saying: "Work to sanctify the world, work for it as my mother did—without words and in silence. Go live among those who know me not; bring me to them, establish an altar, a tabernacle, and bring the Gospel to them and preach from example, not by telling the Gospel but by living it."

Those who had the vocation of Nazareth must bring the Gospel to all men. One had to set oneself to it like Mary, for anyone with Jesus within oneself cannot fail to bring Him to others. And anyone with Jesus within him cannot fail to help others as Mary helped her cousin Elizabeth. To live the life of Nazareth is to put oneself at the disposal of those who do not know Jesus, to live as their servant.

This theme of the Visitation recurs often in 1898. Constantly in his meditations Brother Charles repeated the words "save," "light unceasingly the flame of love." The Gospel of love should be preached everywhere: "Our hearts, like that of Jesus, must embrace

all men; our aim on earth is like that of Jesus and the Church—
to glorify God by improving all men."

What he wanted was to love all men as Jesus had, and to go to
those who had been the most rejected. "Let us occupy ourselves
with the sinners, the poor." "Let us be poor workers as He was, like
Mary, Joseph, the Apostles, the shepherds."

9.
Conditions in the Community of Nazareth

In his life as a domestic servant, he humbly and simply put himself at the disposal of everyone. The urchins of Nazareth made fun
of him and threw stones at him, but Brother Charles said nothing.
One time when he was in the courtyard of the Poor Clares, sorting
lentils, two French monks on a pilgrimage remarked on his house-
wifely occupations, and Brother Charles's face turned red. Having
been served by Brother Charles on Christmas Day, the preacher of
the Poor Clares, full of good intentions, sat Brother Charles in his
place and served him what was left. One day he was asked by the
Poor Clares to kill a jackal that had been killing their chickens.
They borrowed a gun from their neighbor, Karam, and his son
instructed Foucauld how to shoot it. The former officer listened
patiently and thanked him for his help. He spent that night, pre-
sumably on guard, with the gun across his lap, saying his Rosary.
The next morning it was found that the jackal had made another
successful raid, and everyone laughed at the ineffectual domestic.

Those were little things. But hadn't Jesus lived the same hidden life in Nazareth, doing trivial things as other people living around Him did? Wasn't it there that He had learned to live a daily life filled with humbleness and insignificant details? Charles de Foucauld, in pursuing the last place, was not leading a life as extraordinary as did a vagabond such as Benedict Labre. As a domestic servant for a convent, there was nothing astonishing or "original" about his life. Still, though, it was a new method of living the Gospel.

Three months after his arrival in Nazareth, on June 6th, Pentecost, he wrote:

> Think that you will die a martyr, stripped of everything, stretched out on the ground, naked, unrecognizable, covered with blood and wounds, violently and painfully killed . . . and long that it would be today. . . . Be faithful in watching and carrying the Cross so that I can grant this infinite grace. . . . Consider that your life struggles are for this death.

In his little "hole" in Nazareth, Charles de Foucauld saw the death that he was to know in a little less than twenty years.

On January 16, 1898, eight years after he had arrived at the Trappist Monastery, he wrote to his directors, "Tomorrow marks eight years since I entered the Community, years of great memories . . . of voyages! Of changes!"

While he was happy at Nazareth, he was not completely happy. He thought of it constantly while he was there—he wanted to be an "evangelizing worker." He wanted to instruct in the Gospel, to "work in the service of God." He wanted to communicate his happiness in knowing Jesus and the Gospel to others. His heart was opened to the whole world. "I will reach the entire universe by prayers that will embrace all mankind." There was no limit to this love. "Our heart, like that of Jesus, must embrace all mankind."

On July 7th, Foucauld left for Jerusalem carrying a letter from the abbess of the Poor Clares of Nazareth to the abbess of the Poor Clares of Jerusalem. It was a good opportunity for Mother Elizabeth to see the man that the Poor Clares of Nazareth had spoken of so highly. During his four days in Jerusalem, she questioned him and scrutinized him and she concluded that he was truly a saint. Mother

Elizabeth was a woman of intelligence who had already founded three convents. She had very precise ideas about the future of the servant of Nazareth. She wanted him to stay on in Jerusalem and to have, as he wished, companions around him. But he thought he should do nothing without the consent of Abbé Huvelin, to whom he wrote immediately. On September 11th, he received a reply in the affirmative and he returned to Jerusalem. Since there was a young man in Akbès who wanted to follow the same life as Foucauld, Mother Elizabeth sent him to Akbès. It was hoped that Pierre would be the first companion of the would-be founder of "The Hermits of the Sacred Heart." But the voyage to Akbès was a disappointment. Pierre, not wanting to leave his mother, refused, and Brother Charles returned to Jerusalem and continued to live as a servant. "The convent is a little over a mile from the village; my small house is made of green planks placed against the wall of the enclosure—three walls are wood and the fourth is the stone wall of the enclosure. From my door I see Gethsemane, Mount of Olives, the Cenacle, Calvary, and our dear Bethany." He expected to stay in Jerusalem for "at least a year."

Mother Elizabeth was extremely tenacious, she was in accord with Brother Charles's projects for a foundation but she also wanted him to become a priest. If he were a priest, she maintained, it would be easier for him to have companions. The servant's heart burst with happiness as it seemed that his project might take form, and he described anew the brotherhood he wished to found. It would be simple. He did not want the spirit of it to be like the Trappists, "too formal and too narrow." He wanted a "simple" life, free from a multitude of formal prayers. He wanted much poverty and much work, and "an elimination of exterior ceremonies . . . much more prayer, and a deeper inner life, along with the practice of charity toward one's neighbor on all occasions that God offers." He wrote to Abbé Huvelin, "Without even admitting it myself, my secret dream—which constantly appears, though I don't permit it and I even chase it away—which I must tell you about because you must know the secret depths of my soul, even that which I dream involuntarily, is of something resembling the first simple communities that existed at the beginnings of our Church. . . ." The Acts of the Apostles describe those first communities. "The Communities of the Believers had but one heart and one soul. No one called anything that had belonged to him his own, but among all, all was shared. The Apostles had witnessed the Resurrection of Our Lord Jesus Christ and they enjoyed great favor. Also, among them no one was in need; all who had owned land or houses sold them and put the money at the feet of the Apostles. It was distributed to each according to his needs." And the non-Christians, seeing that, said among themselves, "See how they love one another."

After four and a half months in Jerusalem, Foucauld returned to Nazareth and stayed there for a little more than a year.

In 1899 he wrote a new rule for the congregation he wanted to found. The aim was the same: to follow the life of Nazareth in the midst of non-Christians. The great rule is the rule "to see in every human being a soul worth saving and to devote oneself to the salvation of souls, as did Our Lord."

The name "Saviour" was to explain the lives of the Hermits of the Sacred Heart as it explained His life. They must be "Saviours" by the presence of the Holy Sacrament and the oblation of the Holy Sacrifice, by imitating the virtues of Jesus, by penitence and prayer, by good deeds and charity; charity must radiate from the Brotherhoods, just as it radiated from the heart of Jesus.

The lives of the Hermits of the Sacred Heart were to be expressed in two distinct movements: the time of profound intimacy with Jesus and the time when they would take the mystery of Jesus to others. First, they were to look toward Jesus in the Eucharist, the heart of "little Nazareth." Second, through welcome and friendship, carry Jesus to mankind.

For the time being, Brother Charles's life consisted above all in constant adoration of the Eucharist, a life that was hidden and lost in Jesus. Like the seed in the soil, he was buried in community life for the sake of Jesus and the Eucharist. What harvest would this bring? Brother Charles was confident in God. "My life continues to be the same," he wrote in February, 1900, "silent and still more deeply buried."

One month later he wrote to Abbé Huvelin: "I am waiting. God Himself led me here, and through your words He has kept me here.

By His own act, He brought me back. My life is in His hands. When He wishes me to leave—if He should ever wish it, of which I am not certain—He will point the way clearly by our voice, dear Father, or by events. . . ." It was three years since he had arrived in Nazareth.

10.

"Hermit-Priest"

Things took a sudden turn. In March, 1900, he learned that the presumed site of the Mount of the Beatitudes, which the Turks held, was for sale. It was a unique chance, and he wrote at once to Abbé Huvelin, to his cousin, and to his brother-in-law, describing his project and asking for money. As the Mount of the Beatitudes project took form, he thought that he could be a "hermit-priest" there, that he could live alone and lead a priestly life in extreme poverty.

"I shall live in penury, surrounded by all kinds of difficulties, truly carrying the Cross of Jesus and sharing His poverty." He asked Abbé Huvelin to arrange with the Archbishop of Paris that he be ordained as a priest and "hermit-missionary." With great joy and great hope, he considered God and his own poverty. On April 26, 1900, he concluded, as he had ten years earlier at his entrance into the Trappist monastery, "God uses adverse winds to get us into port." "Obstacles are the sign that the event is to God's liking." And again the phrase that is so expressive of St. Paul's teachings, "The weaknesses of the ways of human beings is a source of strength."

He wished to carry forth the love of Jesus everywhere. The multiplicity of his projects shows the passion with which he looked for an exact way to express the universal love of Christ. It was then that he took as a motto for himself, "Jesus Caritas," a heart topped by a cross, "Jesus Saviour by the Cross," Jesus who loves all men and gives Himself to the love of all.

On August 8th, he sailed from Jaffa for Marseille. Mother Elizabeth had urged him to see his director; and to encourage him to go, she had given him a confidential mission to do in Rome concerning her project to found another Poor Clares' convent.

On August 18th, he arrived in Paris, having left it ten years ago. It was Paris of 1900, Paris of the *belle époque*. He went straight to Abbé Huvelin, who invited him to accept the priesthood. On his way to Rome, Brother Charles stopped at Our Lady of the Snows and asked permission to prepare for his ordination there. After his ordination he would return to the Holy Land to live as a hermit-priest.

He went to Rome and then returned to Our Lady of the Snows, where he lived in a tiny cell that looked out on the altar. From his cell, he could attend all the functions without being seen.

In December, 1900, he prepared to become a subdeacon. In retreat, he wrote that he wished to found "the Hermits of the Sacred Heart," first in the Holy Land, because it was the country of Jesus, then at Bethany, because it was one of the holiest of the holy places, and "the most abandoned . . . then, if it pleased God, in the Sahara, where so many souls have no evangelist preacher."

In March, he was in retreat for the diaconate. He meditated on the Gospel according to St. John, especially a verse in Chapter 12: "Unless the grain of wheat falling into the ground die, itself remaineth alone. But if it die, it bringeth forth much fruit."

III

AT THE HEART
OF THE WORLD, 1901-1916

1.

Until the Last Crust of Bread

On Sunday, June 9, 1901, Charles de Foucauld was ordained priest in the chapel of the Major Seminary at Viviers by Monseigneur Montety, a bishop who had been a missionary in Iran. Accompanied by Dom Martin, he returned to Our Lady of the Snows the same night. Having arrived at midnight, Brother Charles spent the rest of the night in prayers before the Holy Sacrament. His heart was filled with immense joy.

During his months at Our Lady of the Snows, and particularly at the moment of his ordination, an evolution took place within Charles de Foucauld. It was a radical rupture comparable to that which had taken place at his conversion. It was a sudden change in his recent and earlier ideas.

His recent ideas had been formed following fifteen monastic years. They were, first, to stay in the Holy Land and then, second, to go to the Sahara. Very quickly, Charles de Foucauld abandoned his idea of Palestine and also his idea of becoming a hermit. What he now wished to do was to go where men were the "most abandoned." In a letter of June 23rd, two weeks after his ordination, he wrote, "To follow the life of Nazareth not in the Holy Land but among the very sick and the most forsaken." "The Divine Banquet which I am to minister will be presented not to the relatives or rich neighbors but to the lame, blind, poor—to the souls who have no priest."

From the moment of his ordination, Charles de Foucauld thought his call was to men who were furthest from the Gospel. At the moment of his conversion, he had been called by God and he had replied by giving himself completely to Him. At the moment of his ordination, he was called by the non-Christians, and he wanted to answer them with all his love.

Thus, there were in Charles de Foucauld two extremes: the absolute love of God and the absolute love of men furthest from God. These loves were joined. Beginning with his ordination, Charles de Foucauld gave himself, with a single love, to the two extremes: to God and to men furthest from God.

Charles de Foucauld felt that there was a loud call from non-Christians, and their cries for help crossed the life of this man like a bright light and illuminated his past. For him, the non-Christians were the men he had met before his conversion—the Moslems, the "believers" whom he had met when he was an unbeliever. "In my youth, I traveled across Algeria and Morocco. In Morocco, large as France and with ten million inhabitants, there was not a single priest. . . . No people seem to me to be more abandoned than they." During the weeks around his ordination, Charles de Foucauld searched his past as a man and as an unbeliever to find his place as a priest, to discover the concrete adaptation of his new state.

When Charles de Foucauld once decided something, he wanted to see it through as quickly and thoroughly as possible. He wanted to realize quickly the decisions he made during the retreats for his ordination. The first person he told about his desire to go to the Sahara was Henry de Castries.

Henry de Castries was a few years older than Foucauld, but he, too, had gone to Saint-Cyr, and in 1873 he had been sent to Africa. Like Foucauld, he had led a gay life in his first garrison of Chambéry, and his family had had him ordered to Africa. Enamored with a part of the world that was so new to him, Castries began to study Arabic. He was interested in the manners and customs of the country. He studied the law of the Koran. He had a passion for everything African. Charged with the creation of a small post at Aflou, he offered hospitality to everyone. He talked with everyone about their travels and even made maps of the routes they had taken. In 1880 he published a map of the South Oran region and the borders of Morocco. When Charles de Foucauld returned from Morocco, after his exploration, he wrote: "By good luck, I had the excellent work of Captain de Castries. It enabled me to follow the basin of the Drar with great precision. No one has ever been more surprised than the natives when I read off to them the road I wished to follow, village by village." In 1881, when Foucauld had returned to fight with his comrades, Captain de Castries had not wanted to see him. But after his exploration of Morocco, the value of which De Castries could well appreciate, Foucauld gained back De Castries' respect. To pay tribute to De Castries, Foucauld gave him a copy of his book, *Reconnaissance au Maroc*. But Foucauld never spoke to Castries about his entry into religion.

Charles de Foucauld's letter of June 23, 1901, to De Castries began, "The silence of the cloister is not the silence of forgetfulness . . . more than once during the twelve years of this blessed solitude I have thought of you and prayed for you."

It is clear why Foucauld wanted to renew his relationship with De Castries. De Castries was the best geographer of the region and he knew a great deal about the South Oran regions that had once before captivated Foucauld and were again tugging at his heart—this time to bring the Gospel of Love to the people there.

Charles de Foucauld told De Castries of his project:

It is for the Good Lord that I have kept silence. It is also for Him that I break it today. Among us are several monks who cannot say, "Our Father" without having sad thoughts about vast Morocco, where so many live without "sanctifying God, being part of His Kingdom, accomplishing His Will, knowing the sacrament of the Lord's Supper." Knowing that one must love the poor as we love ourselves, with the help of God who depends on us, little as we are, we want to bring them the Light of Christ. We would like to do for those people that which we would hope would be done for us if we were in their place. We wish to found on the Moroccan frontier, not a Trappist monastery, not a big, rich monastery, not a moneymaking farm, but a small, humble hermitage where a few poor monks live on a little fruit and barley harvested with their own hands. They would live in a small, narrow enclosure in the penitence and adoration of the Holy Sacrament, never leaving and never preaching, but giving hospitality to anyone who comes, good or bad, friend or enemy, Moslem or Christian. . . . This is Evangelism, not by talk, but by the presence of the Very Holy Sacrament and the offer of the Divine Sacrifice, prayer, penitence, the practice of Evangelical virtues, charity—a charity that is fraternal and universal, sharing the last crust of bread with every pauper, every guest, every stranger who comes, and receiving every human being as a beloved brother. . . .

A few lines later in the same letter he added, "We would give humble hospitality to travelers, to caravans, and also to our soldiers." Charles de Foucauld thought that hospitality was the first way to evangelize this country that he had explored and knew so well.

Charles de Foucauld knew that hospitality was of great importance. In many languages the words "guest" and "enemy" come from the same root, for a stranger can be considered as either an enemy or a guest. Charles de Foucauld knew that fraternity is achieved the first moment that a stranger is received as a guest and not as an enemy and that the whole world changes when the stranger is covered with dignity instead of curses. The first stranger was Cain, "and I shall be a fugitive and a vagabond in the earth; and it shall come to pass that everyone that findeth me shall slay me." The fugitive, the stranger is slain, but the situation is reversed the day that he is received as a guest sent by God.

Charles de Foucauld knew the hospitality of the Semitic, and especially the Arab, world, and he knew the custom that the stranger who has crossed the threshold of the tent becomes a sacred guest even if he had hitherto been a personal enemy. Sharing shelter and, even more, sharing food made a man sacred, and any act of violence or scorn was considered very serious. Because it lacked hospitality, the city of Sodom knew God's wrath, while Abraham, on the other hand, had welcomed the three strangers who asked for hospitality.

Since his conversion, Charles de Foucauld had understood that, above all, the guest was Jesus Christ: "I was a stranger and ye took me in." He understood that Jesus had identified himself with the guest. He was the stranger who came into the world and knocked on doors: "Behold, I stand at the gate, and knock. If any man shall hear my voice, and open to me the door, I will come in to him, and will sup with him, and he with me." He knew that hospitality mysteriously reverses itself and that in reality it is the host and not the guest who receives the most, for it is a grace to receive a stranger.

Perhaps, too, Charles de Foucauld remembered that the Rule of St. Benedict says that guests should be received as Christ himself.

But it was in the Arab world that he found the most concrete expression of his idea, and in De Castries' answer to his letter he found the exact word he was seeking. "You understood exactly what I wanted: to establish a *zaouïa*." This word brought back to Foucauld's mind his Moroccan explorations twenty years earlier when he was received by Jewish communities and also by the Moslem communities called *zaouïas*. The latter struck him especially, for they were small centers of hospitality founded by religious groups, where travelers, pilgrims, beggars, and all who passed found asylum and protection.

Far from perfect, the *zaouïas* preached and often practiced slavery. As Charles de Foucauld told Henry de Castries in January, 1902, "Many slaves: relatively few in the Ksar, where the population works, but they abound among the nomads who are proud and lazy, and for the same reason they are also plentiful in the *zaouïas*." Furthermore, protection in the *zaouïas* was not always certain or free, as Foucauld had learned in December, 1883, when the Mrimima *zaouïa* exacted a good sum of money from him in return for shelter.

But Foucauld remembered these hostels and was aware of the possibilities they offered. He also remembered the favor they enjoyed throughout North Africa. Thus, when he thought of establishing a monastery in Islam, he did not think of a large foundation in the Western style, but of something in the style of the country. Charles de Foucauld did not wish to transplant Western customs to the Arab world, which he respected. His respect and his evangelical inspiration led him to being revolutionary by wanting to adapt to the country where he was establishing himself. He wanted to establish a religious center resembling these small Moslem hostels. He wanted to found a monastery-*zaouïa* that would be both a hermitage and a center of hospitality.

Charles de Foucauld wanted to do for the people of Morocco what they had done for him, they had helped him find God and had offered him shelter. He wanted to give them God and bread, he wanted to be among them always, praying for them and welcoming them like a brother. He did not wish to found a cloistered monastery or a "welcoming center," but to create a place that would by its existence express charity to God and "fraternal and universal" charity. He wanted his life concretely to express divine and brotherly love, "to spread the Gospel, Truth, Charity, Jesus."

After fifteen years of contemplation of the Heart of Jesus, Foucauld was not breaking with the past and throwing aside his faith simply to live in human brotherhood. What he wanted was to live at both poles of charity. His *zaouïa* would be open to all, but it would be pervaded by a feeling of God and it would be free of slavery. His unique creation was not to be a juxtaposition of elements, but a complete intermingling of the total consecration of the self to God and the total consecration of the self to all men. As he put it, Foucauld's *zaouïa* was to be "a *zaouïa* of prayer and hospitality."

Charles de Foucauld followed the Gospel of Love to the letter. From then on, if he wrote to Henry de Castries, the man who knew most about the region, it was to help express in Islam the Gospel of Love. He wanted to use the best means available to men to live, truly, Christ's charity.

2.

The Best-Placed Spot

Now that he was to bring the Gospel to Morocco, he planned his work as precisely, as rigorously, and as scientifically as he had his earlier exploration of Morocco. With the same energy he showed during his first trip, this forty-two-year-old man who was dedicated to God vowed to give himself to those whom he had met on his first trip.

The fact that he used technical terms in writing to De Castries proves that Charles de Foucauld was approaching what even Abbé Huvelin called "his mission" with scientific precision and not as a dreamy and romantic young priest:

> Where to locate this little foundation—the position most favorable to spiritual well-being . . . a place where favorable relations with the Moroccans can be established . . . the best-placed spot to dig in, breach, and later penetrate more and more deeply the flank where Morocco is most susceptible to being evangelized. . . . I think it is the South . . . and so it seems to me that it would be best to be at some isolated watering spot between Aïn-Sefra and Touat.

De Castries sent not only geographical information but also a book on Islam that he had published five years earlier in 1887. Writing to De Castries about this book, he told his friend about his conversion, first congratulating De Castries on having given examples in his book of both Christian and Moslem martyrs: "The examples that you mention, holy examples of our martyrs—Euloge, Flora, Isaac, Bernard, and their companions—and the examples of Moslem martyrs who so often and so admirably showed their virtue—Chikhech-Chârâui, Omar II, Mohammed, fighting and suffering for one God with only a house built with his own hands and a few camels, and of all those early Moslems who were more virtuous than the Christians they were fighting."

De Castries' book also led him to explain with extreme clarity the depths of his soul, the dynamo-like effect of love on his life, the will to make the absolute gift to God and to all men.

With the information that De Castries had given him, Charles de Foucauld was soon ready to present the complete project to Abbé Huvelin, who wrote to the Apostolic Vicar of the Sahara and Sudan and to Monseigneur Livinhac, Superior General of the White Fathers. He described Charles de Foucauld to them: "A sturdy instrument for a hard task. . . . Firmness, a desire to go as far as possible in loving and giving, and to face all the consequences."

The ecclesiastical authorities gave Charles permission to establish himself in Africa. He left France at once, without even seeing his family again. On September 10th he arrived at Algiers, and the Bishop of the Sahara, Monseigneur Guérin, was waiting for him. The bishop granted Charles permission not only to settle in the Sahara but also to gather companions.

On September 7, 1901, he had written his wishes to Madame de Bondy:

> To go south of the province of Oran on the Moroccan frontier to one of the French garrisons that has no priest, and to live silently and cloistered as a monk, having neither the title of chaplain nor priest, but being simply a monk who prays and administers the Sacraments. The aim is twofold:
>
> 1. Prevent our soldiers from dying without having received the Sacraments in a place where fever kills so many and where there are no priests.
>
> 2. Above all, to help the large and forgotten Moslem population by bringing into its midst Jesus in the Most Holy Sacrament, just as the Most Holy Virgin sanctified John the Baptist by bringing Jesus to him.

The Sahara region neighboring Morocco was in the hands of the army which was colonizing it, and as soon as he arrived in Algiers, Charles was once again in contact with the army. While awaiting military authorizations, he returned to the Staouéli monastery between September 20th and October 14th. This stay offered only relative solitude, for at every moment he was receiving letters renewing his ties with the past. On September 24th he even received a visit from a noncommissioned officer in the Spahis who had just spent two years in the Béni-Abbès region and was able to furnish detailed information.

De Castries had recommended Foucauld to his friend General Cauchemez, who had the Aïn-Sefra region under his authority. Commandant Lacroix, a friend of Foucauld who handled local affairs for the Government General of Algeria, got all the necessary papers and passports. Thus Foucauld was tightly bound to his past and was relying on it for help. His past—a time of pride, of expeditions and explorations—was helping to open doors to the non-Christian world. During this time, the news spread rapidly: "Foucauld is back! He wants to settle near Morocco—as a priest, monk, chaplain!"

Having returned from Staouéli, on October 15, 1901, Charles de Foucauld left Algiers by train. From Oran he went to Aïn-Sefra, where he was received with great pomp by General Cauchemez, who greatly facilitated his trip to Béni-Abbès, the spot that had finally been chosen. He was given an escort. "I wanted to go on foot, as a poor monk, but I had to accept a horse and an escort. At every post they fear for my safety ["they" being officers of all ranks], a kindness which touches me and fills me with gratitude to God." At Taghit, an oasis between Aïn-Sefra and Béni-Abbès, the commander of the post, Captain de Susbielle, came at the head of his native troops, telling them, "You are going to see a French Marabout who will live among you in prayer, despising riches." The horsemen dismounted and came to kiss the hem of Charles de Foucauld's robe. And when he arrived at the oasis of Béni-Abbès on October 28th, Foucauld received a warm welcome from the head of the post, Captain Regnault, who was to become a close friend.

3.

A Universal Brother

On November 1st, two days after his arrival, Charles de Foucauld wrote to Abbé Huvelin, "There is a great deal of good to be done— as much for the soldiers as for the Moslems."

The principal oasis in the Saoura region, Béni-Abbès is one of a chain of oases south of Colom-Béchar at the tip of South Morocco. The population of the Saoura is composed largely of *haratins,* Negro Moslems who live poorly on dates and millet, under the constant threat of pillaging Moroccans, who come from the west, harvest the crops, and take slaves.

West of Béni-Abbès lies a somber desert of stones, a *hamada,* and on the other side of Béni-Abbès stretches a desert of sand. Béni-Abbès was a *ksar,* or settlement, of 130 families, located, as Charles wrote to Henry de Castries,

> in the middle of a thick forest of 6,000 palm trees. . . . The oasis is very beautiful owing to its exceptionally harmonious shape, its well-kept gardens, its air of prosperity . . . and beyond this refreshing and peaceful scene one has the immense horizon of the *hamada* losing itself in that beautiful Sahara sky that calls to mind infinity and the God-who-is-almighty—"Allah Akbar." The populace is very gentle; having feared the arrival of the French, the natives now seem content and they seem to realize that now, for the first time in untold years, they can harvest their crops. . . . Not far from the fortress and the oasis I have found a solitary little valley—deserted but fertile, for there is plenty of water in Béni-Abbès—which with God's help I shall transform into a garden. On its slopes the garrison and the Arab officers have, with a charity and grace that touch me deeply, started building me a chapel from dried bricks and palm-tree trunks. It will have three cells and a guest room.

One month after his arrival, on November 30th, the work was finished and Charles de Foucauld moved into his new home. The chapel consisted of four palm-tree trunks supporting a roof of woven twigs and branches. This was sufficient, for it never rained. Between the whitewashed walls it was as dark as the catacombs. Later, Charles de Foucauld decorated his humble chapel, and Lyautey, who visited it some years afterward, wrote:

> On Sunday my officers and I went to seven o'clock Mass at the hermitage. A ramshackle shanty, this hermitage, the chapel is a miserable passage with columns, roofed with rushes, a board serves as altar. The only decoration is an image of Christ on a piece of calico and tin candlesticks. Our feet were in the sand. Well, I must say I have never heard Mass said as Father de

Foucauld said it. I thought I was in the Thebaid. It was one of the greatest impressions of my life.

In the chapel there was also a large Sacred Heart which Charles had drawn himself and which he described as, "The Sacred Heart holding out its arms to embrace, hold, and call all men and giving itself to them by offering its Heart."

Charles himself had no rooms. He slept on the floor, in the sacristy, a tiny nook. He lived on dates and barley cakes. "It costs me seven francs a month," he noted.

Brother Charles, as even the Moslems called him, led a very simple life. "Among the populace surrounding me one can do much good; they are gentle, peaceful, and poor. Kindness and charity may bring them to bless Jesus." Like the image of Christ in his chapel, he opened his arms to all, and in a letter of December 8th, he wrote; "My life is divided between prayer and receiving visitors, which takes a great deal of time—a few officers, many soldiers, many Arabs, many poor to whom I give as much barley and dates as I can."

On November 29th he wrote to De Castries:

The constructions are called *khaoua,* or brotherhood, for *khaouia Carlo* means universal brother. Pray God that I may really be a brother to all the souls of this country. I have had a most affectionate reception from the military of all ranks, and the natives too have received me perfectly. I make as many contacts as I can with them.

On January 7, 1902, he wrote his cousin: "I want to accustom everyone—Christian, Moslem, Jew, or pagan—to look on me as a brother, a universal brother. They are beginning to call the house 'the brotherhood' (*khaoua* in Arabic), and that is sweet to my ears." January 19th was a great cause for celebration: "I have had a great joy: for the first time poor voyagers have received hospitality under the humble roof of 'the brotherhood of the Sacred Heart.' The natives have begun to call it the *khaoua* and to understand that the poor have a brother—not only the poor, but all men."

Spending his first Christmas at Béni-Abbès, he told his bishop, Monseigneur Guérin, about the brotherhood:

It is 1,200 feet from the camp and 3,000 feet from the *ksar,* solitary enough for contemplation but accessible so that Christians may go to the chapel and Moslems may ask for alms or for other help. . . . Not only the garrison but also the natives—settled berbers and Arab nomads alike—have given this poor monk the warmest welcome. A chapel has been built and since December 2nd, the Blessed Sacrament is always in the tabernacle. The garrison consists of about eight hundred men, two hundred of them French. They are sufficiently fervent so that at Christmas the Blessed Sacrament could be exposed all day long before a good number of worshipers. For the first of January we will do the same thing if it please God. Each night a number of soldiers come to the chapel for their evening prayers. . . . The natives come at all hours to ask for alms, while others come to pay friendly calls. God seems to have wanted to make the road to the chapel a familiar one.

Brother Charles was happy to be warmly received by the soldiers as well as by the natives, but it was above all he who was receiving them with open arms. He was interested in everyone's life and welcomed the problems of Captain Regnault and the other officers as well as those of the natives of Béni-Abbès. He received each person as a friend, and for everyone he was the man with the big heart who spoke of God as Love.

In his hermitage at Béni-Abbès, Brother Charles was living at a crossroads. He found himself involved in colonial conquest and he did not withdraw to the ivory tower—on the contrary, in fact. He wanted to go beyond colonization to fraternization. He placed himself in the midst of the population of Béni-Abbès which had once known marauding plunderers and which now knew the army. He put himself in the midst of the army of which he had once been an active colonizing member. The Heart of Christ, as he understood it, was not a pious image, an easy and sentimental love, but the concrete realization of universal brotherhood.

At the dawn of the twentieth century, Brother Charles, with all his mystical and realistic love of Jesus and of mankind, let himself be tied to and sheltered by nations, classes, and races that did not know one another. His politics were the politics of love. He opened his arms to all in peace and love. Like Christ on the Cross, he was to know the greatest meaning of Love, face all demands, and suffer all consequences.

4.
"I Do Not Want to Be a Bad Shepherd"

On his arrival in Béni-Abbès, Brother Charles made the monstrous discovery that, despite the presence of the French, slavery continued to exist. Slaves had been freed in Algeria, but, in order to spare the feelings of local chieftains, nothing had been done in the Sahara. Not only had the French tolerated slavery; they had also confirmed the *status quo*. On January 8, 1902, Brother Charles wrote to Madame de Bondy: "Here, alas, slavery flourishes as it did 2,000 years ago, under the eyes and with the permission of the French government." Three days later, when writing to a White Father, he repeated, "Here slavery flourishes openly and unhindered, on entering the country the French authorities boldly announced that it would remain in force . . . slaves are extremely numerous."

The question of slavery was of great importance to him. "At present it is the most urgent and important question," he wrote on January 19th. Four days earlier he had written to Henry de Castries, "Slavery is this country's greatest affliction."

Fighting with all his might against this oppression, he first examined the problem carefully. He compared the relatively harmless position of the slaves he had known in Morocco with those he now received each day. Undoubtedly the warm and fraternal reception they got from Brother Charles helped him to learn the real truth from them.

The truth was terrible. Clearly and soberly, Brother Charles described the slaves' condition to Monseigneur Guérin:

> After exacting all the work from them that they require, their masters do not feed or clothe them or shelter them, but let them prowl around idly, telling them to shift for themselves. Slaves can own nothing, so they can never buy their freedom; their material misery is extreme and their spiritual misery is greater still; more or less without religion, they live in hate and despair.

In another letter to Monseigneur Guérin he wrote, "The slave question is extremely serious." Giving his bishop his humane and spiritual reasons for wanting to do everything possible to end slavery, he added that he hoped to found the first Christian community for them: "I think that finally, with patience and goodwill, we can form the first Christians from the same group as most of them were formed in Rome: the slaves. . . . I bless you, my Father, for having shown to the insignificant what you have not shown the wise and the prudent!"

Seeing in the fight against slavery his first task at Béni-Abbès, Brother Charles was realistic and provident:

> This seems to be the first problem because of its urgency, because of the extreme abandon in which such a great number of these poor souls find themselves. . . . It is also the first problem because of the hope that it will give . . . and it is the first because of its difficulties, for we must expect contradictions from every side and great disappointments (contradictions and difficulties with the French authorities and Arab rulers; disappointments from the poor).

Brother Charles not only saw the situation clearly, but made definite plans. "For the slaves," he wrote in the same letter, "I have a little room where they find shelter, welcome, bread, and friendship." He added that the room had been finished January 15th and that since then he had had slaves "at the fraternity every night." Further, he wrote, "Sometimes I see twenty slaves a day." He ended his letter to Monseigneur Guérin with an urgent request for advice.

Please have the goodness to give me a line of conduct for the slaves. Until I hear otherwise, this is what I am doing: far from preaching flight or revolt, I preach patience and tell them to stay where they are, for in time God will give them liberty and comfort; that the better they serve Him the more He will comfort them; that they should seek God and that in return they shall have justice and everything else in abundance. But at the same time, I do not hide from my French friends my view that this slavery is unjust, that it is monstrously immoral, and that it is their duty to do their best to end it. . . . In Madagascar, with a single stroke of the pen, General Gallieni ended slavery in one day, although there was a huge slave market and some people owned 800 slaves. The officers here and at neighboring posts (Taghit, and others) are agreed in wishing the end of slavery, but the order must be given from on high, for it is by order of General Risbourg (an order confirmed by Colonel Billet) that slavery here is maintained: when they came here they announced that no changes in the condition of slaves would be made. Furthermore, an officer in the Arab office was forced, when a slave who had escaped from the Marabouts of Kerzaz sought refuge with him, to return the slave to his masters *by command* of General Risbourg. With such precedents, the Arab offices dare not act, despite their wish for emancipation and justice. . . .

I am putting the problem in your hands. Pass it on, if you wish, to Monseigneur Livinhac. If there is a chance of approaching the Chamber of Deputies or the Senate through Catholic deputies or senators, you and Monseigneur Livinhac will let me know what to do. We are not charged with the responsibility to govern, but we are expected to "love thy neighbor as thyself" and "do unto others as you would have others do unto you," and by extension we must do whatever is necessary to bring relief to the unfortunate: "That which we do for them, we have neglected to do for Jesus." We have no right to be silent dogs or silent sentinels.

We must cry out when we see evil: *Non licet* and *Vae vobis hypocritae*. (That is not permitted, and Shame on you, hypocrites!)

Direct me . . . tell me what I should do about the slave question. It seems to me that one should not condone evil, but that one should fight it with all one's might.

Brother Charles continued to shout the truth. On February 7, 1902, he wrote to Dom Martin, Abbé of Our Lady of the Snows:

In helping them in every possible way, it seems to me that the duty is not done and that it is necessary to say—or to have said by those who have the right to speak: *Non licet . . . Vae vobis hypocritae*. You, who put "Liberty, Equality, and Brotherhood"— the Rights of Man on your postage stamps and all around. You also put slaves in shackles. You condemn counterfeiters to serve on convict ships, and you permit children to be stolen from their parents and sold at public auction. You punish for the theft of a chicken and you permit a man to be stolen. (In effect, nearly all the slaves in this region are children who were born free and who were taken by force from their parents.)

Then, it is necessary to "love thy neighbor as thyself," and to do for the poor souls as "you would have others do unto you"; and we must prevent anyone whom God has entrusted us with from being lost—and he has entrusted us with all of the souls of our territory. . . . One should not meddle in government affairs —no one is more convinced of that than I—but one must "love justice and hate iniquity." And when the government commits a grave injustice against those who are, to some extent, entrusted to us (I am the only priest within 180 miles in any direction), we must speak up. For it is we who represent justice and truth on earth, and we do not have the right to be sleeping sentinels or silent dogs of indifferent shepherds.

I am asking myself (we are in agreement about our behavior vis-à-vis the slaves) whether a voice should not be raised, either directly or indirectly, so that everyone in France will know of this injustice, of how slaves are stolen in our territories. Shouldn't we say, "Look what is happening." . . . I have informed the Apostolic Prefect—maybe that is sufficient. It is far from my wish to talk and write, but I do not wish to be a traitor to my children, nor do I wish to fail to do that which Jesus—whose spirit lives among us—would want, for it is Jesus who is in this unhappy condition:

"For that which you do unto one of my children, you do unto me." I do not wish to be a bad shepherd, nor do I wish to be a silent dog; I have fear that I might sacrifice Jesus for my peace and my preference for tranquillity and because of my natural cowardice and timidity.

On February 8th, he wrote to Monseigneur Livinhac: "I must inform you that the conditions of slavery in the valley of the Saoura could not be more lamentable. There are many slaves and they are badly treated, and the French government has grandly declared that slavery will not be abolished, but continued."

The same day he exposed the situation to Father Voillard in the same terms and at length.

Monseigneur Guérin told him that he was eager to see the situation for himself. "I feel the need to study the question thoroughly."

To that, Brother Charles replied: "As for this serious question of the slaves, I am most eager that you see this country, whatever discontent such a visit would cause—for the idea of justice in this matter may be obscure, even among the good souls, and it would seem to me unlikely that you would not stir matters up. There will be difficulties but 'it is better to obey God than to please man.' "

June 15th: "I have a great need to talk with you on the question of slavery—a question that weighs heavily on my mind. I implore you not to let summer pass without coming here."

But Monseigneur Guérin returned to France to raise funds for his "mission." Brother Charles continued his activity. He wrote to Henry de Castries. He told him of the effect the complicity of certain French authorities with slavery had produced:

In permitting it, in supporting it, we will breed contempt—the natural fruit of injustice. The natives know that we condemn it and that we do not permit it at home and that we have forbidden it in Algeria; then they see that we lend ourselves to it here and they say, "They don't dare, they are afraid of us," and they *despise* us. They are right. It is right to despise those who know they are doing wrong and who, through mortal fear, act against their consciences. No human power has the right to put shackles on these unhappy men whom God created as free as he created us. To permit their so-called masters to hold them captive, to chase them down when they escape, to sell them when, hoping in vain to find protection and justice, they throw themselves at the feet of the French authorities—is to deprive them of undeniable rights. . . . It is justice that the natives should despise us for condoning this out of our own fear.

Henry de Castries responded to Brother Charles's outburst by offering to present the problem to Denys Cochin.

Brother Charles wrote to Monseigneur Guérin on June 28th:

One of my friends has proposed that he should put this matter in the hands of Baron Cochin, a man who is fervently against slavery and who works on antislavery problems in the Chamber of Deputies. I have not accepted this offer for the moment, preferring to leave the matter in your hands. . . . But during your visit to France, wouldn't it be a good idea if you were to see M. Cochin. Perhaps you know him. If not, my cousin Madame de Flavigny could certainly introduce you.

Brother Charles worked out this method to present, work, and resolve the problem: "To enter into the details of how badly treated the slaves of the Saoura and the Oasis region really are seems to me to be a bad approach. They are badly treated to be sure, but whether they are badly treated or not the great injustice lies in the simple fact that they are in bondage."

Brother Charles went right to the heart of the problem: the law that permitted slavery. It was in the declaration of General Risbourg. "That is the 'Black Code' in the Saoura, and it is the Law." He repeated, "That is how a master is permitted to 'force' people into slavery; and it is that which prevents the officials of the Arab offices from protecting the slaves when they have asked for protection."

Brother Charles continued to explain that that law not only sanctioned slavery but also put a stamp of approval on kidnaping and gangsterism:

> Slavery here is all the more unjust—it is always unjust. We are all the sons of Adam and we should "do unto others as you would have others do unto you." But aside from the enormous and monstrous injustice of slavery, there is a particular point to be made about slavery here: very few of the slaves are the sons of slaves; almost all of them were stolen, when they were five, ten, fifteen years old, from Soudan or Touat. . . . Horsemen would go from here to Touat and lie in wait near a village. Then when the women and children from the village left to go to the woods, they would seize them, take them away, and sell them when they got back here. (This no longer happens since the French occupation, but they are still able to enjoy the fruits of their earlier raids.) But that is the way that most of the slaves of Saoura became slaves. It is not only slavery but the kidnaping of children that the French authorities are sanctioning.

If someone claimed that slavery was indispensable to the Saoura for economic reasons, Brother Charles had an answer:

> We are told that the slaves are necessary to the country . . . that they are needed in agriculture . . . without them, the oasis would perish. That is inexact. Many oases, and the most prosperous ones, have no slaves at all or very few. . . . It is the nomads and the Marabouts who have great numbers of slaves, for they never work and they spend their life in total idleness, and they would revolt against us at the first opportunity. If we freed their slaves, we would force them to work a little, and that would help them.

But Brother Charles did not base his reasoning on opportunism: "But even if it had no true advantages but only inconveniences, we still must free the slaves because it is just."

On his return to France, Monseigneur Guérin visited Maison Carrée. The young bishop wanted advice from a man of great experience, Monseigneur Livinhac, Superior General of the White Fathers. Monseigneur Livinhac, for whom Brother Charles had high esteem, advised silence. This was the advice that Monseigneur

Guérin imparted to Brother Charles: one cannot "dream of an official denunciation of acts that take place in this country."

To that, Brother Charles, on September 30th, sent this reply: "I will follow to the letter the conduct you have prescribed." Nevertheless he added, "To say it for the last time, the reasons do not leave me without regretting that the representatives of Jesus must be contented to defend a cause of justice and charity with 'a whisper and not a shout.' "

Brother Charles had wished to alert the public officials, and he had wanted to launch an offensive in broad daylight. Because the hour had not arrived and the atmosphere was not ripe, he would have to continue to work as well as he could, day by day, fighting against slavery. Truly, Brother Charles was a man alone. No one listened to him, and his voice was muffled. However, he pursued his task without being discouraged. He used the money that permitted him to live so meagerly to buy up slaves one by one. As of January 9, 1902, he told his cousin that he had been able to give one of them his liberty. But he went broke from his purchases and he had no money left to pay for the land for his fraternity. Further, he saw that these liberations made one by one could not resolve the over-all problem. In January he had asked his cousin, as he had asked all his good friends, to start an information campaign that would result in a law:

> Each day I am offered slaves to buy. It breaks my heart to have to leave them with their masters. Try to make people understand to what degree authorized slavery reigns here, slavery permitted by the French authorities. There should be a government act that would destroy with one sweep this injustice. Or charitable people should furnish the means by which the most unhappy of the slaves could be bought away from their masters. The first solution would be better, because slavery is an abomination.

But since the first method, true and radical, failed, his only choice was to pursue the second method with increased intensity. He wrote on July 4th: "I have had the pleasure to buy and free a slave; for the moment, he will stay with me as my guest, working in the garden. He seems to be about twenty-five years old."

A few days after, he had added a three-year-old boy. On September 3rd:

There is one slave I am trying to buy so I can put him back with his children; this young head of a family with children at Tafilalet (Morocco), thirteen miles from here, was stolen two years ago (the men steal men as if they were cattle), and sold here. . . . Days seem like centuries to him; he wants to be with his wife and children; I am going to try to buy him and keep him as a guest in the fraternity until such time as I can safely send him to his family. . . . This is not a soul that I can hope to introduce to the goodness of Jesus, but this is in obedience to the words of Jesus: "Do unto others as you would have others do unto you." . . . It will be a joy to me when I can return this poor man to his children.

He succeeded in freeing him on September 14th, and the same day saw a young fifteen-year-old man freed—Paul Embarek—who was never to be catechized but who was, finally, the only witness to the death of Brother Charles at Tamanrasset.

On February 27th, there was another Paul, as evidenced in this moving document:

I, the undersigned, have purchased from Mohammed and Rziq, sons of Ombarek bou Rziq (of the Tenemma tribe in the Saoura Oued), one Paul Bonita to whom I have given freedom for the love of Our Lord Jesus Christ. To Him, Glory forever. Written in Béni-Abbès, Saoura Oued, February 27, 1903. (*Signed*) Brother Charles of Jesus.

Perhaps it was the result of Brother Charles's acts that enabled him to write to Henry de Castries on December 15, 1904, in this manner:

In common accord, the chiefs of the annexes of the oasis have taken measures to suppress slavery. Not in one day—that would not be wise, but little by little so that in a short time, there will be no more slaves. Already, literally speaking, slavery no longer exists: the sale of slaves is forbidden; and slaves themselves cannot change masters; if they are badly treated, the chief of the annex sets them free. . . . It is a huge step . . . a wonderful accomplishment. . . .

Slowly, gradually, the rest will materialize with the help of God. Pray—let us pray, my dear friend—that all of the souls of this country will be delivered not only from slavery, but from a more cruel and sinister slavery of evil, vice, and error that separates them from the good and the true, from everything that separates them from knowing God while they are on this earth. . . .

Brother Charles had completely open arms. He never ceased to welcome. The time he had left for prayer was diminished:

I am so busy with outside duties that I no longer have a minute to read or to meditate. The poor soldiers come to see me all the time. The slaves fill the little house that was built for them, and travelers come straight to the "brotherhood," as well as the poor. . . . Every day there are guests to feed and put up. We are never without guests, and sometimes there are eleven in one night, not counting an old cripple who has become a permanent fixture. I have between sixty and one hundred visitors every day.

He began further building, not in order to receive companions, but to enable him to welcome more guests.

He was overwhelmed; indeed, he had every reason to be overwhelmed, even with his special capacity for activity. On February 4, 1902, he described a day to Monseigneur Guérin:

I meet with twenty slaves, welcome thirty to forty travelers, hand out medicine to ten or fifteen people, and give alms to about seventy-five beggars. Often I see sixty children in a single day. . . . The "brotherhood" is very quiet during the night and from 10:00 A.M. to 3:00 P.M. (the time when many people sleep and others don't go out). But it's a beehive from five until nine in the morning and from four in the afternoon until eight at night.

In August, 1902, he wrote his cousin that he saw people continuously "from four-thirty in the morning until eighty-thirty at night" and that, despite having taken the precaution to say Mass before daybreak, he was constantly interrupted during the ceremonies. One of the principal resolutions of his retreat in June, 1902, a year after his ordination was this: " *'Order and Activity'* in a manner that will economize on time and that will provide a contemplative life, at the same time serving everyone in a manner to give Jesus to all."

So the "Nazareth" of Brother Charles was not at all a house where one lived apart from other men and "spirit to spirit" with Jesus; it was a place for prayer and a place where all men could find a friend, a brother; it was a simple place where anyone could come to know Jesus. This *"zaouïa* of prayer and hospitality" was a place where each could enter to participate in Brother Charles's life.

He welcomed one and all, without making any distinctions. He shared his meals with each. At the same time, he respected the tastes of his guests. He understood that they had different customs. "It is absolutely necessary to have different lodgings for the men who are free and for the slaves. They cannot live well together, and one does not have the same things to tell the two groups." In the same letter of February 4, 1902, to Monseigneur Guérin, he spoke of the crippled and the homeless old people. He suffered because he was able to receive only

> those who get along well together, because of the lack of space. . . . The poor travelers find at this "brotherhood" a humble asylum and a meager meal, but with a kind welcome and with a few words to help them along and to take them to Jesus. But the place is small and the virtue and know-how of the monk is smaller still. More virtue, intelligence, and resources would help make it possible to do more good.

He was living a life vastly different from the life he had lived only one year earlier. It was vastly different from the little monastic cell he had had at Our Lady of the Snows, where he had prepared himself for the priesthood. Brother Charles had plunged headlong into adventure. He devoted himself completely, without retaining anything of his former way of thinking, to an incessant welcoming of everyone. He regarded everyone who lived at Béni-Abbès as brothers; above all, he wished with all the strength of his love for Jesus, and for all, that each person would look upon him as a true brother.

He especially wanted the slaves to approach him as they would a brother who awaited them, understood them, and welcomed them. He wished to share his bread, his roof, his life with them. As if he were guided by a strong evangelical sense, soon after his arrival at Béni-Abbès, Brother Charles sought out the lost sheep who were the most completely lost—the slaves: the slaves and the children.

At Béni-Abbès he was situated between the French garrison and the Arab village. He wanted to establish a line of peace between the two. Also, and perhaps more important, he wanted to welcome into his "brotherhood," to the heart of his friendship and tenderness of Christ, the poor, abandoned people whom the village and the garrison turned away—those who had no family, no country, those who were alone and without hope in the night, those who had had their freedom taken from them. It was to them—the poorest of the poor—that he opened his arms.

5.

The Roman Army

Brother Charles's love was boundless. He refused no one. He received everybody. On July 14, 1903, he wrote to a White Father: "In evangelizing the poor, the rich should not be neglected. Our Lord did not neglect them; nor did St. Paul, His imitator . . . because of their influence, their improvement is good for the poor. Their sincerity is less to be doubted. There is less danger of their being 'soup Christians,' listening to Christian truths only for their material gain."

Brother Charles also opened his house to the soldiers and officers of the garrison. He thought particularly of the most deprived of the soldiers—those who were sick. He wished that a military hospital could be constructed at Béni-Abbès. "It would not be a hospital only for this garrison but a sanitarium for all the garrisons of the region, for Béni-Abbès is remarkably healthy," he wrote to Monseigneur Guérin.

He saw his brotherhood as "a center for soldiers and officers, a place for conversation of Moslems and Jews." Again he wrote to Monseigneur Guérin about what he wanted to do for the soldiers: "To create love among them, to teach them, to help them with services, and to provide get-togethers for them when they are off duty—Sundays and during the week—to help get everyone to know each other . . . and to do it all so that they will begin to accept our house as their own."

Brother Charles also had frequent contact with the officers. This is what he proposed to do for them: "To be a friend to all and, if possible, become their friend and confidant, to teach them and lend them books that they want to read and to guide them imperceptibly toward Jesus."

Captain Regnault, head of the post at Béni-Abbès, quickly became a friend of Brother Charles. He went to see him almost every day. The *Khaoua* soon became a meeting place for Captain Regnault and the other officers.

Brother Charles, constantly sharing the life of the officers and soldiers, saw clearly their good qualities, and had no illusions about their faults. Although he loved "the good Captain Regnault," and congratulated himself on his deeds—"acts of peace" realized out of "goodness and courage"—he also realized the lamentable consequences caused by the presence of certain soldiers. "One of the great mistakes of our occupation of the South is to use in certain posts (Béni-Abbès, Taghit, Igli, and so on) companies of the African Battalion. While the officers of the Arab Bureau strive to gain the respect of the natives by justice and goodness, these unhappy *joyeux* openly practice every vice, rendering themselves the most wretched of men, which makes France and the French despised. They should be confined at Khreider, at Macheria, and at other such posts far from the native population, and hidden so that no one would see them. . . ." That was the picture he presented on July 13, 1903, to Henry de Castries.

With such a close relationship with the French garrison, Brother Charles of Jesus may then have had some thought of becoming a missionary and quietly following the army during its penetration, so that he could baptize people who were conquered. Brother Charles was loyal and he was a realist. He had been an officer, and he was French with every fiber of his being. He knew the region thoroughly. He was not a servant of the army; he was a servant of the poor—a brother of the poor. And he compared the French Army stationed at Béni-Abbès to the Roman Army that occupied Palestine at the moment Jesus was born. In April, 1903, he wrote to Monseigneur Guérin, "Everything possible should be done to extend the reign of Jesus and His Evangelists, an extension which will come to pass whether France likes it or not; when Augustus ordered the census, little did he know that it was to bring Mary and Joseph to Bethlehem."

In the advance of the French Army, he saw but one possibility, completely related—"the birth of Jesus and the presence of His Evangelists in this country."

He further wrote to his cousin on May 18, 1903, "Human events touch us only by the glory they bring to the HEART of Our Husband —by the salvation, the sanctification of souls which they have prepared and favored."

6.

The Mission to Morocco

In the first months of 1902, the Moroccans were responsible for a series of raids and lootings. Brother Charles condemned these misdeeds for the suffering they brought to the poor *haratins* (the semislave laborers). He wanted the army to protect them. According to him, that should be its only role, and when he demanded a suppression of the misdeeds, his aim was to protect these people.

In March, 1902, Captain Regnault made an expedition to the Southwest:

A very interesting exploration has just been made of Tabelbalit by Captain Regnault, head of the post at Béni-Abbès. . . . With fifty *mekhaznia* (native soldiers) he went quickly—and in a peaceful and friendly way—to visit that oasis. The *ksoura* chiefs received him very peacefully and told him, *"Bledna bledek"* (Our country is your country); the Berbers, knowing of his visit, did not try to stop him. The importance of this place, between the Dra and Tafilalet, can be seen from a glance at a map. The Saoura and Touat are also more important than one would have known.

In this letter to Henry de Castries, after explaining the interesting points about Tabelbalit, Brother Charles wrote (and it is surprising to see how enterprising the monk of Béni-Abbès could be):

A favorable place for defense, as the width of the valley makes it possible to see great distances and to shoot from afar; it is a unique position from which to watch the roads of the Saoura, Gourara, and Touat and to put up a shelter for the *harkas* (partisan troops); it is a unique position from which to threaten Tafilalet and the Dra, if necessary; it is a unique position from which we could strengthen our peaceful relations with the Draoua and the tribes from the extreme west; supply lines also make

Tabelbalit the strategic place of the Saoura annex. Following this remarkable exploration of last March—which I hope will interest you and which I have told you about immediately—I sincerely hope that Tabelbalit will be the established center of the annex. If you want more information, Captain Regnault will tell you anything you ask.

It is evident that Brother Charles instigated Captain Regnault's expedition to the Southwest. A little farther to the west were the Dra, Mrimima, Tisint—places where Charles de Foucauld had explored earlier, places about which he thought more and more often.

Proof of that is in this letter of April 13th, which he wrote to Henry de Castries: "I would like to ask you a favor, dear friend. Could you send me your study on the Dra? Pardon my indiscretion. For months we have tried to get it here without success. I thank you in advance with all my heart." Obviously, Brother Charles had not stopped thinking of Morocco since his arrival at Béni-Abbès. Béni-Abbès was for him a point of departure for Morocco.

Brother Charles was impatient. On June 16th he wrote to Henry de Castries that he had not yet received his study. Through De Castries, he had been put in touch with an English explorer named James E. B. Meakin, who had written several books on Morocco. Henry de Castries had told him that Meakin was writing a book on the history of Morocco.

In June, 1902, Brother Charles wrote to Meakin, explaining his precise wishes:

It is good news that you have undertaken this immense work. No one could do it better. . . . What a task! There is one point that interests me intensely: What role has Christianity had in Morocco? How far south had it extended during the time of the Romans? And at that time, to what degree had it reached the people of the mountains . . . then what was the Christian anguish during the time of the Moslems? . . . Later, when the Fathers of Mercy and other religious men traveled through Morocco to comfort and buy up the Christian slaves, where exactly did they go and what was their accomplishment and their influence? What was the Christianity of Morocco during the centuries when European slaves were so numerous? . . . Those are the questions—the history of Christianity in Morocco alone would require long research. . . . The people of the country south of the Atlas Mountains always speak of the Christian occupation before the arrival of the Moslems. I found a Hebrew manuscript (Arabic language in Hebrew alphabet) which devotes several pages to this subject and affirms such an occupation above the Dra all the way to Dabaïa. . . . I have also been told of "inscribed stones" from the Christians a few miles south of the Dra, directly south of Tisint. But all of this is mixed with legend and fables. . . . My companion, Mardochée, assured me that his father had read inscriptions on Hebrew tombs at Mhamid el Rozlan, where he was from, that predated the destruction of Jerusalem by Titus. . . . Here, in the Saoura, between Béni-Abbès and Kerzaz, there are three *ksours* in ruins which have the name of *ksours* in Maçara; Captain Regnault's excavations have not brought forth any new discovery. [Brother Charles concluded:] Divine grace is powerful enough to enlighten all men. What is impossible for human beings is possible for God; he ordered his disciples to go to all men: "Go forth into the world to preach the Gospel to all living creatures." And St. Paul added: "Charity never loses hope." With all my heart I, too, have hope for the Moslems, Arabs, and heathens of all races.

It was, then, Brother Charles who invited Captain Regnault to go to the west, and he was also careful to tell De Castries and the influential Commandant Lacroix about the expeditions: "I draw your attention to the great importance of the exploration of Tabelbalit made by Captain Regnault."

If he was inspired by the "good of the country which is so dear to us," it can be seen from his letter to Henry de Castries that he was most of all interested in the evangelization of Morocco. On January 22nd, he went further, and asked Commandant Lacroix to give full permission for the entry into Morocco: "I would like you to give the Arab Bureau of Béni-Abbès once for all instructions necessary for Captain Regnault and for me, if I should want it one day, to make a discreet trip to Morocco with facility."

Thus, Brother Charles, who gave Captain Regnault all kinds of strategic advice, asked for the chance to penetrate into Morocco, not in an army convoy and not as an explorer, but as a man alone, unarmed, a disciple of Jesus.

In August, Captain Regnault went on leave, and did not return until Christmas, 1902. Brother Charles wrote to De Castries on December 5th: "During his absence, the officers of the Arab Bureau, very few in number, had made no efforts at reconnaissance."

There had been the expedition in the west in March. But another event made Brother Charles look more intensely toward Morocco— the extension of Béni-Abbès, which was becoming more and more the crossroads of the caravans. On December 16th, he wrote to De Castries:

> This is to tell you that here in the Sahara, so close to Morocco— are we not at the gateway to Morocco?—both of which you have studied so much. We will pray for you with all our hearts all night long on Christmas and New Year's. . . . Béni-Abbès is growing in importance in front of our eyes; it is a pleasure to see. . . . Each day, attracted by the good welcome, the security, and the advantages they receive here, more and more caravans and travelers from Morocco arrive. The Berbers are beginning to come for commerce, furnishing us with barley and sheep. They were very frightened at first. Day by day, their confidence grows. We hope that the day will come when the border will vanish and that the Magreb will belong to France and above all to Jesus.

In the same letter, he spoke again of Morocco: "What dark night and veil of mourning covers all of Morocco. No priest and no Tabernacle—Christmas night will pass without a single Mass being said and without a single prayer to Jesus. Deeply moved, I pray for it." The same refrain appeared in a series of letters written in November and December to Monseigneur Guérin: "Christmas Day and the following two days I was visited by two Moroccans of Tafilalet. I thanked God for them. Let us pray for poor Morocco!" Was it not Jesus who, on that Christmas Day, signaled him to go to Morocco?

While waiting, he prepared himself. The thought of the many, many Moslems in Morocco made him love Jesus all the more and to live but for Him. "To say good things about the Moslems, one would first have to convert them, and I have not done that . . . the history of St. Pierre Claver shows it . . . to convert them, one has first to convert oneself and to be a saint."

A few weeks earlier, on September 30th, he had written to Monseigneur Guérin:

Everything that happens to me—it is the foundation of my soul —brings me always the same two things, sings to me the same two songs, the same two anthems, if I dare to say: the first is Joy, for in everything there is some glory for Jesus, something which glorifies His name, something which helps communion with Him . . . the second is: *Sanctify yourself, convert yourself! Conversion!* Everything tells me to convert myself, everything sings out to me of the necessity of sanctifying myself. Everything repeats to me and cries to me that, if good which I wish does not materialize, the fault lies within me and I must hasten to convert myself.

In mid-January, 1903, Captain Regnault was ordered by telegram to Algiers with Lapperrine. He left immediately. At Algiers he met Monseigneur Guérin, and on February 15th, Monseigneur Guérin wrote to Brother Charles: "It seems clear to me from all of your past experience—military, exploratory, and religious—that the Good Lord has destined you for a mission at the border of Morocco and in Morocco itself: you are now beginning this work—you will have to continue it—and I do not doubt that the circumstances in several years will lend themselves to your having greater access to this region." Monseigneur Guérin told Brother Charles that Laperrine and Regnault had been called to Algiers to "carry out a program of diverse actions in the center of the Sahara." For Monseigneur Guérin, as for all of the missionaries of this period, there was no doubt: "The Evangelists are interested in having this country truly penetrated as soon as possible."

During Captain Regnault's absence the "Moroccan tribes . . . raid time and again at our expense." Brother Charles was very anxious about this, and wrote of it to Monseigneur Guérin. At the same time, with no thought of danger, he wished to go to Morocco, and he asked Monseigneur Guérin for permission on March 9th. On March 20th, he wrote to a White Father, "The Saoura is not remarkable or important except for its proximity to Morocco."

Near Easter, Brother Charles planned the project for a mission in Morocco. He wanted to establish a commission whose objective was to interest a number of priests, monks, and nuns in going to Morocco. He wrote:

> I think the best thing for the conversion of Morocco would be to organize a small legion of priests dedicated to contemplation and good works who would live meagerly from the work of their hands and whose simple rule could be summarized in three words: Perpetual adoration of the Holy Sacrament, imitation of the hidden life of Jesus of Nazareth, life in the country of the mission. This small mission would be an advance troop, prepared to launch itself in the fields of Morocco.
>
> What we want as evangelical workers are priest-apostles . . . prepared to die with and for Jesus, to sacrifice everything with and for Jesus.

In this "project for a mission in Morocco," which was probably destined for several superiors of religious congregations, Brother Charles wrote: "Since my arrival, I have made contacts with the natives and above all with the Moroccans. Every day many natives visit the Brotherhood of the Sacred Heart and, among them, there are Moroccans."

It is clear from his project that Brother Charles did not plan to enter Morocco with the French Army; he wanted to enter it with the Moroccans. A poor and humble brother, he wished to accompany them, to be admitted by them, respecting them with all his heart:

> I would like to be able, in the near future, to go with a few Moroccans to their country. I would go there first for a few days, then a few weeks, then a few months and buy there a small piece of property where a new "Brotherhood of the Sacred Heart" would be founded. One would go closer and closer. Charity, hospitality, purchase and liberation of the slaves, and more—the offering of

the Divine Victim will reconcile the hearts and open the way to public sermons. The sermons will come more quickly the more numerous and fervent the silent advance troop. I am alone, and as embarrassing as it is, considering the short trip I plan to make to Morocco in a few weeks, it would be useful to me to have a select companion to help me in my misery and to help avoid any indecency or sacrilege. That should tempt many because of the dangers being great, it is nearly glory that is offered. Despite my desire to have companions, I would rather be alone than have anyone who has not been called by Jesus and who is not a true disciple of His Heart.

Always it was evangelism by love and hospitality. On March 30th, he wrote his cousin:

To come back to the subject of Morocco, you understand that if I came here to Béni-Abbès on the border, it was in the back of my mind to spread the Gospel, not to cease being silent and contemplative, which is my vocation, and to penetrate with the Gospel not by going out to preach like the first holy disciples of St. Francis— which is not my vocation and which does not seem to me to be the way to know and love Jesus—but by forcing myself, after having founded at Béni-Abbès a poor monastic colony of priests who worship the Holy Sacrament, to found others nearer and nearer Morocco. This must be planned ahead through relations here with Moroccans, getting them to accept me there by offering them hospitality here.

No more was heard of Brother Charles's project either from civilian or military quarters.

"I am still alone," he wrote on April 15th, to Madame de Bondy. "Several would like to join me, but there are difficulties, the principal one of which is that the civilian and military authorities have forbidden all Europeans to travel in the region for reasons of security."

He had converted no one; but his project was not to convert someone for the sake of having made a conversion, but to make everyone know that Jesus is Love and that all men are brothers. Brother Charles lived in great expectation.

On March 3, 1902, he wrote to his brother-in-law:

It is true that conversions of the Moslems are rare, but it is certain that, like anybody else, they are called to the Gospel, that they need both it and the possibility to embrace it. It is also certain that the Church must preach "to the entire universe and to all living creatures" the religion of Jesus. Consequently, there is nothing to do but try, adding our work to that of our predecessors. What will be the success? That is God's secret. But one's duty is clear and evident. . . . One should not forget, though, that evangelical workers sometimes accomplish more after their deaths than during their lives; also, their accomplishments are in proportion to their holiness. If there are not many Moslem conversions, perhaps it is because we missionaries are too tepid, not fervent enough, too little men of prayer and sacrifice and detachment. . . .

7.
Missionary Methods

Monseigneur Guérin made Brother Charles very happy by paying him a visit on May 31, 1903, the feast of Pentecost. He suggested that Brother Charles devote himself more to the evangelization of the world of the Moslems. Brother Charles's apostolic conclusions were revolutionary for a missionary of that period:

The mission of evangelical workers in Moslem countries is not only to teach Christian principles to children, but also, and above all, to work toward converting adults. . . . So it was with St. Paul and with the apostles . . . the children could not germinate the evangelical seed sown in their souls if the surroundings in which they lived were not a little prepared, a little predisposed;

for the apostolate to bear fruit with children, it would have, also, to reach adults.

Brother Charles refused to accept the principle—which was not very evangelical—that held that the Moslem world was closed to the message of Jesus.

For the "evangelization of grown men," Brother Charles believed that the best method would be by "loving conversation about God and religion in daily life." He thought that getting the natives to work would be helpful to them. But there was a problem in getting them to understand the importance of work, unless they had help from "good monks, poor monks who were laborers and who lived from the work of their hands, who lived the life of Jesus of Nazareth."

Brother Charles thought not only of the "brotherhoods," such as that of Béni-Abbès, in the work of evangelization. In addition to establishments, he thought "that missionaries should travel constantly in their efforts to spread Christianity. They should spend a few days in one place and then go back to it often, and be seen often talking first to one person and then another, becoming a true Apostle who, little by little, spreads the Christian spirit—the natural truths first, the others following—by friendly conversation with everyone."

The visit of the Bishop of the Sahara made it a true Pentecost, reinforcing and illuminating. After the departure of Monseigneur Guérin, the little universal brother of Béni-Abbès, feeling lonely, wrote to him, "I felt *alone* for the first time in many years Monday night as little by little you disappeared in the shadows." After the visit, he searched with renewed ardor for concrete ways to bring Jesus to those who lived at Béni-Abbès and to those who lived in his beloved Morocco. He revised his life, his apostolic methods, his poverty. Little incidents helped him, and he paid great attention to them. On June 3rd, he wrote to Monseigneur Guérin, who had left two days earlier, of something that happened:

Yesterday, two men from Tafilalet, both Marabouts, visited me. They had heard about you, and they asked whether you had gone to Tafilalet.

"No. He will go another time."

"Merhaba!" [Welcome to him!]

"Is he traveling on foot?"

"No, by camel. . . ."

This question, asked by the Marabouts, made me think. . . . They go by foot, leading their donkeys. . . . We are the disciples of Jesus. We want Jesus to exist within us; we talk endlessly of poverty. They are the disciples of Mohammed, their questions make me think. We have the examples of our Fathers, the Apostles. As were St. Peter and St. Paul, we are in a heathen country. If we want to follow their works, we should also follow their example. Everything tells me that.

Another event caught his attention:

Commandant Laperrine has written me that at the time of the massacre of the Flatters mission there was a noble Touareg woman who had refused to kill the wounded and had cared for them in her home and refused to admit Attici, who had been wounded in the battle of Amguid against the Dianous, and who wanted to kill the wounded himself. After she had nursed the wounded back to health, she sent them back to France by Tripoli. She is now between forty and forty-three years old, supposedly has a great deal of influence, and she is famous for her charity.

Later in this letter of June 18th to Monseigneur Guérin, Brother Charles wrote: "Jesus is the King of the Universe. . . . Jesus is King and Father of the Touaregs." And he concluded, "It would be good to enter into closer relations with the Touaregs and to try every door."

The charity of the Touareg woman interested him. As it was not possible to go to Morocco at this time, Brother Charles asked himself a new question:

Because I am still alone and no door toward the west is open to me, wouldn't it be better for souls—and more pleasing to the Heart of Jesus—if I asked my friend of the Oasis [Laperrine] permission to establish myself at Aoulef or farther south if possible, as near to the Touaregs as possible, in a place where, in solitude, I could learn the langauge of the Touaregs and translate the Gospel into it? . . . If it is agreed, I will . . . put myself in a cell, six feet by six feet, with an oratory six feet by fifteen feet and lead a solitary life, though uncloistered, and devote myself to:

1. Developing closer relations with the Touaregs (visiting them as often as possible).
2. Translating the Holy Gospel into their language.
3. Visiting each post at least once a year.
4. Communicating as much as possible with the natives by short trips.

It counted above all with Brother Charles to show the love of Christ to those who did not know Him. He was prepared to go to Morocco or to go somewhere else; he was ready to live in his cloister, or to leave it; he was ready to change his life and his manner of living; he was forever willing to do anything in the name of Jesus Christ.

On February 27th, he wrote to Monseigneur Guérin:

I am miserable without end; I have searched myself without finding any other desire than this: "That Thy Kingdom will come! that Thy Name will be sanctified!" . . . You ask if I am prepared to leave Béni-Abbès to spread the Gospel: For that, I am prepared to go to the ends of the earth and to live there until Doomsday.

It is evident that an astonishing evolution took place between the monastic life of Brother Charles of Nazareth and the missionary life of Brother Charles of the Sahara, a universal brother who wished to be a universal apostle. At the Trappists and at Nazareth, he was interested in the writings and the work of St. Paul, evidenced by a notebook that he filled with St. Paul's works in 1902.

What were the first methods of evangelization that Brother Charles wished to use? To take Christ to the people who knew him not, to be an apostle in the manner of St. Paul, Brother Charles selected two ways that, in his eyes, were inseparable: he wished to share the lives of the people of the country and to speak their language. In due course, having established a brotherly relationship by sharing the life, language, and customs, he would translate the

Gospel—adapt Jesus to the life, language, and customs of the people of the country. Brother Charles was not satisfied with words, he knew that to deliver Jesus to those he wanted to evangelize, he would first have to deliver himself, to give up his own life and live the life of the people, offering himself as nourishment to them.

8.

The Mysterious and Fascinating South

For what deep reason did Brother Charles want to go south? Why did a cloistered monk, which he was, wish to become a wandering apostle? Why this complete change in his life? There were several interwoven reasons. Above all, these reasons were "human events," which called Brother Charles, and a spiritual situation that engulfed him.

During June, July, and August of 1903, the situation around Béni-Abbès had become critical. It was so critical that on August 14th, he wrote his will.

On July 29th, he had written to Madame de Bondy:

We are at war around Béni-Abbès. There were two violent battles on the 16th and the 23rd between our native cavalry and strong troops of Moroccan looters. Captain Regnault returns tomorrow, the victor, but not without pain. He was slightly wounded, and a large number of his men were wounded and killed. The number will probably grow. But I do not think that the garrison at Béni-Abbès, which is very strong (nearly five hundred men), will be attacked. There were several very brave men among those killed . . . they all leave wives and children. A few days ago they were full of life, and now all is ended. Unhappiness comes quickly! And where are their souls? This is the saddest of all.

The battle that Captain Regnault survived had been in the open desert. Brother Charles wrote:

I should like to have been with those who were attacked, for it is there that a priest is the most vital, and I am the only one in the region. . . . I have told you—between us—that I might some-time spend time in the Touat region—Tidikelt—Gourara, until such time as Monseigneur Guérin can send more priests. There are eight or ten garrisons that *never* see a priest. And Monseigneur Guérin will not be able to send any there for some time. I have offered myself, but I have not had a reply from Monseigneur Guérin. . . . In the Regnault encounter, we had about a dozen killed and as many wounded, all natives and Moslems.

Brother Charles wished to go where there had never been a priest, to help the soldiers who were wounded in battle. But in the same letter, Brother Charles told that the wounded and dead were Moslems. What really attracted him in these lost places in the South were the garrisons that had no priests—but above all, the Touaregs. He was living in a battle zone. Although Brother Charles wished to be among the poor who were being attacked and the soldiers who were being wounded, he wished above all to be in a region where there was no fighting, a region of peace, a place that waited for the Gospel and had never heard of Christ.

On June 30th, he had written to Monseigneur Guérin a letter in which he had taken a very strong position:

I wish simply and clearly to go—waiting for Morocco to be open, if it is to be open—to the Touaregs, in a place where I could have sufficient security. . . . I have no companions, and Morocco is closed. I could not do better for the salvation of souls, which is our purpose here on earth, as it was the purpose of Jesus our Saviour, than to go forth and sow the seed of the divine doctrine to as many souls as possible—not by preaching, but by conversing, and above all to go, to prepare and to begin the evangelization of the Touaregs by establishing myself in their country, learning their language, translating the Gospel and making relations with them as friendly as possible.

One other circumstance pushed him toward the South.

In March, 1903, Henri Laperrine had arrived in Béni-Abbès. In 1901 he had been put in command of the Sahara oases. Brother Charles had known Laperrine well, and they renewed their friendship. What Brother Charles admired most in Laperrine was his directness; deception was the one thing that Laperrine could not forgive. He loved truth. He had a high respect for everyone he met; he did not wish to humiliate or exploit. He wished to reconcile the natives with each other, to be on an equal footing with them, to establish a complete friendship between them and the French. To accomplish that, Laperrine did not hesitate to assume his responsibilities; he fought for the good of the natives. Laperrine was anything but a follower. He had unkind words for those he called the "big chiefs," who, far away, knew nothing of the situation. Since 1902, Laperrine had been on the scene. "As for the 'big chiefs,'" he wrote on March 10, 1902, "I make a habit of telling them what I think and I believe they think of me as a holy terror." And again the same year, "I hope, despite all the obstacles, that we will come out in the clear. I am becoming a 'militarophobe' when I see the blunders made in the name of regulations."

Laperrine told Brother Charles in confidence that he wanted to move southward, toward the Hoggar. He made Brother Charles look at the immense South with its limitless, infinite horizons.

Brother Charles was braced by the directness and the loyalty of Laperrine. He knew that with Laperrine there would be no risk of a brutal colonization, but only a real desire respectfully to discover new countries and to bring progress to its people. Brother Charles wanted to know and understand people who had never heard the words of Christ, for whom Christ was unknown. Laperrine and Foucauld met on the same point: respect for people, and an ardent desire to enter into friendship with other human beings.

Laperrine worked to convince Brother Charles to look toward the South instead of toward Morocco. After his departure, he sent a young officer to convince Brother Charles of his views.

Nieger recounted:

It was in April, 1903, when I met Father de Foucauld. After a first sojourn in the Sahara of thirty months, my commanding officer [Laperrine] gave me freedom of movement. I was given one express order: "You will pass through Béni-Abbès. You will see Foucauld. He is working as a mason. He is building a hermitage, which he does not leave. He doesn't eat. He lives on public charity and still he finds means to buy up Moroccan slaves. He thinks only of Morocco, obsessed by memories of his youth. There is nothing to be done about that, for he is hardheaded. We must make him decide to come and join us. . . ."

In June of 1903, Laperrine wrote to Brother Charles; he spoke again of the Touaregs; he again told him about the woman who had saved the wounded French after the massacre of the Flatters mission. That woman, that stranger—wasn't she like the Good Samaritan of the Gospel, the stranger who understood better than the Jews the meaning of charity as preached by Christ? Once again Brother Charles reviewed his past. The massacre of the Flatters mission in the Sahara had been in 1881, the year Foucauld had re-entered the army in order to share in the dangers of his comrades; it was also the year Foucauld had quit the army to go to Morocco. Foucauld recalled what a loud reverberation the Flatters mission affair had had. Why was it that Colonel Flatters was headed toward the Hoggar in 1881? The reason was that an engineer named Duponchel had advanced an idea that met with immediate success: in America a transcontinental railroad had been built that resulted in farms and towns and civilization suddenly appearing along its route all across the country. Why couldn't France do the same thing by crossing the Sahara? Duponchel proposed to start the line in Algeria and run it across the Sahara where 100 million inhabitants of darkest Africa were waiting for French merchandise. *L'Illustration* and other magazines published maps of the Sahara—a Sahara no one had truly explored—covered with a complete railroad network!

The Minister of Public Works, Charles Freycinet, obtained credit to send three exploratory missions across the Sahara. Lieutenant

Colonel Flatters was charged to explore the area lying farthest east. That was how Flatters, performing a useful service, went toward the Touaregs and the Hoggar. To approach the country and the inhabitants, Flatters had only the advice of Henri Duveyrier, who had been there to explore the foothills of the Hoggar in 1860 and who had met the Touaregs. With a naïve enthusiasm, he judged them to have a mentality very like ours.

Henri Duveyrier was the astonishing man to whom Napoleon III gave, in 1860, a reconnaissance mission to the Ajjer Touaregs. A student of Saint-Simon, Duveyrier was fascinated by the East, which he had studied in Berlin. His attitude toward the natives was inspired by the principles of Father Enfantin, to whose daughter he was engaged. He was totally frank, seeking no disguise. He inspired confidence in his adversaries. He used no trickery, showing his hand clearly. This attitude netted him many strong friends. It was this man, then, who produced the first ethnographical study on this section of the Sahara, *les Touaregs du Nord*.

But when the Flatters mission was massacred, he was criticized for having pictured the Touaregs as dignified men in whom one could place confidence, and he was held responsible for the massacre. However, it was the Hoggar Touaregs who had been responsible for the massacre, and not his friends, the Ajjer Touaregs. Profoundly upset by the massacre and by the unfair accusations, Duveyrier shot himself in 1892.

In 1886, Charles de Foucauld spoke of Duveyrier as his "only friend." It was Duveyrier who had read the account of Foucauld's exploration of Morocco before the Geographical Society. At Akbès, Brother Marie-Albéric had been deeply affected by the death of Duveyrier. Brother Charles was preparing to go to the very people who had exterminated Colonel Flatters and who, in an indirect way, were responsible for the death of his friend.

Flatters had been betrayed by the Touaregs. The massacre of part of his party, the attempt by a handful of survivors to return to Ouargla—nine hundred miles of solitude—was a tragedy of the Sahara that profoundly upset people. All the newspapers told of the frightful march toward Ouargla: one day the survivors met a group of Touaregs on the road. The Touaregs agreed to sell them several pounds of crushed dates. But mixed in with the dates was a deadly poison—the powder of *bettina*—that drives men crazy and to their deaths in a frantic state of drunkenness. The man who had poisoned the dates was a man named Attici, who was eventually named Amenokal (chief) and who remained chief for twenty or thirty years, making the name of Hoggar synonymous with terror.

The past was made alive by his memory: again, the death of a close friend. In 1896 the Marquis de Mores, who had been a fun-loving companion of the Foucauld of Saumur, had taken his turn at adventure by a visit to the Touaregs, toward Rhadamès and Rat. He had been assassinated by the Iforass Touaregs, his guides, on June 5, 1896, before the Tripoli border.

Brother Charles wished to follow in the tracks of Duveyrier and Mores. He wanted to avenge their deaths, but in his own manner. On March 18, 1905, he wrote to the Marquis de la Roche Tulon:

> Yes, I am among the people who killed my friend, avenging his death by giving good for evil and trying to give them eternal life. My dear Mores, of whom I think, for whom I pray each day, helps me. In heaven, in the bosom of Eternal Life, bathing in immense charity, he has nothing but prayer and love for those Moslems who spilled his blood and may spill mine. We work together. He, above, glorious, and I, here on earth, have the same work of salvation and love.

Bringing the past alive pushed Brother Charles toward the Sahara. On June 21st he decided to write to Tarichat, the Touareg woman. His letter is admirable in its respect and comprehension. It was a work of the heart:

> In loving thanks to God for having seen you practice great charity toward mankind, we write this letter to tell you that in the land of Christians hundreds of thousands of souls, men and women, take vows of celibacy, renounce earthly goods, and dedicate their lives to prayer; to meditate on the words of God and to practice goodness, all of the monks, priests, and nuns who have heard of your goodness will bless you and thank God for your virtues and will pray to Him to give you a full measure of blessings in this

world and glory in heaven. . . . We also write to ask you to pray for us, for we are sure that God, who has given you the will to love Him and serve Him, will listen to your prayers. We beg of you to pray for us and for all men, so that finally all of us will love Him and will obey Him with all our souls. To Him, glory, blessings, honor, and praise, now and forever.

He sent a copy of this letter to Monseigneur Guérin and asked for permission to go, on foot, to pay a visit to Tarichat.

On July 5th Abbé Huvelin invited him to leave for the Hoggar. "Go where your spirit takes you." On June 24th Monseigneur Guérin told him the same. On July 22nd Brother Charles received the military authorization from Laperrine, but he was piqued to learn of the circumstances under which it was given. It was not an official authorization, but a purely personal one. "My dear Comrade," Laperrine wrote to Regnault on August 19th,

I authorize Foucauld to come to Tidikelt. I do not have the right, but I hope, as usual, to get by with nothing more than a few insulting and menacing letters from the subdivision, backed up by the top echelon. It's curious. One gets used to the kicks in the . . . , it doesn't bother me any more. I have a special place in the files for them, that's all. If you have any special things you want Foucauld to do, please tell me so that I can assume the responsibility and ward off the insults.

In August, new battles began around Taghit. Captain de Susbielle was attacked by nine thousand men. Brother Charles wrote to his cousin on August 22nd:

Having foreseen this attack, I wanted to go to Taghit, as I told you. Despite my efforts, I could not; I try every day, but I have found no one to take me, and it is absolutely necessary to have a guide, for there is not a trace of a road, and anyway, because of the enemy bands, one must take roundabout routes. I am governed by circumstances and possibilities. In another letter I will give you the details of my projects for the South. It could happen that the Taghit attack (which was supposed to enable us to get our hands on Morocco) would hold me here, or it could take me toward the West. Whether I am here or elsewhere, my line of action is: first, to seek to convert the heathens and, second, to give spiritual help to our soldiers.

But on August 29th Brother Charles got Monseigneur Guérin's authorization to go south. And on August 31:

An excellent opportunity to leave has presented itself: a military convoy in this country will leave here probably on September 12th (this convoy is made up of several soldiers under the command of a junior officer and of a number of camels carrying supplies for our troops). As the country is safe toward the South, this light escort is sufficient.

On September 2nd new fighting broke out, and Brother Charles wanted to go quickly to the front. He got the authorization, took a horse, and rode for twenty-three hours to get to the field hospital at Taghit, where he spent the month comforting the wounded. A new convoy was scheduled to leave for the South on October 15th. Brother Charles, thinking of the possibility of fresh fighting, hesitated.

"Will I be able to accomplish my projects in the south if I wait until later? I don't know. . . . I live from one day to the next." In November he was called back to Taghit to the gravely wounded soldiers. He returned to Béni-Abbès on December 6th. A new convoy to the South was announced for the beginning of January. Could he follow it? He felt "more and more drawn to this trip." He wrote an urgent letter to Abbé Huvelin. By January 13, 1904, he still had not had an answer, and the convoy was about to leave. Brother Charles packed up the reserved Host of the Tabernacle and left for the South with the convoy and with him was Paul, the young Negro slave he had freed.

9.
Saharan Marches

Brother Charles allowed himself to be led by circumstances. "I am always ready," he said. "I shall do what I think the circumstances call for." Again he wrote: "Let us go where we can, and when other doors open we shall go there. Sufficient unto the day is the evil thereof; let us do the best we can at the moment; at each of the moments that follow each other and form our lives let us profit from present blessings and from the means the Lord has given us." "I live from day to day." "Love always obeys when God is its object." "I let myself be driven, as if in a vehicle." His road was to lead him to the Touaregs.

At Béni-Abbès he had received all the poor who came to the brotherhood, and he followed the same principle on his travels. When he arrived in each village he asked to be directed to the poor and the sick so that he could give them alms and medicines. "I have given out more medicines in a week here than in two years at Béni-Abbès, and yet there I gave to several people each day." On January 21st he wrote to Madame de Bondy, "They are giving me a good reception." That was all he wished, for this wandering apostle was really a beggar, begging for the friendship and confidence of those he met.

On February 2nd Brother Charles arrived at Adrar, the capital of Thouat, where he saw Commandant Laperrine, who told him that of the six tribes who form the Touaregs, three had surrendered to him a year ago. They included the Hoggars. Brother Charles wrote to his cousin and told her the information that Laperrine had given him, noting that he was especially impressed by the chief of the Hoggars ". . . the most important and warlike of the six tribes, the chief who murdered Colonel Flatters and has until now been the Christians' arch-enemy is in In Salah right now with eighty Hoggar notables to surrender both himself and his tribe. This is important news, for it indicates that the Touareg region, until now closed to Christians, will be open from now on."

Laperrine offered to accompany Brother Charles on the tour he planned to make of the Hoggar. "I doubt that he would do this for other priests and so I accept, thanking God for the good that he is enabling me to do and begging Him to keep my faith. Perhaps on the next tour that will begin in five or six weeks Laperrine will push on to Timbuktu. If he does, I shall go with him, for the more I travel, the more natives I see and the more familiar I shall become to them. I hope to win their friendship and their confidence." With his technical knowledge and experience, Brother Charles began to search for the best spot to begin. "The best spot to study the language is Akabli, where everyone speaks it and where there are many Touareg caravans. So it has been decided that I shall go there and devote myself to study with all my energy."

Noticing that Brother Charles was well satisfied with his trip, Laperrine wrote Captain Regnault:

Foucauld is well. He is studying the language as hard as he can. Here he has gone through my archives and has been very sensible. He has agreed to eat with us, has been very gay, and has even agreed to sleep in a bed. Moreover, he has left on a camel, but carrying a pilgrim's stick instead of a lance. I have promised to take him on a tour, and if I see that he gets on with the Touaregs I shall give him more scope. I am sorry he didn't arrive two weeks earlier, for he would have seen Moussa Ag Amastane at In Salah and could perhaps have left with him.

While Laperrine dreamed of making him the first priest of the Hoggar, Brother Charles was interested in immersing himself in the Touareg world. In the same letter to Captain Regnault, written while traveling on February 19th, Laperrine explained that the Arab is the Touareg's natural enemy. "We are troublemakers, on the other hand, the unknown quantity."

Having lived between the French garrison and the Arabs in Bénis-Abbès, Brother Charles was now headed south in search of the Arab's enemies. A stranger to them and friend of the Arabs, he went to them in friendship. He carried no arms.

When he arrived at Akabli on February 20th, Brother Charles stopped living as an officer. He no longer shared their mess or slept in a bed. He led the life of the Touaregs, to his great joy. "Among other pleasures," he wrote on March 5th, "I have one that I have asked from Jesus for a long time. That is to live in a similar state of well-being out of love for Him as I lived in for my own pleasure when I was in Morocco. Here it is quite similar."

The tour resumed on March 14th, and on March 23rd he noted in the little book, in which he entered all the events and geographical details of the trip, that he had met Aziouel. Aziouel was "the chief of the Taïtoq (about forty years old), very intelligent, very energetic, a great fighter and plunderer, and a longtime enemy of Moussa Ag Amastane." Brother Charles had wanted to meet Moussa and had met Moussa's enemy. As the trip progressed, Brother Charles continued to study Touareg. "I am studying Touareg with all my energy so that I can help my brothers in Jesus." He was deeply content with his many encounters with the natives. "It is a great blessing from Jesus to be able to make contact, to become acquainted."

An important incident occurred on April 16th when Laperrine's group arrived at the well of Timiaouin and came up against a French group from Timbuktu, commanded by Captain Théveniaud, who forbade the group from Algeria to enter the Adrar. As he noted in his diary for April 16, 1904, Brother Charles was shocked and outraged by what he learned:

Stopped tonight at the well of Timiaouin (desert,—five miles). There we met a French party from Timbuktu composed of twenty Sudanese sharpshooters, ten Kenaka auxiliaries, Captain Théveniaud, Lieutenant Jerosoloni, military interpreter Pozzo di Borgo, Combe-Morel, a telegraph functionary. . . . Since they have been among the Iforass they have raided, pillaged, mistreated, robbed as they went; they seem only to have come here in order to punish the Iforass and perhaps the Hoggars and the Taïtoqs for having surrendered to France through the intermediary of Algeria. . . . In any case, their brigandage makes me blush before the Touaregs. Well received by the Iforass who came to them submissively bearing gifts, they have behaved like savages. Every moment we hear of another act of brutality or theft. Having given them a fraternal handshake on arriving, I shall leave tomorrow without saying good-bye, for I do not wish to enter into a compact with such infamies. I shall not address a word of reproach to them: (1) because it would be profitless for them, (2) because it would only remove them still further from religion, (3) because it could start trouble between them and Laperrine's officers. The intention of this sad outfit was to go to Timissac; they are carrying a letter from the lieutenant colonel who is in command at Timbuktu, forbidding Algerian troops to enter his territory and, should they insist upon crossing it, urging them to travel with Captain Théveniaud and not to have any contact with the natives. They recognize neither the surrender of the Iforass nor that of the Hoggars. . . . Since Commandant Laperrine cannot allow the Iforass, his charges, to be robbed and mistreated before his eyes without defending them, and since he has no hope, despite repeated efforts, that Captain Théveniaud will stop his pillaging, he does not wish to defend his charges by taking up arms against another Frenchman, and so he prefers to return and to inform the authorities as quickly as possible. Captain Théveniaud, for his part, also agrees to turn back and to stop pillaging the Iforass until the Council of Ministers decides whether they are under the jurisdiction of Algeria or Timbuktu. . . . What I see of these Sudan officers saddens me; they seem to be pillagers, bandits, freebooters. I fear that this great colonial empire, conquered for some time and capable of giving birth to so much good, moral good, true good, might soon become a source of shame for us that will make us blush even in front of savages; that it will make the word "French" cursed and, alas, the word "Christian," too; that it will make people who are already miserable more miserable still.

On June 4th he asked Monseigneur Guérin in a letter, "Will the natives know to make a distinction between soldiers and priests, to see in us God's servants, ministers of peace, soldiers of charity, universal brothers? I do not know."

In a letter of April 16th to Madame de Bondy, Brother Charles told what Laperrine planned to do:

> We will leave for In Salah tomorrow morning. It is very likely that I will not go to In Salah. My good friend Henri Laperrine will, if he can, put me in the hands of the natives at some convenient point along the way, and I will, to the best of my ability, do the work of Jesus among them; it is a great privilege.

Thus Laperrine wanted to turn his friend over to the natives, not as a hostage, but as an unarmed friend and brother. Brother Charles was happy to accept this plan.

As the march in the desert continued, Brother Charles began to discover the Touaregs and to become passionately interested in them. "The Touaregs appear to be very open and affectionate." He wrote to Monseigneur Guérin:

> I try everything to establish good relations, confidence and friendship with all the Touaregs. If all goes well, my friend will probably leave me on the way back at some point where I will be in the midst of these newly governed people. In order to establish good contacts, I will stay alone for a time. . . . I am studying Tamashek day and night. . . . How long shall I stay alone in the midst of our brothers? As long as obedience to Jesus permits it. . . . Don't speak of this to anyone . . . we must be silent in order not to attract attention and get my friend in trouble, which would put obstacles in front of God's work. . . . I beg of you not to speak of my trip . . . silence is good for the works of God.

For this trip Brother Charles accepted Monseigneur Guérin's suggestion, and chose a name the natives could call him. "I have taken the name of Abd-Isa." Abd-Isa means "servant of Jesus."

On Pentecost, May 22nd, two principal Hoggar nobles, representing Moussa Ag Amastane, Chief of the Hoggars, called on Laperrine. "Many good things are said about Moussa Ag Amastane. He is said to be a fervent Moslem, pious, brave, intelligent, a lover of good and of peace, and a man of his word." Moussa was sick and unable to call on Laperrine himself.

Brother Charles—Abd-Isa—learned that the Taïtoq and Hoggars had long been at war.

On June 7th the company set up camp near the tent of Tarichat Oult Ibdakane, the woman who had received and saved the French who were wounded at the massacre of the Flatters mission. There Brother Charles wrote in his diary a summary of the first five months of his journey. Above all, it reveals much about him.

First, he wrote of his vocation, "a vocation established for years." "This vocation has not changed." It was "to follow the life of Jesus of Nazareth . . . to be as humble and poor as Jesus of Nazareth." The differences existed only in the methods of living, and so Brother Charles decided "not to look for ways to give charity, as in Béni-Abbès; to give commensurate to what there is, as did Jesus, Mary, and Joseph of Nazareth; not to give, as a lone man, charity and hospitality as would a brotherhood of twenty-five."

His projects were far less rigid than at Béni-Abbès:

> When in doubt, I will always conform to the ways of Jesus of Nazareth. Consequently, the first thing I must do is to build an oratory four feet by six feet as a shelter for Paul and me. I will choose the best place for the present, without looking for a permanent location for a future brotherhood. Next, I must find work that will give us our daily bread. With that done, there is left but the prayers at night, the work by day, the full and constant love and contemplation of Jesus in poverty, holiness, and love. And we must give our neighbors all the spiritual and material help our limited means permit. . . . Prayer, work, hospitality—these are the essentials of a brotherhood.

The principle for establishing a brotherhood is always the same. It was the same for Abalessa: "Not in the heart of the village but near it—a little remote, to combine the silence of a retreat with the proximity of people." Of Abalessa he wrote, "It's not only the center of the Hoggars, but of all the Touareg country . . . the principal market for everyone." He wanted to live at that crossroads, but a little aside from it, so that he could live there in silence and with hospitality:

> Silently, secretly as Jesus of Nazareth and with the same obscurity . . . to live on earth unknown, as a voyager in the night . . . poor, diligent, humble, gentle, and with goodness as He lived,

defenseless and silent in front of injustice, like Him, and allowing myself, like the blessed Lamb, to be shorn and sacrificed without a word, imitating in all Jesus of Nazareth and Jesus on the Cross.

On July 4th he wrote to Monseigneur Guérin: "There are three things I need desperately, and for them I ask your prayers: (1) the conversion and salvation of the Touaregs, (2) saintly evangelical workers to concentrate on this, (3) my own conversion. For if I convert myself I shall obtain the first two."

Passionately impatient to show that Jesus *is* love, he wrote to Abbé Huvelin on July 15th, "With all my strength I try to show and to prove to our poor strayed brothers that our religion is all charity and all brotherhood, and that its emblem is a HEART." Knowing that this aim of friendship was hard to accomplish, he wrote to Monseigneur Guérin "that the brothers I meet are still very touchy, defiant, and sometimes full of hatred."

During this period Brother Charles was finishing an exhausting translation, and on August 17th he was able to tell Monsiegneur Guérin, "I have completed the translation of the four Gospels into Tamashek. Now I am correcting and recopying them."

Once again at the end of October Brother Charles found himself uncertain of what the future would bring. "I am completely ignorant as to my future," he wrote to Abbé Huvelin on October 25th. "Be it as Jesus wishes." On November 11th he arrived at Ghardaïa, Monseigneur Guérin's residence, to make a retreat and to ask advice. "I cannot see the future clearly; it will be for you to decide. . . . I am still studying Tamashek and am prepared, having seen you, to leave immediately for the Hoggar."

On November 26th he wrote a White Father about his trip, saying:

In countries so poor where life is so simple, the missionaries, in order not to build a wall between themselves and their flock, in order not to alienate those whom they hope to attract, in order not to gain an unpleasant and unevangelical reputation for wealth, will be obliged to live in great poverty. At the same time these missions will ask for little in the way of expenses. . . . The language of the Touaregs is very easy, one hundred times easier than Arabic, which is another advantage.

Brother Charles had in mind missions to which four or five missionaries would be attached. "Two or three would remain on the spot while the others would always be moving from camp to camp in the surrounding country." With the Touaregs above all, he felt that this plan of four or five missionaries, with two always traveling, to be absolutely essential.

Brother Charles hoped that White Sisters would accompany the White Fathers among the Touaregs, for he had noticed that women in the tribe were privileged. "What good they could do among the Touaregs, where the women are as free as in France and have as much influence, but where they do not use it as they do in France because they have no religion."

10.

To Unite in Brotherhood

But Monseigneur Guérin had decided to create foundations in the South, and so Brother Charles had no more travels to make. "I shall return to Béni-Abbès and resume my solitary life," he wrote at the end of his retreat on December 13th. On January 24, 1905, he was back at the brotherhood of the Sacred Heart. "Here I am back at Béni-Abbès for a long time, forever if God pleases, with no work except to live the life of Nazareth and to imitate the Divine Model with all my heart, with every bit of strength and love that is in me."

Early in January, while he was traveling, Brother Charles had received through the French consul in Casablanca and his friend Lacroix, Director of Native Affairs, a letter from Hadj Edriss ben

Omar, one of the men who had helped him most in Morocco, and a close relative of the head of the *zaouïa* of Bou el Djad.

This letter, dated August 16, 1904, said in part, "The French consul here tells me that you have been in Jerusalem in the Holy Land in the honest service of God and that you have sacrificed your time to the Eternal. I congratulate you and I am certain that the world no longer interests you." Brother Charles wrote to De Castries at once, briefly identifying his correspondent, telling how he had been treated as a brother at the *zaouïa,* and asking him to reply to Hadj Edriss.

The letter made him look back to the Morocco he had explored: "This letter, received after over twenty-one years, gives me great pleasure. It shows that there are people turning toward us, regarding our long-expected arrival as imminent, and hoping that we will bring the peace and security that Morocco has lacked for so long." In his letter, Brother Charles added: "Forgive me for writing this long business letter. I would rather write to you of God, but this business concerns Him. *Deus caritas est,* and everything that unites souls in brotherhood and love is His affair."

Answering the letter he had just received, Brother Charles wrote: "It would be sweet and agreeable to me to go myself to renew my friendship with you at Bejaad, but I cannot do so. I send you my best friend, my brother, my kindred spirit, the Count de Castries, and I ask you to receive him as you received me and as you would receive me today were I able to see you in person.

On March 23, 1905, Hadj Edriss answered: "I love you for your greatness of soul, for in the priesthood you will continue to be as good to the poor and suffering as you were in the fields of Maghreb. Good memories of you constantly come to my mind. It would give me pleasure to send you anything you might need or that might give you pleasure."

Morocco was a topical problem of the day, and if Britain, Italy, and Spain admitted that it was within the French sphere of influence, Germany was formally opposed. Wilhelm II decided to strike, and on March 31, 1905, he debarked at Tangiers during a Mediterranean cruise and called on a representative of the sultan, declaring himself ready to help defend the independence of Morocco.

The situation became tense. In France, Prime Minister Maurice Rouvier learned that the army, shaken by the Dreyfus Affair, was unprepared. Germany demanded an international conference, and Théophile Delcassé, the French Minister of War, was forced to resign when he refused.

Between 1905 and 1912 French, and even European, diplomatic history was dominated by the problem of Morocco. France wanted to occupy it and to assert her independence in so doing, for Morocco was a place where her energy and initiative could be expressed. Germany's aim was to humiliate France. On January 16, 1906, the three-month-long Algeciras conference began. Germany accepted France's primary role in building the Moroccan state bank. France and Spain were to share in organizing police forces in Moroccan ports.

Further incidents occurred between 1907 and 1911. On July 1, 1911, Germany notified France that she had laid up a gunboat, the *Panther,* in Agadir in South Morocco "to protect German nationals from the menace of Moroccan anarchy." This was a repetition of the Tangiers blow, and on November 4, 1911, another treaty was signed that gave France free rein in Morocco in exchange for territory in the Congo. In 1912 Lyautey was named Resident General in Morocco.

In national affairs, as in international affairs, the years 1905–1906 —during which Brother Charles waited at the edge of Morocco— marked an important turning point. There was an explosion of ideas and research; the world was swinging to a new era. In 1906 Léon Bloy wrote, "We are at the prologue of such an extraordinary drama as has not been heard of in centuries, and I invite you to practice a certain degree of meditation."

France in the early twentieth century was a country that doubted herself and her vitality, a country living on its nerves. The national sport was politics, "pure native art," as Paul Morand called it. "Little Father" Combes resigned as Prime Minister early in 1905, and in 1906 Clemenceau took power.

During these years a real religious war had taken place. The Carthusians had been expelled in April, 1903, and in December, 1905, the Law of Separation took effect, solemnly condemned by Pope Piux X. At the same time, there was a strong revival of

Catholicism; if in 1905 only three or four students at the *École Normale* attended Mass, forty, or one-third of the student body, did so in 1912.

Wilhelm II's Tangiers blow awakened French patriotism, and the wish to colonize Morocco came from a sense of oppression. In 1905 Maurice Barres began his series of *Bastions de l'Est,* Charles Maurras published *Kiel et Tanger,* and Charles Péguy brought out *Notre Patrie.* In 1906 Henri Bergson conquered the public with *Creative Evolution,* became one of France's glories for his method of philosophy, and was regarded as an answer to the German techniques that had been so admired since 1870.

Regardless of the interest in Africa and Psichari's Mauritanian campaign of 1903, France remained self-occupied. The small population increase of scarcely 1 per cent between 1906 and 1913 indicated that dreams of foreign expansion had no counterpart at home. Besides, although people dreamed of Africa, no one did much about it, and in February, 1914, when the Governor of Algeria came to Paris to discuss the Algerian question, he found himself in front of twelve members of the French Parliament—and 587 empty chairs.

On January 28, 1905, at Béni-Abbès, Brother Charles received an impromptu visit from General Lyautey, who arrived with a number of Native Affairs officers. The subject of the conversation was Morocco. "For Moroccan and African problems, we call endlessly on his research," said Lyautey of Brother Charles.

This might mean that Brother Charles would finally go to Morocco. In the meantime, however, he recorded his observations on the Touareg country in the same careful manner that he had taken notes on Moroccan explorations. "I spend my monastic and silent life replacing manual labor by translating Touareg and working on the studies made in the year's travels," he wrote to Madame de Bondy on February 18th.

In that life of solitude and prayer, Brother Charles was surprised by two letters, April 1st and 8th, from Laperrine, inviting him to leave in May to spend the summer in the Hoggar. Brother Charles replied that he could not leave Béni-Abbès before fall. But, on April 15, 1905, he wrote in his diary:

I am perplexed. . . . The Oasis and the Touaregs have no priest and no priest can go there; not only am I permitted to go, but I have been invited; the most backward and forsaken of countries is without a priest and I have been asked to go; I alone could go there, and I refuse! . . . A great expanse of land without prayers and Masses and there is no one to offer the Holy Sacrifice except me, alone, who has not only been given permission but who has been asked. . . . Is it truly the will of Jesus to have me refuse? . . .

He wrote to Monseigneur Guérin and Abbé Huvelin. With the advice of Abbé Huvelin, Monseigneur Guérin sent Brother Charles a dispatch urging him to go. Brother Charles received it on Good Friday. A choice had to be made; he could not hesitate; it was the command of Jesus, and he must obey. He quickly wrote to Laperrine to find out whether it was still possible for him to leave. On May 3rd Laperrine answered in the affirmative, and Brother Charles left at once for Adrar. The caravan was composed of several French government officials, including M. Étiennot, Inspector of Post Office, Telephone, and Telegraph.

11.

According to the Circumstances

En route to the Touaregs, Brother Charles thought about the future, and he wrote to Abbé Huvelin of what he envisaged. He planned to divide his time between Tamanrasset and Béni-Abbès. He was guided by God, God who so often showed His will by events. "This life of Nazareth will be led according to the circumstances; at Béni-Abbès, with the Touaregs or somewhere else . . . the circumstances will show the way."

He wrote the letter at Akabli on May 18th. From then on he placed his life in the hands of the Father; he looked constantly toward Jesus and followed His life from day to day. He did not wish to use the Rule as if it were a directory. "The life of Nazareth can be followed anywhere; follow it in the place where it is most helpful to your neighbors. It is the call of the neighbor that is the law that should be established among men in command."

On May 30, 1905, Charles joined the Dinaux caravan, as arranged with Laperrine. Later, Dinaux wrote:

> It is the end of the calvary suffered by Father de Foucauld since the departure from Adrar. I have had immediate echos. The high official from the post office, filled with his own importance, red-faced and fat, could feel only contempt for the poor emaciated hermit who followed wearily, pulling his camel by the bridle, and who isolated himself from the camp at night in order to meditate and who ate only dried dates and roasted barley. . . . He called him "Brother Charles," and he spared him no sarcasm; the camp was often astonished at the lewd songs he and his assistant sang as they opened their food and flasks of absinthe.

Dervil, another witness, told what happened in June, while the caravan was traveling:

> Just before we got to In Ziz, a sandstorm brought the temperature to 55 degrees centigrade in the shade for four days. It was impossible to see six feet in front of you and we had to find water. What a hideous thirst! I had never been so certain that I was watching death approach. The fat official, wild with fear, kept away from us. Father de Foucauld's goatskins held the last drops of water that he had been saving for a sickness or an emergency, as had occurred before. He offered it to Monsieur E. who gulped it down and then said, "Pooh, it smells of tar. . . ." "Thank you!" the father replied simply.
>
> Some days later, the official was idly roaming around the camp while everyone else was tending to his own business. He approached the tent of the father, who was poring over his manuscripts. "Well, Brother Charles," he said in a sarcastic voice, "still silent. . . ."

Father de Foucauld raised his bespectacled eyes and said softly, "That's because I have a horror of windbags, Monsieur! . . ." The camp went up in laughter!

In the Dinaux company there was a man named E. F. Gauthier, an explorer and geographer who wanted to go to Gao, and also a writer named Pierre Mille, who had this to say about Brother Charles: "His extraordinary passion for the desert made us laugh a little. With the carefreeness of youth, we said among ourselves that he was like someone who still found the streetcars too close by."

On June 5th Brother Charles found Aziouël "completely changed in a year, more hopeful." The journey continued. "I see many Touaregs, and I am happy; they are more friendly, more trustworthy than a year ago." He rejoiced to see the officers so close to the natives. "The journey is peaceful, the officers are amicable; furthermore, the relations with the natives are excellent, and for that I rejoice," he wrote on June 16th to his cousin.

Dinaux described his side of the trip:

If this stage was especially painful, he did not forget to cover the camp, visiting the French officers and men in their sleeping bags, giving out occasional quinine tablets, drops of Mass wine, and comforting words. Nor did he fail to learn from the meharists [camel riders] about the natives who needed care. He was loved by everyone. After two hours of marching in the morning, everyone would mount. But the father would continue on foot to the point of exhaustion, saying his Rosary and reciting prayers; he pushed himself to keep up the pace in the most difficult terrain. Beginning at 5:00 A.M., the sun beat down and the temperature in the shade varied from 40 to 50 degrees centigrade; we each drank from two to two and one-half gallons of water a day, and what water! Often it tasted of magnesium, when it had not been drawn from pools where herds had been wading. And always the Father, walking quickly, followed behind until a storm blew up or until one of us said, "Father, if you don't mount, I will dismount and walk with you," and then he would give in, smile, and talk of various things until the next stage.

On June 25th Brother Charles wrote in his notebook, "To be a friend of everyone, good or bad, is to be a universal brother." That day the French officers and the Arab meharists * expected the arrival of Moussa at any moment. What would he have decided? Suddenly there were troops on the horizon. It was Moussa and the principal members of the Kel Rela; they advanced calmly, and exchanged solemn salutations. Little by little, the atmosphere became more friendly. There between the officers and the Touaregs, Brother Charles asked Moussa for hospitality. Dinaux says:

It was June 15th, 1905, at the wells of In Ouzel, that Moussa Ag Amastane presented himself to me, made honorable amends for his attitude for the past two years, and accepted, in the name of all adherents to peace, the principles of absolute submission and of payment of taxes. He made an excellent impression, which was confirmed during the days that followed. From then on, I no longer considered Father de Foucauld's project to settle in the Hoggar as foolish fancy. . . . I presented him to Moussa as a "marabout who served God alone," passionate about solitude, eager to study the language of Kel Ahaggar, ready to render great service to the people, and capable of giving him useful advice. During numerous meetings, we finally chose Tamanrasset as a place for the father to live.

The Amenokal † accompanied us for two weeks, which gave Brother Charles the chance to know him better and to find him "a very intelligent, very open, very pious Moslem who, as a liberal Moslem, wished for good."

Dinaux tells how Brother Charles, placed in the middle of a group mixed with French and Touaregs, lived at that time:

Following the contact with Moussa Ag Amastane and the notables of the Kel Rela, there were a series of conferences on France's politics, the benefits of peace, the question of taxation, the cessation of vandalism, the Amenokal's role in governing, and so on. . . . Father de Foucauld never missed a meeting. Squatting at

* Native camel-mounted troops.
† Chief, the rank of Moussa.

my feet, wishing to be humble and refusing even a camp stool, he followed the exchange with great interest, in that way perfecting his knowledge of Tamahaq, the dialect of the Touaregs, and showing his good will to the people around him. When the encampments were close enough, accompanied by an interpreter, he would distribute medicine and useful objects to the tribe.

Brother Charles wrote to his brother-in-law:

I have not written to you for a long time; I have little time. Most days we are on the march and the marches are often long. When we get to a stopping place, one would like to write, read, or work; but usually we have to rest in order to have strength for the next day's march. Also, the natives have a right to my time, and it is my duty to study the language in order to make the work easier for those who follow me.

On July 10th Moussa left the company and went back to his life as a nomad. Brother Charles continued toward the South, dividing his time between "relations with the natives" and "putting together a small Touareg dictionary and an elementary grammar."

On August 6th they began to approach the center of the Hoggar:

I will stay for several months, maybe longer, in this region at the town of Tamanrasset. I tried to settle here last year, without success; this year, it seems that I may make it; I think I must take advantage of this possibility and not let this half-opened door close. In all probability I will be here for summer, fall, winter, and maybe longer; I have no definite plan.

This is what he wanted to do at Tamanrasset:

I will quickly build a hut and live meagerly. I will live a retiring life with the Holy Sacrament which, if luck is with me, I will have in a small Tabernacle. Here I will be, until a new order comes, trying to imitate the Divine Worker of Nazareth. . . . I am trying to make each moment better, without specific projects. . . . Pray for me that I will be faithful to God who has put me among these people who, until now, have been so far from us. Pray that good comes from it and that the reign of the Heart of Jesus has begun.

12.

In the Heart of the Hoggar

Brother Charles, as he met officers and soldiers, chiefs and semi-slave laborers, looked then as he would look for the rest of his life. Devril, who had lived close to him at Béni-Abbès and who had been along on the Laperrine expedition, wrote:

I can still see him as he appeared to me then—his head covered with a sort of white linen cap with a neck covering, wearing a *gandourah* [Arab robe] with a bleeding Sacred Heart, and a large beaded rosary hanging from his waist. Thin from the privations of the life in the Sahara, he had much resistance and was trained in the hard school of the *bled*. From his emaciated face, framed with a spotty, short beard, his eyes shone with profound intensity, showing both gentleness and firmness. Seldom loquacious, willingly lost in his own thoughts, he was rarely animated. He had little to say about his past life in Morocco or France. He was neither morose nor haughty, and he often laughed at the jokes of Laperrine. . . . During the long trips, the three or four Frenchmen pooled their food and ate together: balls of minced meat fried in oil, rice, game, and tar-flavored water was their menu. Each one had his own mug and chipped plate, and they squatted on the ground and talked of the Sahara, Touaregs, maps, and so on. The father ate well, in silence. When arguments began, he would let them rage to a point, then put a finish to them with one word that would calm everyone. . . . While digging a well in the Hoggar, I thought I had discovered a vein of gold. Triumphantly, I brought back samples. All that glitters is not gold! . . . I was wrong. But the father said, "That would have been a true catastrophe for me. If gold were discovered in the Sahara . . . where else in the world would there be for me to hide! . . ." He went on foot as long as possible and mounted his camel only when fatigue and heat forced him to. One afternoon, a scorpion, hidden in the packsaddle, stung him on the middle finger of his right hand. I quickly gave him a massive injection of permanganate. Of bad quality or rusted, the needle broke in the joint. Despite the pain, Charles de Foucauld simply said, "There is nothing to do but try again! . . ." His hand and arm became enormous. He began to run a fever, and we were afraid of phlegm. Without a single complaint, and under a sky of molten lead, he persisted in walking in mortification. At the stop, he installed himself in his little tent and took his notes on the Touaregs whom he had met, and worked on his Tamashek-French dictionary. . . . For several months, I lived in the company of a saint without realizing it. It is only now, in reliving my memories, that I can see the true proportions of his character—a character so perfect that its perfection didn't show and didn't disturb his entourage.

"That is where I want to live," he said, when he saw Tamanrasset. We left him on the threshold of his little hermitage of mud-mortar and thatch—alone with his piety, his goodness, and the silence! The silhouette of him with a few sacks of dates and flour and a few cans of milk was gradually obliterated by the glaring light.

On August 11th Brother Charles wrote in his notebook:

I choose Tamanrasset, a village of twenty hearths, high in the mountains in the heart of the Hoggar and of the Dag-Rali, the principal tribe, away from all the important centers. It seems that there will never be a garrison, telegraph, or even Europeans. Nor will there be a mission for some time to come. I choose this abandoned spot and I will establish myself here, praying to Jesus to bless the establishment, and taking as my only example the life of Nazareth.

The mission having arrived at Tamanrasset on August 13th, Brother Charles wrote to his cousin, "I will stay here, the only European; the authorities are convinced that there is no danger." On the 26th: "I am here not with Laperrine, but under his command, and I will see him from time to time, once a year. He is a fine friend. We keep in constant touch by letter—as constant as is possible here. . . . The detachment with which I came will stay on here for a few days . . . then I will be alone and very happy to be alone with Jesus, alone for Jesus."

Installed in his tiny Hermitage, his hut, as he was at Béni-Abbès, he continued his work on the Touareg language. Manual labor was replaced by his work on the dictionary. It was very difficult for him, as his eyes grew weaker day by day, and he was obliged to wear glasses. "I even have to wear glasses to write letters, and I will have to have them changed now and again."

Like Béni-Abbès, the brotherhood was in the heart of the country, but apart. Although there were only about sixty inhabitants at Tamanrasset, many people passed through. "I congratulate myself for being in this country and this particular spot," he wrote on September 16th:

There are few inhabitants—twenty poor huts scattered over almost two miles, but there are many nomads in the vicinity. It's the heart of the strongest nomadic tribe of the country. The nomads and the residents have already got in the habit of coming to me to ask for needles and medicines, and the poor occasionally ask for a bit of grain. I am overburdened with work in my effort to finish the Touareg-French and the French-Touareg dictionary quickly. It is going slowly because I am constantly obliged to stop work to see the natives or to attend to something. Much as I would like to, I work very little with my hands. I am a monk, but at the same time I am a priest, sacristan, and missionary. And at the moment, it is vital that I work out the basic elements for learning the language of the people. I am eager to finish this work of writing so that I can take up the tools of Jesus and Joseph.

13.

General Interest

When Moussa Ag Amastane and Brother Charles met again, they formed a close friendship. On October 23, 1906, Brother Charles wrote in his notebook:

Moussa has asked my advice about what he should tell the Colonel [Laperrine] on Sunday about his trip to Adrar. Jesus, inspire my answer. Guide me. . . . The more perfect one is, the more one puts general interest before individual interest (Rule of St. Augustine). Moussa must not, then, consider his special interest but only the general interest. Whose interest? First, of the Kel Ahaggar and, second, the other Imouhar.

Brother Charles drew up long pages of advice for Moussa. First, he wanted Moussa to understand something of the will of God. To do that, the mind should be developed. "Science increases the power of the mind, and we better understand the will of God when our minds are more developed." He concluded his first point:

Ways to help the understanding of the will of God and to develop the mind: (1) *Teaching of children,* boys and girls, and it is important to teach girls because of the influence women have in the family (by bringing men and women teachers here); (2) *Adult education* (by friendly relations in their own country with men and women who are capable of teaching truths; by traveling to Algeria, France, Mecca; by learning French and Arabic to make their travels easier; by the development of commerce, agriculture, industry which will establish relations with outside peoples and which will require a knowledge of foreign languages and which will develop learning in all branches; (3) *Prayers of the saintly* fervently asking God that the Touaregs can better know His will.

137

Brother Charles did not stop with general principles. He gave precise, concrete advice. He gave advice on education, family life, work, on the development of outside relations, on justice, external peace, and peace at home. On the subject of work, for example, he wrote:

To honor work—contests with annual prizes should be held for the best livestock and the best products from industry and agriculture;

—honor, favors, and preferential treatment should go to those who work and who help create work and those who honor it;

—gardens and model works should be established in the Hoggar by Moussa with the help of the Government.

To establish justice and peace in the Hoggar, he proclaimed: "Honor, favors, and authority should be used to the advantage of, and should be given only to, men of intelligence and virtue. . . . Only merit counts. Nothing else should be considered."

His precise counsel is followed by varied observations:

The best way to win the affection of the colonel is for one to open one's heart to him as if he were a brother, as if he were the person in the world one loves the best and has the most confidence in.

Truly, whether among Moslems or Christians, there is no friend who is truer, surer, better, or more objective than the colonel. He can have full confidence in him. . . .

May Moussa be assured that he has no better friend among the French—or among any people—than myself and the colonel, myself because I love him as God has ordered me to love him and the colonel who loves him because he is good.

That Moussa asks for nothing out of his own special interest.

The more open, friendly, and willing Moussa is, the more open, friendly, respectful, and willing the Hoggar will be, and then everything will roll along better with Moussa and the Hoggar; one should go less to the Hoggar and intervene less, leaving more in the hands of Moussa.

Let Moussa not ask the *Hakem* [soldiers] to come to the

Hoggar. It would gain nothing, and the request would be displeasing and would have a diametrically opposite effect. Contrary to that, if he would ask to send some French people to the Hoggar—a doctor, several families to teach farming, weaving, caring for the sick women—he should beg that, whether Hakem or other French, only *very, very, very good* people who could help strengthen the friendship of the Touaregs for us be sent. . . .

If the colonel wishes, and if my sheikh [religious chief] advises it, and if Moussa wishes, I could offer, as a private individual, to take Moussa and one companion to France where he could spend one or two months with my sister and my friends, providing I don't have to have anything to do with the Government: the Marabout is *dead* to the world and lives only for God and His will. . . .

The three most essential things to the development of the people of the Hoggar are: *education, habit of working,* and the *family* unit.

After a relationship of several months, this is Brother Charles's appraisal of Moussa, the young chief who was then thirty-five years old.

He is a very intelligent man, full of good intentions, who is searching for the good of the Moslems and of the Touareg; with great spirit, he is devoting his life to creating peace among the Touaregs, to protecting the weak from the violence of the strong. From that, along with his generosity, his piety, his affability, and his courage, he is acquiring a universal worship from In Salah to Timbuktu; the good that he does, his work for peace and justice, extends beyond the Hoggar to the neighboring tribes. . . . his moderation, his spirit of peace, his constant protection of the poor and oppressed from injustices are remarkable. His is an open mind, wise and moderate; if God lets him live, his influence will be great and lasting. . . . My relations with him are excellent. I did not see him last year; this year I haven't been without him for almost four months now. He is here at the moment. He has no residence. He is a nomad, as are all of his compatriots. . . . It seems to me that he has enough true pity to let the general good come before any other interests and that he has enough intelligence to enable him to correct the bad and the false he has in his ideas and in his heart.

That letter is extremely interesting because it shows what an enormous respect Brother Charles had for human virtues. One can see from it that Brother Charles relied on man's own natural qualities to open his mind and his heart. He believed in the natural riches of the men whom he met. He was not an ascetic who thought only of penance and abstinence. His abnegation did not signify an escape from life, or the stifling of life. He wished to be small, to enter into human existence. He wanted to live with the most forsaken to give them hope and faith in their destiny.

Brother Charles expressed this confidence in life in his notebook on October 23rd:

> The more one knows, the more one loves; the more one loves, the more faithfully one performs . . . all science strengthens the power of the mind, and the better developed our minds, the better we will understand the will of God . . . science makes possible not only the Law of God but of all things. The first thing that is absolutely necessary for the Touaregs is that they grow and that they learn of the Law of God and that they develop their minds.

The "universal brother" wanted progress for all mankind. At Tamanrasset, he was especially concerned with the Touaregs. There with Moussa—in front of the Moslem—he wore his *gandourah* and on it the Heart and the Cross of Christ. It was in the name of Christ and out of his love for Christ that Brother Charles was there. For Moussa, Brother Charles was a man of God, a man who prayed and man who *lived* hospitality. For Moussa, Brother Charles was a servant of Jesus.

Brother Charles spoke to Moussa passionately of God and of the adoration that one must give him. He showed Jesus, too, but silently, Jesus of the Gospel whom he loved and who is his God but whom Moussa sees only as a prophet. Realizing what Brother Charles was, Moussa welcomed him, the servant of Jesus, the universal brother. Not only did he welcome him; he—a fervent Moslem —asked the Christian Marabout to become his spiritual guide.

Brother Charles had great respect for the evolution of Moussa's heart, and of all the Touaregs whom he met. In his conversation, he adhered to a plan of the natural evolvement of religion:

You want to know what I can do for the natives. If we started speaking to them about Our Lord, they would surely flee. We must first get their confidence, make friends with them, do small things for them, give them good advice; out of friendship with them, we can discreetly get them to follow *the natural religion,* proving to them that Christians love them.

14.
"Follies, War, and Insane Contradictions"

The Touaregs accepted Brother Charles for what he really was. On October 26th he wrote to Monseigneur Livinhac: "Last year I tried on several occasions to settle in the Hoggar without success. The natives were suspicious and thought I was a government spy. This year I tried again, and from the first moment I have succeeded without the slightest difficulty."

Brother Charles had a number of projects planned for Moussa and the Touaregs. To accomplish them, he thought, would require imagination. On October 26, 1905, he wrote to Monseigneur Guérin and asked him for advice about a trip he planned to take with Moussa to France (telling him that he had also written to Laperrine on the subject):

"It would be good for the spirit of Moussa Ag Amastane and

for the spirit of his people, I think, if he lived with a French family for a few days and made friends with them."

He had, of course, spoken to Moussa of this:

I proposed this to him this afternoon, and he was pleased. I made the condition that, if I send him on this trip, he is to go as a private individual, as a brother traveling for his pleasure with his brother, and not see the Hakem of Algeria or of France, with whom I have nothing in common. If you think it is the will of Jesus that I make this trip, would you consult with Monsieur Huvelin and send me his opinion as well as yours?

But, having recognized Brother Charles as a man of God, Monseigneur Guérin wanted to leave the decision to him, and on November 30, 1905, he wrote to Brother Charles that he did not wish to give him any advice at the moment:

I put my confidence in the Divine Traveling Companion to whom you have entrusted yourself. He is the Master; you are his *sokhar;* it pleases Him to visit His domain with you and to bless His poor, unknown, and unsuspecting children. It has pleased Him to spend the winter at Tamanrasset. Perhaps as a good nomad who loves travel and change (if, in all respect, we can so speak of Him) in the spring or summer He will wish to put His encampment in another place. I don't know, I don't try to know—you don't have to ask yourself this now—certainly, when He feels that the time is right, He will show His wishes. With all my soul, I ask of Him but one thing, and that is, remaining true to His daily blessing, that you will be able to spread around you His presence and His name.

On November 30, 1905, Brother Charles wrote to Monseigneur Guérin of still another project:

Every day I think of the White Sisters and of the good they could do here. If they could found an almshouse (native style —huts made of rushes), it would soon be full. There are many black slaves. As they get old, their masters free them and they are completely without resources, with no husbands and no families, and they live among the goats. As long as they are able to work, the slaves of both sexes watch the flocks and pair off like their animals. The children don't know who their fathers are and they soon forget their mothers. You can see the misery . . . one must have patience, great patience . . . it will be a long time before the seed germinates. Patience must be used with the widest and surest ways, even though they are slow. One must be patient and work with all one's energy despite failure, obstacles, contradictions, and uncertainty. At the same time one is patient, one should make the greatest possible effort with the means one has and one should create new methods for that which is lacking.

Laperrine wrote to one of his friends:

General Lyautey finds that I am too occupied with the Touaregs and has asked that I be removed; he never answered my personal letters, and he spent three days with Gautier (*Herr Professor,* at the Hôtel de l'Oasis), talking on the following theme: he adores me, he likes me very much, he finds me perfect, but he wants to hear no more of me as his subordinate and he declares that he has dropped me. *Alors?* One would have to be Bourget * himself to understand people like that who are so complex.

Brother Charles was working in another direction. He persisted in increasing his knowledge of the language of the country. In December, 1905, he wrote to Motylinski, an old friend and director of the Constantine Médéria, "to spark his interest in the Touareg." He wanted Motylinski, who was an excellent interpreter and linguist, to work on the Touareg language. "He is better able than I to compile a good dictionary and grammar."

Brother Charles, in summing up his first weeks at Tamanrasset, gave priority to two tasks. On October 26, 1905, he wrote to Monseigneur Livinhac:

It seems to me that the two most urgent and necessary things to be done in the Hoggar are education and the reconstitution of the family. They are so ignorant that they are incapable of knowing

---

* Paul Bourget, fashionable novelist of the turn of the century.

the difference between what is true and what is false and the slipping away of family life—followed by immorality and many divorces—leaves the children to grow up like animals and with no education.

On April 3, 1906, he wrote to his cousin Louis de Foucauld:

Our civilized nations—who have people who are just as savage, just as ignorant of elementary truths, and just as violent as the Touaregs—are guilty of great wrong in not bringing light, in not spreading good and in not bringing learning to countries that are so backward. That should be so easy, but we consume ourselves, instead, in follies, war, and insane contradictions.

On December 30, 1905, he gave Father Voillard a clear picture of the material, moral, and religious state of the Hoggar, and he explained his viewpoint on his apostolic studies:

To sell cretonne or blue cotton at reasonable prices is one good, simple way to get people to come to us; . . . those who sell should be good people so that a good impression is made, to have good friends in a country is the beginning. . . . If, lacking something better, you could find a few good souls to do this business, who would work in obscurity for the love of God—what a good thing that would be! . . . Small businessmen from France who are honest would be welcomed by the authorities who are embarrassed by their compatriots in the South; there is no Frenchman in the Oasis who is not there to deal in alcohol—it is disgraceful. What we want is Christians like Priscilla and Aquila who quietly do good while living the lives of poor merchants; . . . they would be respected and loved by all. If only you could send us a few merchants like that! They would earn their living without difficulty and the authorities would receive them with open arms; if only you can find them.

And he told him of the situation as he saw it:

The Hoggar seems to have 1,000 to 1,200 Touareg families, totaling perhaps 5,000 to 7,000 people; to that, you can add 3,000 to 4,000 *haratins* or slaves. . . .

The slaves are in a good material position. They are well treated and they have much liberty. But they are in a bad state morally. They are so free that they live like the animals they tend, with no thought of establishing a family. They mate like animals and they are violent and ill-tempered.

The Touaregs stay apart from us, following their centuries-old prejudices that will need time in order to disappear. Still, they are more naturally open than the Arabs; gay, curious, without a closed family, they become quite familiar as soon as the first ice is broken. They are closer to us than the Arabs with their harems. However the ice is difficult enough to break because they have heard many bad things about us; the *Ikoufar* (the pagans), they call us; we have to go to them, for they will not come to us. But once we have met, good relations are quickly established and they are with the entire family.

They are so ignorant that they are at the mercy of anyone who talks to them. They are incapable of distinguishing true from false. Without education, it would take nothing less than a miracle to lift them out of their present state.

Theirs is a patriarchal life, like all nomads, and certain family ties are very strong. But frequent divorce eats away at the family structure. One can come and go with equal ease; these idle people love pleasure. There follows a great instability in their unions, and this is the true plague.

Pure nomads, they have their land—a lot of it, but they could use more—cultivated by *haratins* and their flocks tended by slaves, and they themselves have nothing to do in the way of work except to keep an eye on their flocks and to move about a bit as nomads do. The women make goatskin bottles, weave, and work in leather . . . men and women alike work very little, having little regard for work.

Everyone has equal need for education; work is scorned by the nobles; the tribes of Israel (free but of inferior condition) are better workers.

On January 15, 1906—the 15th of January was the anniversary of his departure from Paris for the Trappists in 1890—he wrote:

January 15th has become, for me, a day of retreat when I look at the past and the future—a day of resolutions. My resolution today is to work with all my energy on the dictionary, grammar, and translation of the Holy Bible, the purpose of which is to make easier the work of those who follow me as the Father of this family. Then I must make several visits to the villages and encampments to see those who do not come often enough to see me. Then I will accept the long trips into the Sahara that have been proposed to me again this year, which I will make in the company of officers. It is the best way to see the natives better. I will do as I think best, but I think this year will again be a year of travel.

It would be a mistake to think that the relations with the Touaregs were easily established. Two months later, Brother Charles said; "In winter, the Touaregs, cold and badly dressed, move about very little. They are not in a great hurry to visit me. The ice must be broken, and it will be in time."

The Touaregs, whom he had around him, were handsome. The "pure" nobles were tall and broad-shouldered. It was not unusual for them to be nearly six feet tall, and their faces were very aristocratic. However, their faces were often hidden with a veil called a *litham,* which was a strip of very expensive fabric made in Nigeria. Only the men wore it. As a protection from the wind and the sand and the sun, the *litham* was practical, but it was also romantic and it served as a mask that frightened people during raids. It also had a mystical purpose—to protect the wearer from evil spirits that might otherwise enter his nose and mouth.

The men of the desert hated sleeping under a roof. Not too far from water, they would pitch their tents, build *zéribas* from branches and reeds, and put their animals to pasture. They would stay in one spot until the wells were dry and the pasture eaten. During these weeks, they did nothing. The women put up the tents and carried the water. The slaves took care of the animals and gathered the wood. Well-born nomads were forbidden by tradition to work. It is easy to see that Brother Charles, who lived on the level with the poor and who wanted to work, would pose a problem to them.

The princes of the desert put the women in a very special place and gave them a principal role. According to legend, the Touaregs were descended from Princess Tin Hinan, whose mausoleum on the banks of the Balessa River was the true capital of the country. It was the women who produced the sons. A child did not belong to the tribe or to his father's class. He was the child of his mother, and, according to her, he would be a noble or a vassal. If the woman was not officially in command, although she could hold power, she had the same rights as a man and was the superior. It was the woman who possessed the traditions of her people. She was well read and cultivated. She wrote in *tifiner*, the ancient written language of the Berbers. She was the source for poems, songs, and legends. She inspired them and she wrote them. At the *Ahals*, courts of love where the women reigned, Love and Death were portrayed in curious literary jousting.

Brother Charles soon saw that women held a primordial position in the Sahara. On April 20, 1906, he wrote to Madame de Bondy:

> Would it be possible for you to find me some "lay" nuns—lay in costume only, for all their hearts must be with Jesus. They would have to be full of devotion to Jesus and for Jesus to come so far . . . without their religious habit, but with the work, the truth, and the spirit of a religious life, complete and lost in God? For ardent spirits, this should be tempting.

The social classes were very precise. At the top were the aristocrats, nobles, recognized by everyone. Under them came the Marabouts. Next, in third place, were the vassals, the Imrad. The Imrads were a mixture and were more privileged than the artisans or the slaves (for both the Marabouts and the vassals could own slaves). Most of the slaves were blacks who had been taken captive. The Touareg nobleman was a nomad. The *haratins*, when they were not slaves of the Touaregs, were sharecroppers who got four-fifths of the crops. These sharecroppers had no way to defend themselves except by dissimulation and marauding. They had the cowed attitude of the slaves. People have spoken of the "merciless feeding by the beasts of the desert on the Sahara's few green spots."

Brother Charles wrote,

Their character is very different from that of the Arabs. It is gayer, less fanatic, and less believing, even though they are Moslems in name and faith. They are ignorant of their religion and are concerned only with the easy work of their nomadic life, which is simplified to a degree unknown among our Arabs, and with their pleasures. There aren't many Marabouts, and those that are here are of the Arab race and come from other places—some from Kounts in the Sudan, others from Tidikelt. Most of them are reduced to the role of secretaries to the big chiefs. The Touaregs who have had no relations with the Christians are very defiant and touchy owing to the lies they have heard about us since their infancy and which have been repeated to them and amplified by the Marabouts. As soon as they enter into relations with us, they see that they are wrong, and they become more open.

Brother Charles did not hold the Marabouts in very high esteem. The *cheurfa* were rich and lazy. They owned all of the land, but they didn't work it. They passed a lazy life smoking kef and drinking tea. So he looked more to the *haratins*. "Berbers mixed more or less with the Sudanese—poor, dying of starvation, enslaved by the *cheurfa,* possessing nothing, working until they are literally nothing but skin and bones to till the soil for the whites. . . . The missionaries meet much antipathy from the rich *cheurfa*. But it seems certain that they would soon have the sympathies of the poor *haratins,* who make up the majority of the population."

Brother Charles pinned his hopes of evangelization on the *haratins* and Touaregs. "It seems certain that there is more hope for the harvesting of souls with the Touaregs and *haratins*."

Brother Charles had made a choice. In 1881, when Flatters went south, he led ten Europeans and seventy-eight natives across the dunes. These natives were from the Chamba and were traditionally hostile to the Touaregs. The Chambas had actually meant their ambush for the Touaregs who were with the French. In 1902, Lieutenant Cottenest, with the Chambas, crushed the strong fortress of the Hoggar in just a few weeks. In the following years Laperrine, working to establish peace, formed the famous company of meharists, which was made up largely of the Chambas commanded by young officers. These events remained fresh in people's memories. Brother Charles, alone at Tamanrasset, was the friend of Laperrine and the Chambas who were with him. At the same time—and it seemed a sort of gamble—he was a friend of Moussa and of the Touareg princes. But he was first a brother of the poor, of the *haratins,* and it was with them that he shared his life.

What Flatters had tried to do with arms, Brother Charles accomplished alone and poor. A Universal Brother, he held his arms open, and his heart was full of all of the problems of the contrasting lives of the men of the Sahara.

15.

Preliminary Work

Was Brother Charles's main purpose to convert the Touaregs? Or did he wish only to learn their language? One should not separate things that Brother Charles did not wish to separate. He wanted the Touaregs to keep their language, their customs, their way of life. At the same time, he wanted to introduce Christ to them. His love for the Touaregs made him want to develop the good that was in them, to preserve their personalities, and to work to know them thoroughly. His love for them demanded that they be shown the person of the Lord God, Jesus Christ.

In order to present the Gospel, Brother Charles saw that he must have an orderly, progressive plan:

To prepare a translation of the Gospel into Tamahaq. This translation would first have to be read to them. There is no reason to teach Arabic to the Touaregs; that would bring them closer to the

Koran, and we would rather guide them away from that. It is better that they learn Tamahaq. It is an excellent language and easy to learn. We should start with words that are indispensable to explain religious ideas, Christian virtues. And we should improve the written language, without changing anything . . . we must read them the passages which touch on natural religion, or on morality, such as the parable of the Prodigal Son, or of the Good Samaritan, or of the Last Judgment, or of Jesus, as a shepherd. . . .

In January, Brother Charles had good news:

I may have with me all summer, from mid-April until the end of October, my good friend Motylinski, who once came to see me in Paris. He was once a military interpreter, one of the most knowledgeable men in Algeria. He has asked to study Touareg with me. Pray a little for him. It will be a great sacrifice for him to leave his wife and children for eight months.

Motylinski had worked as a military interpreter during the campaign against Bou Amama. A Professor of Arabic and of Berber, like Brother Charles, he was attracted to the Touaregs. It was a great joy to Brother Charles to think that, thanks to Motylinski, the Touaregs would be better known, understood, and loved.

Motylinski arrived on June 3rd, Pentecost. Six days later, Brother Charles wrote, "Motylinski's being here is a good thing. His goodness, his gentleness, and his knowledge of the natives make them love him."

During the summer of 1906, Brother Charles felt very tired. He thought he was nearing the end of his life. Looking back on his past, he thought he had been weak and useless. "I go along without getting anywhere or producing anything." He felt that he was not being sufficiently obedient to Jesus, who had asked him to give his life to the Touaregs: "Love is not just in saying, 'Lord, Lord,' nor is it in having rapture through prayer (they are blessings, and not love). Love is obedience, obedience at all costs. 'He who loves Me, obeys Me.'"

On June 25th he wrote to his cousin about his future, "I think of the workers whom the Father will send into the fields and of this preliminary work that is necessary for them." He was tired, but quiet and full of hope:

> Confidence in the love and power of the Good Shepherd who, though he has given liberty to the poor blind sheep, is the Master who can call them back at any moment. . . . Let us pray and offer daily sufferings for that. . . . I have no sufferings; I am not worthy of them; not able to bear them. "God protects the shorn lamb from the wind." No doubt the absence of sufferings and the moving away from them is permanent. But that is made better by the thought that the will of Jesus is being done.

In the same letter, dated July 15th, he told his cousin that all his days were spent studying the Touareg language with Motylinski. He said that Motylinski worked "for knowledge." Brother Charles worked for knowledge and for Jesus:

> St. Paul has taught us that hope is charity. We must hope, work, and pray while improving ourselves. . . . When one loves, one gives without measure and does all that one can do. Also, at all times, we owe ourselves equally to Jesus. If there is one thing that could make us be and do more perfectly that which He wishes, and to convert ourselves fully, that would be to convert the souls of my brothers.

At the beginning of August, Brother Charles and Motylinski started for a trip north. They wanted to meet nomadic tribes on the way, and Brother Charles wanted to see Monseigneur Guérin. He had almost abandoned his dream of founding a congregation of paupers, and now he hoped that he could have one companion with him. That was all that he would ask for then—one companion!

He wrote on December 3, 1905:

> What I am looking for at the moment is not a swarm of souls to enter into the framework of a fixed life following a kind of existence that is planned. . . . No, at present I look for a person of good will who would share my life in poverty and obscurity with no fixed rules. He would follow his interests as I follow mine. I

ask only three things: profound and absolute good will and a
desire to be one with Jesus—joyful acceptance of extreme poverty,
dangers, humiliations, fatigue—willingness to follow my advice,
not for interior things, but for exterior relations with the world
(in order to do good instead of bad, one needs to have had much
experience in these surroundings).

A young Breton who was in Algiers had answered the appeal of
Brother Charles and wished to join him. On October 7th Brother
Charles and Motylinski arrived at El-Goléa, and separated. Motylinski went toward Constantine, where he lived (and where he died a
few months later, in March of 1907, of typhus). On November 7th
Brother Charles arrived at Béni-Abbès, where he had established
himself five years earlier. He was very happy. "In coming here, during the last days of the trip, the natives welcomed me and showed,
despite my long absence, that they remembered me and had confidence in me. I myself don't exist. It is the Marabout, as they call
me, the Christian priest, they know."

On December 1, 1906, Brother Charles was at Maison Carrée.
Brother Michel had decided to follow him. With Monseigneur
Guérin, Brother Charles decided that he should divide his time
between Béni-Abbès and Tamanrasset—summer at Tamanrasset and
winter at Béni-Abbès. . . . On that date, December 1, 1906, Brother
Charles had exactly ten years to live.

On December 10th Brother Charles and Brother Michel left
Maison Carrée for Béni-Abbès. Between Colom-Béchar and Béni-
Abbès, they were, according to Brother Michel, escorted across the
desert "by five or six native troops commanded by a sergeant. The
soldiers always walked a few steps ahead of us, carefully searching
all the bushes and indentations of the land to see that no caravan
looters were hiding for us. After three days and no incidents, we
finally arrived at Béni-Abbès, where the father had established what
he called his first Hermitage, and there we were supposed to rest
for a few days."

Brother Charles wanted to stay at Béni-Abbès for the Christmas
holidays so that the entire garrison could be present at Mass on that
day.

On December 27th Brother Charles and Brother Michel started out for the Hoggar. "After an exchange of good wishes and warm handshakes, the officers left us with two native soldiers for our protection. At the moment of parting the father gave the key to his Hermitage to the captain, and said: 'Take good care of the House of God. I entrust it to you.' "

On January 4th en route, Brother Charles met Laperrine. Brother Charles had never broken with his past, with the officers of his country. At the same time, their friendship did not stand in his way when he wanted to go and share profoundly the lives of men whom he considered free, men whom he considered as brothers: the people of the Sahara. He asked for prayers that he would truly be the "Universal Brother" amid the Touaregs:

> Pray for me that I will be what I must be for the Touaregs to whom I return so that a little good will be done among the souls for whom Our Saviour died. . . . This Africa, this Algeria with its millions of infidels, Moslems, calls for holiness which alone can obtain their conversion.
>
> Pray for me that I may convert and sanctify myself and that the other priests—so few in number, alas—may do the same. May they receive the Good News at last and may the last to arrive present themselves at the Manger to adore Jesus in their turn.

On February 9th they reached In Salah, where they spent a month continuing their studies of the Touareg language and where Brother Charles had found an excellent tutor, Ben Messis. He settled in In Salah in his usual way, buying a house and making it into a small chapel "right in the native quarter, that is to say within the reach of the poor and of the entire Moslem population."

Brother Michel fell sick. A strong young Breton of twenty-three, he was unable to stand the hardships of Brother Charles's way of life, and returned to Algiers. Looking back at this period of his life, Brother Michel later sketched a portrait of Brother Charles:

> To be entirely truthful, I must mention one imperfection common enough among men who have long exercised authority. Every so often, when things didn't go his way, he would become im-

patient—although he would immediately repress this mood. . . . He loved Jesus Christ, his God, his Brother, his Friend, passionately. He wanted to give Jesus Christ the greatest proof of affection and devotion that a friend can give by dying for him. . . . This former student of Saint-Cyr was the humblest of men; I never heard him praise himself. One had to question him in order to find out about his past, his family, his successes. One day I asked him how many pagans he had converted and he replied, "Only one, that old mulatto woman whom you saw at the Hermitage of Béni-Abbès."

"No others?" I asked. "Oh, yes, I did baptize a little dying boy who had the joy of quitting this earth almost immediately after and flying to heaven. Also, I baptized a thirteen-year-old boy, but it was not I who converted him, for he was brought to me by a French sergeant who had taught him the catechism and had prepared him to receive the Sacraments."

He liked—in fact, he sought out—snubs, insults, and derision by making his appearance extravagant. He always wore clumsy sandals on his feet, which were cracked by the cold, and he wore an unbleached muslin cassock, too short and often stained and torn. He cut his own hair and beard without using a mirror. He didn't care what people thought of him: as long as he pleased God, men's judgments did not concern him. . . . On trains he always rode third class and he always crossed the Saharan sands on foot, although he was a fine horseman. . . . Giving unstintingly, he was generous to the point of prodigality. When he entered a village, which we did once a day usually, and sometimes twice, the natives, having heard of his saintliness, would come to meet him in great numbers, led by their chiefs, and they would crowd around him to see him and listen to him. They hailed him with veneration, kissing his hand and calling him Sidi Marabout. Brother Charles believed in earning his bread by the sweat of his brow, and there was never an empty moment in his day. In the desert, instead of taking a siesta or resting, even when exhausted by a long march in the sun, he worked on his dictionary, which he hoped to finish before his death in order to ease the task of future missionaries.

Ben Messis, Brother Charles's language tutor, was one of the most intelligent and sympathetic men in the Sahara. Son of a Chamba father and Touareg mother, he was considered by the Touaregs as one of them. He was astonished, and fatigued, by his pupil's will to work.

Laperrine arrived at In Salah on March 4th, bringing Brother Charles news of the death of their mutual friend, Motylinski. Thus Brother Charles had lost not only Brother Michel but also another companion who had been of great help in understanding the Touaregs.

Leaving In Salah on March 8th, Brother Charles, more alone than ever, traveled with a group commanded by Captain Dinaux, working without stint along the way. Ben Messis accompanied the group, and Chernach, a Negro courier of Moussa Ag Amastane, was the guide. In order to collect material, Brother Charles offered Chernach one sou for each verse he recited. "What a wonderful stimulant for the memory!" one of the officers wrote. "All day long, Chernach recites verses, and he might even write some for less."

On April 6th, at Tit, Moussa Ag Amastane visited the officers. Brother Charles decided to go to his Hermitage at Tamanrasset, accompanied by Lieutenant Cortier who wrote that he was "happy to have this supplementary trip to Koudia and to have the chance to live on more intimate terms with a man whose beliefs command respect and whose knowledge commands admiration."

They arrived at Tamanrasset on April 9th, Lieutenant Cortier noting that Brother Charles had told him "delightful things about the ancient history of the Touaregs, the origins of Islam, and Mohammed's penetration of Babylon, Koufa, and Baghdad. He knows how to talk about the results of his research with a precision and charm that delight the mind."

Having visited the Hermitage at Tamanrasset, Brother Charles continued to travel among the Touaregs with the group. "Sometimes we march part of the night, leaving at midnight or one o'clock or any other suitable hour. When my time isn't occupied with talking to the Touaregs, I study their language. It's hard work for my old head."

On May 6th Brother Charles wrote to Father Voillard, "I am

getting on in years and I should like to see someone better than me replace me at Tamanrasset and at Béni-Abbès."

On May 31st he wrote to Monseigneur Guérin:

I have promised a small sum for the poems that are brought to me. This promise, given in a poor country, has sufficed to give me enough to fill my tent for a month. I have also been told that neighboring *douars* wish me to come so that their women can give me poems. So I have been to the *douars* several times, spending hours under a tree or in a tent amid women and children, writing verses and giving small gifts.

His aim was to "make an end to prejudice, repulsion, defiance." He hoped to finish his Touareg-French dictionary during the year 1907, hoping out of love for the Touaregs that his work would give them a recognized position. From humility, he wanted his work to be anonymous:

I have begged Laperrine to have published by whomever he wishes and as something belonging to him, the military chief of the Oasis, the Touareg grammar and the French-Touareg dictionary, which are already finished, as well as the Touareg-French dictionary that I am working on and the poems I am collecting. My only condition is that my name not appear and that I remain unknown. Next year I do not wish to do anything except correct my translation of the Gospel and selected texts from the Holy Scriptures. After that, I hope to have no other work than be an example of the life of prayer and manual labor—an example which the Touaregs so badly need.

16.

Charles Becomes a Native

Brother Charles returned to Tamanrasset. Until now, thanks to the French members of the group, he had never lacked a server at Mass, but now he wondered what he would do, for a priest must have assistance in order to say the Mass, and for Brother Charles the Mass was the very source and center of life.

A few years earlier he would not have hesitated, but would have lived in a place where he could have an altar boy (Paul, whose function this had been, had left him some time ago). But now Monseigneur Guérin gave him his choice, and Brother Charles answered on his way to Tamanrasset, on July 2, 1907:

I have often asked myself the question you have asked: Is it better to stay in the Hoggar unable to celebrate Holy Mass or is it better not to stay? Since I am the only priest who can go to the Hoggar, while many priests can celebrate the Holy Sacrifice, I think it best after all to go to the Hoggar, leaving to the good Lord the means to celebrate Mass if He wishes (up until now this has always been the case, in the most diverse ways). I used to make a sharp distinction between the *Infinite,* or the Holy Sacrifice, and the *finite,* or all that is not He, and I always gave up everything in order to celebrate Holy Mass. But this reasoning must be imperfect in some way, since, from the times of the Apostles, the greatest saints have in certain circumstances sacrificed the possibility of saying Mass in order to accomplish works of spiritual charity or to travel or for other reasons. If it turns out that I shall have to remain at Tamanrasset for a long time without celebrating Mass, then it would be best for me to stay there for shorter periods and not to limit myself to traveling with military groups, *which is not at all the same as living alone.* Living alone in the country is a good thing; one can act, even without doing much, because one becomes one of them. One is approachable, because one is "so small" alone.

Letting himself be led by circumstances, Brother Charles arrived at Tamanrasset on July 6th. "I was well received, much more affectionately than I had dared hope. Little by little they seem to trust me. It is only a very, very small start, small and miserable as I am, but I thank Jesus for this start, small as it is."

The region was experiencing great hardship when Brother Charles arrived. "It hasn't rained for seventeen months. In a country that lives mostly on milk and whose poor live almost entirely on milk, this means famine. The goats are as dry as the earth, and the people are nearly as dry as the goats," he wrote to his cousin on July 17th.

Feeling exhausted, he wrote his cousin nine days later, "I feel old; I have lost my strength and it lessens each year. More and more I feel myself declining." On the second anniversary of his arrival in Tamanrasset, he wrote in his diary, "No Mass, for I am alone." He had, however, kept the Holy Sacrament with him. Two months later, on November 18th, he wondered:

Does my presence do any good here? Contact with the natives helps to lessen the feeling of strangeness, tames them, and slowly makes taboos and prejudices disappear. It is very slow, a very little thing. . . . It is painful to see the reign of evil all around, the lack of good, the enemies of the Lord who are so enterprising, the friends who are so faltering, and to see oneself so miserable after so many blessings. However, one should not be sad but should look above it all, to our Beloved Lord. For it is He whom we love and not ourselves, and it is His good that concerns us. Hope is a duty—charity hopes for all—hope is but faith in the goodness of God. He is good and all-powerful. Unquestionably, He leaves us free, and often we use our freedom lamentably, but while leaving us free, He still remains the master and can at His will send a grace so powerful that it overwhelms everything, transforms everything. He has already done enough for us to make us believe in His love. . . . For the Sahara, which is eight or ten times the size of France and which, without being heavily populated, is inhabited everywhere, there are only twelve or fifteen priests, all at El-Goléa or at Ouargla. . . . There are difficulties of all kinds and on all sides.

Despite his fatigue, Brother Charles was thinking very carefully about the future of the Hoggar. Continuing to work closely with Moussa, he wrote a long letter to his friend Lacroix:

Like me, Moussa has chosen Tamanrasset as his capital; it is a central point between the largest tribes, it is an arrival and departure point for Aïr and Adrar, communications with Touat are good, and above all it is a good spot for grazing. . . . He has erected his tents a few miles from here and has undertaken considerable agricultural work right here. He intends to build a house and has already started building a mosque . . . he is an extremely interesting man. It is astonishing that so open a mind should be combined with such ignorance. It would be most desirable for him to make a trip to France—a serious trip for his enlightenment, to give him a correct outlook, not a stupid trip where he would be given absurd honors and where, while being shown off like a strange animal, he would see only beer gardens and braying fools. . . . We must be good to him, for he deserves it on his own very real merits, which are astonishing in an illiterate lost in a desert. What we do must be in his true interest and for the public good; that is, we must try to improve him by correcting his opinions and enlarging his knowledge.

He is probably the only one in the Hoggar who is a true, sincere, and firm Moslem, having had this religious fervor instilled by Bei, a Kounti Marabout who lives at Attalia. I have heard only good of Bei, who leads a retired life removed from politics and never concerns himself with politics except to preach submission to the French and to peace. He has made himself an apostle of peace and moderation, blaming Abidine for not remaining in his role of Marabout and criticizing all the uncompromising Moslems who oppose us in the name of Islam. His word is law from Gao to here and throughout the Hoggar; his influence is wide and salutary.

Thanks to Bei's advice, Moussa is what he is. In his youth, Moussa, who is now forty, was known as a pillager, and he had made a great number of successful expeditions against the Ioulliminden and the people of the Aïr. Since meeting Bei he has become a man of peace and prayer, renouncing pillaging raids and using his strength only to help the oppressed. When we, the "pagans," arrived in the Hoggar, his first thought was to sell his possessions and to go live in Constantinople or Mecca, which the Touareg consider an earthly paradise, almost a heaven. Bei made him give up the idea, telling him to work for the good of his compatriots and to try to save them by making peace with the French. Moussa's fervor has helped him to do very fine things, and it has but one drawback: Bei is not always around to give him wise counsel, and in his fervor and ignorance the good Moussa turns to whichever Marabout of Touat he finds (and they are usually the worst of men, having all possible defects and vices, ignorant and hostile to us). He trusted them blindly. However, until now his intelligence and good sense have always helped him out of trouble. As far as the French are concerned he is very good, very loyal, although basically as a good Moslem he despises "pagans." It is extremely interesting to see this combination of great natural gifts and deep ignorance in a man who is a savage in some ways and who, in other ways, is worthy of all esteem. His sense of justice, his mercy, his courage, the nobility and generosity of his nature make him without equal from Touat and Rat to the Niger. . . . This is why I want so much that he make a trip to France, a serious trip with a good companion, not a joker or lowly elephant driver.

17.

Christmas Night

Christmas came, and Brother Charles suffered because he could not say Christmas Mass. Writing to Monseigneur Guérin he said, "I find it hard to spend Christmas without Mass." He hoped that perhaps some Frenchmen would pass by, but none came and Brother Charles was alone. "Alas, no Mass today," he wrote. "Until the last minute I hoped that someone might come, but no one did, neither a Christian traveler nor a soldier nor the permission to celebrate Mass alone. . . ." Five years earlier he had been thinking of Morocco, where he wanted to go—Morocco, where "Christmas night passes without a Mass." A year ago he and Brother Michel had celebrated Mass in Béni-Abbès, leaving the next day for the south. What a difference! His heart had been so filled with hope five years ago, one year ago, but now he was in Tamanrasset alone. "Tonight no Midnight Mass for the first time in twenty-one years," he wrote in his notebook, "may the Lord's Will be done."

For Brother Charles, Christmas, 1907, was a terrible time, worse even than that dark night of waiting in January, 1897. All that he had hoped to build seemed to have collapsed like a house built on sand. He had no companions, and the natives around him were in a pitiful state. Lost in the heart of Africa, Brother Charles examined the situation on the Continent of which France occupied a considerable part.

Deprived of Mass, he saw the world deprived of love. Looking southward, he had been given news of the Sudan, which he conveyed to Abbé Huvelin:

> I have heard what's being done there and the principles being spread by those who have come. Everything indicates that they seek only low personal interests and that they stop at nothing to accomplish their ends. In that immense colonial empire acquired over several years and which could be such a source of good for

backward nations, there is only greed, violence, and disregard for the good of the natives.

[Looking north, to Algeria, he noted:] In our Algeria we do almost nothing for the natives. The civilians try only to increase the natives' needs in order to make bigger profits. They seek only their own interest. The military takes care of the natives by letting them go their own way, without trying seriously to help them progress. . . . So for more than seventy years we have had more than three million Moslems in our charge, for whose moral good we have done nothing and from whom the million Europeans living in Algeria have completely separated themselves, making no attempt at penetration, ignorant of their lives, living without any contact with them, and considering them still as strangers and, generally, as enemies as well.

In 1902, Brother Charles had undertaken his first combat against slavery. He began a second campaign on Christmas, 1907. For five years he had been walking across Algeria and the Sahara; he had seen much, and he wanted to proclaim his indignation. He sought the most effective way to inform French Catholics and bring them to action; he wrote to Abbé Huvelin:

For months I have been wishing for a good book, attractive and easy to read, written by a layman in order to attract more readers, a book that would penetrate everywhere and that would reveal (not in the form of a dry treatise but in a way that would move men of good will and good heart) our obligations to our backward brothers. A book that would not only show the way, but that would push those who can be moved.

Brother Charles looked for an author who could express the truth in such a way that it would be listened to, a writer who was famous and admired. He hit upon René Bazin, whose patriotism was well known, and he wrote again to Abbé Huvelin, fearing that his previous letter might not have arrived:

I repeat the request that I made concerning a much-needed book that would give the right impetus and the right tone to making known our considerable duties toward the millions of souls that inhabit France's colonial empire. I beg of you to take the necessary steps which you can do so much better than I. . . . If you do not think you should, please guide me, advise me, tell me to whom I should address myself, and, incapable as I am, I shall do so. . . . If you think that I shouldn't take these steps, then as an obedient child I won't. . . . But you must believe your child who has become an old man, who lives in the midst of incalculable miseries which no one does anything to remedy and which no one wants to remedy. In a position to do so much good and morally obliged to do so, we are instead worsening the moral and intellectual condition of these people, seeing in them only a source of material gain. What the natives see in us, Christians who profess a religion of love, what they see in unbelieving Frenchmen shouting the word "fraternity" from the rooftops, is neglect or ambition or greed. Almost everywhere, alas, they see indifference, hate, and callousness.

Brother Charles was ill at Christmas, 1907, and his heart was crushed by the evil he saw around him. He felt poor, alone, unarmed against the black night of selfishness, against the lack of love. He saw French Catholics who were indifferent, French unbelievers who talked of brotherhood and practiced injustice. He saw Moussa working ambitiously and Arab Marabouts preaching hate. It was all too much. On January 2, 1908, Brother Charles, worn out, collapsed. His end seemed near. He was obliged to interrupt all work and remain immobile.

The Touaregs came to him who was the poorest of the poor. Amid the terrible drought they looked for milk for him; they took care of him and saved the life of the man who wanted to be their friend. In the midst of their own misery, they did all they could to take care of the foreigner whom they had welcomed and made one of their own.

Christmas of 1907 was perhaps after all the most beautiful of Charles's life, for on Christmas night he had cried out louder than ever before the message of Christ's love and he had tried with greater strength than ever to establish a real universal brotherhood.

On that Christmas, Brother Charles's heart was fuller than ever with love. He understood Christ's heart and he saw that He had expressed His message of love by being the last of the humble, the most deprived of all. Abandoned and near to death, Brother Charles understood that the Cross was the crown on the life of Nazareth. He looked upon Jesus with love—the poor little boy of Nazareth, the pauper of Galilee and Judea, the Calvary—and he wanted with all his love to go, like Jesus, to everyone, to shout out the truth in the same way, disarmed and in want.

In this state of mind he wrote, on January 15, 1908, of

the means that Jesus had given us to continue the work of the salvation of the world. . . .

His methods in the cradle, at Nazareth, and on the Cross were: Poverty, Abjection, Humiliation, Abandonment, Persecution, Suffering, Crucifixion. These are our arms, those of our Divine Spouse who asks us to let Him continue His life in us, He who is the only Lover, the only Spouse, the only Saviour, and also the only Wisdom and the only Truth. We will find none better than He, and He has never aged. Let us follow this "unique model" and we shall be certain of accomplishing much good, for thenceforth it will not be we who are living, but He who lives in us. Our acts are no longer our own, human and miserable, but His, divinely effective.

On January 1, 1908, sending his New Year greetings to Monseigneur Guérin, Brother Charles had written:

May Jesus, who has made you an apostle and charged you with lifting the stone from the tomb and reviving the dead, direct you and live in you as He did in Peter, Paul, and their disciples. Your work is similar to theirs, your mission is like theirs, given from the same mouth, just as true and accompanied by the same powers and blessings. . . . May Jesus accomplish His Will through you, may His Spirit guide you, may He live in you so that in you and for you He may continue his work of salvation on earth in these regions desolated by death and darkness.

18.

Centuries May Pass

Despite his exhaustion, Brother Charles was more aware than ever of the problems of his friends the Touaregs. On January 15th he wrote to his cousin, asking for

> a stereoscope, a very ordinary one like the ones we had as children, to give to our big children the Touaregs. They are crazy about them, and it is a teaching method that we shouldn't ignore. Would you send a lot of photographs to use with it—people, landscapes, fields, and towns, not too many monuments, for that would mean nothing to them, but mostly landscapes with a person or animal. It would help enlarge their ideas for them to see fine fields and beautiful forests.

In the same letter he wrote of Moussa:

> He has received a great deal from God, but his extreme ignorance (he cannot read or write) makes it difficult to push him as far as one should. What I must do for the present is to become as friendly with him as possible. He had his first child, a little girl, a few days ago and would be very touched were I to give her a small gift. Could you send me an inexpensive little necklace for little Marnia—something strong and durable that could be put around her neck now that she would still be able to wear when she is grown up, something in agate perhaps, or false amber, or even good cut crystal; plain beads on a string, no metal or chain or coral, for only slaves wear coral here. The main thing is that it be long-lasting and that there are enough beads for it to be wound around her neck several times, as is the fashion here.

Brother Charles was happy that certain kinds of Frenchmen who were allowed in Algeria and the Sudan were unable to come to the Hoggar:

It is forbidden for anyone, French or otherwise, to penetrate the South beyond a certain limit without special authorization from the Governor General of Algeria. This measure is a good one, for without it the region would be full of adventurers who would profit from their position as Europeans and from the natives' ignorance, behaving badly, treating the natives like conquered people, and doing harm to our honor and reputation.

On January 31st Brother Charles learned to his great joy from a letter from Laperrine that Monseigneur Guérin had received papal permission for him to say Mass alone. He wrote in his diary for January 31st: "*Deo Gratias!* How good you are, O Lord! Tomorrow I shall be able to celebrate Mass. Christmas! Christmas! Thank you, Lord!"

His health grew better, and Laperrine sent him food, having previously told Monseigneur Guérin by letter, "I shall give him a good scolding and shall quote you when I tell him that penitence to the point of slow suicide is not allowed." Shortly afterward, Laperrine went to Tamanrasset and wrote to Monseigneur Guérin on February 11th:

He was much sicker than he admits. He had fainting spells, and the Touaregs, who nursed him very well, were most anxious. He is better now. I gave him a stiff lecture because I suspect that exaggerated penitence accounts for much of his illness and that overwork and the time he spends on the dictionary account for the rest. Since my lecture couldn't do everything, I also sent three camels laden with food, condensed milk, sugar, tea, and various preserves. In any case, he knew that he had to supplement his diet of boiled barley, for he asked for some milk. On his next trip north I think it most necessary that you get hold of him and keep him at Ghardaïa or at Maison Carrée for a month or two so that he can replenish his hump—if you'll excuse me for using a desert expression.

On March 25th Brother Charles wrote to his cousin:

Pray for these poor people. Amid an ocean of evils, the two worst ones seem to me to be lack of instruction and lack of education.

Ignorance makes them incapable of distinguishing between true and false and often between good and evil. We should be able to swamp them with missionaries, who by friendly conversations rather than other means would be able to correct their views, little by little, on many things.

He wanted nuns to come also, but "among a thousand other difficulties, there is a grave one particular to the Touaregs, and that is extreme moral laxity. They are Moslems in name only and it is hard to imagine the degree of laxity that they have reached." Confronted with problems, he continued to hope. "What men cannot accomplish, God can. Charity hopes for everything," he wrote to his cousin on June 4th. "I remember well a beautiful little sermon by our father (Abbé Huvelin) on Mary Magdalene, I think. He compared men who are so rigorous and inflexible toward certain sins to God who is so merciful, so tenderly forgiving, and he showed the basis of this difference. Men can forget a fault but never erase it. God can erase it as if it had never existed and make the soul as pure as if it had never sinned."

During the same month, Brother Charles wrote:

The Dear Lord has helped turn to the good Moussa's efforts to organize the Hoggar into a regular and believing Moslem community. These efforts failed utterly and pitifully. Not only did they fail, but they produced the opposite effect. He appointed a *cadi* and gave him large sums for the building of mosques and *zaouïas,* imposing a tithe throughout the Hoggar. Within three months his *cadi* had made himself hated by all, had spent all the money that was given to him, and hadn't built a thing. The tithe made everyone angry, so that now the only result is the memory of an unpleasant adventure, and a horror of *cadis* and the tithe. Let us pray and do penance.

Brother Charles's joy was for progress of good; it was not a joy of personal triumph. He felt that more than ever he had to pray and convert himself. As for the means of making Jesus known, Charles knew that they were poor and slow. Speaking of the Touaregs, he wrote to Monseigneur Livinhac on February 7, 1908:

As Moslems, they belong to those masses of souls who, short of a miracle, will come to truth only very slowly. This is no reason to be discouraged; on the contrary, it is reason to work with even greater ardor, since the task requires greater and longer efforts. To establish close relation with them, to get to know them and be known by them, to be esteemed and loved enough to remove their prejudices and build up their confidence by this relationship, to straighten out their ideas on natural religion and morality, to try by word and example to bring them a better life in harmony with natural religion, finally, to improve the quality of teaching, to improve it a great deal and make it equal to our own so that they may judge the false values of their religion and the truth of our own—unless I am mistaken, this is the triple task of the workers in this part of God's fields. Centuries may pass between the spadework and the final harvest, but the sooner we start and the harder we work, the more He "who gives to him who asks" and "opens the door to him who knocks" will bless the work of His servants and will cause the fruit to ripen.

Brother Charles respected the faith of the Touaregs. He refused to look for ways to convert them, desiring instead that they judge the truth of the Gospel and Jesus for themselves. He also respected the slowly advancing workings of grace:

I don't think the Lord wants me or anyone else to preach Jesus to the Touaregs [he wrote to Monseigneur Guérin on March 6, 1908]. It would delay their conversion rather than advance it. Instead of bringing them closer, it would make them defiant and harder to reach. What I must do—I, who believe in the vocation of the cloister and who live cloistered here—and what others must do, I have already suggested in my letter to Monseigneur Livinhac. We must be prudent, quiet, we must get to know them and make friends with them. Then, later, and little by little, we can go further with a few privileged souls who will have come and who will have seen more than the others, and who will serve to attract others. Above all, we must instruct these poor souls. Let us pray and let us work.

This sense of respect was present in all his deeds without ever causing him to betray his own religion. An acquaintance wrote:

> Laperrine told me this with his customary verve. He was on night duty at the time, the subject of controversy, since he had crossed the border. This is what he told me. Moussa Ag Amastane was the amenokal of the Aaghar Touaregs, a kind of important feudal chieftain with only a few thousand subjects. He owed a great deal to Laperrine and Foucauld, especially to the latter. His aunt was dying, and although he was a practicing Moslem he asked his Marabout friend to come to see her. The old lady died succored by Foucauld. As Laperrine put it, "That so-and-so, he confessed old Tihit."
>
> No one who has seen Foucauld at work should be surprised that he would push charity to the point of offering Tihit the balm of his presence. . . . I am sure that he remained in perfect accord with Catholic orthodoxy in giving this last sign of affection. "Ouksed Massinin—Fear God" was his formula. He often used it in his relations with the Touaregs. Laperrine himself told us a story that showed clearly that the Touaregs took Brother Charles for what he was, "a Christian Marabout." Laperrine told us that a noble Hoggar woman, who felt deep gratitude to Brother Charles because he had saved her five children in the famine of 1907, once said to him, "How dreadful it is to think that such a good man will go to hell when he dies because he is not a Moslem." She and her friends prayed to Allah every day for the Marabout's conversion to Islam.

In the eyes of the Touaregs, this Marabout was, despite his Christianity, a brother. He lived among them, sharing their lives, and his friendship had proved to be deeper than mere words. This sharing of lives was like cement between them, and by "shouting the Gospel from the rooftops" by living among them, he became their spokesman.

Brother Charles was the Touareg spokesman from every viewpoint. In June, 1908, Moussa and his men went with Brother Charles to see Laperrine and had a long conversation with him in Charles's presence. Laperrine spoke of the customs that must be maintained and those, like the *razzia,* that should be abandoned. There was a rumor that their "courts of love" would be banned, and Laperrine wanted to deny this rumor, but he did not know the language well enough. While Laperrine looked for an interpreter, Brother Charles started to laugh. Then, telling Laperrine that he was forcing him to do a most uncanonical translation, he transmitted Laperrine's message, to the great joy of the natives.

Laperrine worked in the same spirit as Brother Charles, sharing his desire for trust from the natives. Considering the fact that the Flatters episode was not in the distant past, he was extremely audacious.

He wrote of his 1908 trip:

> During my stay in Tamanrasset, I lived near Father de Foucauld's Hermitage. Moussa came to see me daily and insisted each time he left that I visit his camp, about two and one-half miles away. One day I decided to surprise him and show my complete faith in him. . . . We left for his camp unescorted and unarmed, carrying no rifles, sabers, or revolvers. We were four, Father de Foucauld, Lieutenant de Saint-Léger, Lieutenant Sigonney, and me. As long as I live I shall never forget Moussa's radiant expression. When he saw us arrive as we did, he was overcome with joy. I had no need to go further; he understood at once that I wanted to give a sign of my confidence and esteem.

Neither Laperrine nor Brother Charles treated the Touaregs as children. They were aware of the natives' pride and of their feeling toward the French. Writing to his brother-in-law, Raymond de Blic, Brother Charles said:

> If we treat them as savages they will treat us as savages. They have the same feeling of scorn toward us as the French have toward the cannibals of central Africa. They consider us "pagans" or "savages." One of the most intelligent among them asked me for information not long ago on those of us who live in central Africa and eat human flesh; they make no distinction between cannibals and us.

Happy at the work that was going on in the Hoggar, Brother Charles wrote to Monseigneur Guérin at the end of October:

The further we go, the better prepared we are for the arrival of our priests. The work that the officers are now doing is all one could ask for; it opens doors, establishes contacts, ensures security, and makes a good impression, for Colonel Laperrine, Captain Nieger, Monsieur de Saint-Léger and the rest are incomparably kind to the natives. Wherever an officer has passed, the populace has become friendly instead of hostile and suspicious. . . . The constant presence of one hundred soldiers in the Aaghar has demonstrated the resources of the land. All the vegetables of France are harvested; their quality is excellent. Water and soil abound and one could plant even more: only labor is lacking.

Looking to the future, it seemed as if his place was at Tamanrasset. His method of making contacts was extremely discreet. He wrote to Monseigneur Guérin on June 1, 1908:

I am doing more good here. Knowing that I am always here, people come to see me, for they are sure of finding me. We get to know each other little by little, and just to the desired extent, without anyone having reason to accuse me of being indiscreet, for I never leave the hundred-yard radius of my chapel. I think I see more people here than by traveling. This discretion seems to me the best possible start. Once wide acquaintanceship has been established, traveling will certainly be useful, but I wonder if I am the one whom God wants for this task? I have had no signs of it. To the contrary, my most recent annual retreat made me reaffirm my cloistered life. . . . To remain faithfully in my cloister here and at Béni-Abbès, except for necessary journeys, is one of the resolutions made on my last retreat. I have kept it and I can only congratulate myself for having done so: from the Touareg standpoint, it has done nothing but good.

Writing again to Monseigneur Guérin on December 16th, he affirmed that he thought a good start had been made: "Nothing new with me. Health is good. But I am feeling the weight of my fifty years. My road seems simple and clear. I need only continue, doing better each day and avoiding a thousand daily pitfalls."

19.

"Let Us Return to the Gospel"

During January and February of 1909, Brother Charles made a trip to France, embarking at Marseille for Algiers on March 7, 1909. His luggage was filled with everything imaginable, including dolls. "Your dolls have had an unexpected effect," he wrote to Madame de Bondy on June 14th. "Before I gave them away they excited such admiration that I kept them for a while to show visitors. Everyone, big and small, asked to see them, so I have become a sort of doll exhibitor!"

As he headed toward Tamanrasset his inventive gifts continued to work to the benefit of his friends. On March 4, 1909, he asked Madame de Bondy to send La Fontaine's Fables: "The simplest possible, with a picture at the beginning of each fable. . . . As you might guess, it is for the Touaregs." Writing to Monseigneur Guérin on May 29th, he brought up a problem that he was trying to settle to the advantage of all concerned:

An Ioulliminden slave, brought to Touat, freed because her masters mistreated her and living since then with Corporal D. of the Sahara company at Ksabi . . . is awaiting with terror the day (about two years from now) when D. will return to France. She does not want to stay in the land where she suffered so much, and she fears the Arabs. D., despite his way of life, is a Christian (he comes from a Christian family in Toulouse), and he has taught the basics of religion to this woman, saying that one can consider them of the same religion. She is grateful to him and believes in him while fearing the Arabs. He is frightened for her and is attached to her, and he wonders what to do when he leaves to be sure that she is safe. She is calm and hard-working, about thirty years old, with an intelligent and kindly manner. I have hired her and I ask you to accept her in your workshop at Ghardaïa. He will take her there and she will remain there, living with the sisters—a good recruit, for her appearance is good and D. thinks highly of her and cares deeply about her. Furthermore, we would be saving her soul and making a real Christian of her. I am telling you all this so that if D. writes to you, you will be up to date. I think that from every point of view it would be best for you to have her taken in by the sisters. Since she was freed her life has been proper. D. took her in his charge and since then she has always been irreproachable in conduct.

He also found "a simple way" to help the Touaregs to pray. On May 11th he wrote his cousin:

I should like to ask you for about twenty ordinary rosaries, solidly mounted in iron or copper and long enough to pass around the necks of people with large hairdos. A little medal, and not a cross, should be at the end. It is for the Moslems, whom I can teach to pray by saying "My Lord, I love you" on the small beads and "My Lord, I love you with all my heart" on the large ones.

On June 11th he was finally back at Tamanrasset after an absence of five months. "Upon arriving I was well received by the Touaregs and especially, to my great astonishment, by the *haratins*. They have never been so warm to me. I thank the Good Lord for it," he wrote on June 29th.

There had been several changes at Tamanrasset. Moussa—and this was good news—had had a big house built from bricks cooked in the sun and dried mud. Several of his relatives imitated him. Furthermore, the Hermitage had grown; soldiers from the newly constructed Fort Motylinski, thirty miles away, and *haratins* from the village had transformed his hut, and a young officer had brought a cot. Brother Charles accepted the gift and for the first time in twenty-seven years he had a bed to sleep on instead of the ground.

He and Moussa resumed their long talks. Moussa had as his secretary a young man who was brought up at Tlemcen and who spoke French; Brother Charles hoped that the new secretary would destroy the evil influence of the ignorant and fanatic "thalebs" who came from Rat.

He had more hope than ever:

Today is the feast day of St. Peter and St. Paul. It is nice for me to write to you on this day. Let us not be frightened by any difficulty. They have conquered many, and they are always there. Peter is always at the helm of the barque. If the disciples of Jesus could be discouraged, what causes for discouragement would the Christians of Rome have had on the night of their martyrdom. I have often thought of that night. It was sad and all would have been lost if they had not had in their hearts such faith! There will always be struggles, but even in apparent defeat, the Cross will triumph.

Brother Charles continued to follow his life of the "universal brother." A few months earlier Abbé Huvelin had given him advice which he followed and which he wrote in his notebook:

My apostolate must be one of goodness. I must make people say this when they see me: "This man is so good that his religion must be good." If someone asks me why I am gentle and good, I must reply, "Because I serve One who is much better than I am. If only you knew how good my Master, Jesus, is." I want to be so good that people will say, "If that is the servant, how, then, is the Master?"

The priest is a monstrance. His role is to show Jesus. He must disappear and make Jesus seen. I must leave a good impression on all who come to see me. I must be everything to everyone. I must laugh with those who laugh, cry with those who cry to lead them all to Jesus.

On December 3, 1909, he wrote to Monseigneur Livinhac:

The situation here remains the same: there is political and material progress every day. There is growing contact, and inroads are being made gently but with persistence. This is done to clear the way for the missionaries and to make their tasks easier. They will find a country that is more reliable with people who are already accustomed to Europeans and who have lost some of their prejudices and gained some respect for Europeans. . . . My life is the same, occupied with work on the Touareg language which will make the work easier for those evangelists whom my heart calls. I am still alone, and I cannot imagine where he will come from—this companion whom I long for. Even though I don't often leave my Hermitage, I still see many Touaregs. They come for medicine, alms, small gifts, or just for a friendly visit.

Brother Charles wanted to "clear the way." That was his vocation. He was a pioneer, a man who opened and crossed frontiers, a man who put no limits on his explorations. But Brother Charles's progress was toward the discovery of that which is Jesus and of the last place that He took. Brother Charles was interested only in discovering Jesus. All his beliefs were in Jesus, and he wanted a profound understanding and realization of the Love which is in the Heart of Christ. Brother Charles seized upon the grace that was offered to him. But it was Jesus who had first seized Brother Charles and had opened his heart to all mankind and had transformed his views and made them visible in God's light to a point where he could recognize the Master in a Touareg woman, in a *haratin* of the Hoggar, or in a French officer, and to a point where he would want to introduce Him in the forgotten land that was the Sahara. Brother Charles wrote to Abbé Caron on June 30, 1909:

Let us return to the Gospel. If we do not abide by it, Jesus will not live in us. Let us return to poverty and Christian simplicity. During nineteen days in France, what struck me most was that all classes of society—above all the least wealthy class and also the Christian families—have increased their tastes for costly and useless things. Carefree, worldly, and frivolous distractions are out of place in such grave times, in times of persecution, and they are not in accord with a Christian life. *The danger lies within ourselves,* and not within our enemies. Our enemies can only lead us to victory. The bad we receive is from ourselves. Return to the Gospel—that is the salvation.

Brother Charles was not an abstract idealist. He made concrete observations on the stages, transformations, and evolution of human societies: the Touaregs, French, Arabs, nobles, and the Imrad.

Brother Charles argued his point not as an economist or a politician, but as one arguing in the light of the Gospel. He looked at everything in the light of justice and the evangelical brotherhood. What the Touaregs saw, without knowing it, what the officers saw, sometimes knowing it, was a man whose actions were based on the Gospel, the Gospel with its absolutes—a man whose hopes for a brotherly city here on earth had begun to be realized. Brother Charles wished to incarnate Gospel truths in the human truths of history.

Brother Charles did not cut himself off from the conditions of the times in which he lived. The Church existed for him wherever he was. The Church had no borders: there were men of God in the countries of persecution as well as in Christian countries, in colonial countries as well as in invaded countries.

Brother Charles was, in the good sense of the word, an adventurer —an adventurer of God. He, like an adventurer, was alone, available, ready for anything and ready to leave anything, a man who never stopped. He set strict rules for himself and he wanted to follow them with precision, but he was forever obliged to ignore the letter of his Law and to live it in spirit. The heart of his Rule was obedience toward people and events. More than a starting place, or a harbor where one could safely return in a storm, his Rule was a star, constantly over him. His Rule was to keep his eye on his mission to establish unity between all men, and at the same time he was to allow himself to be guided by the circumstances and by the daily life of his fellow men.

Brother Charles believed that the blessings of Christ were not only within the Church, but throughout temporal society. He believed that the world of men was under the eye of God. His faith demanded that he participate in life. His religion did not mean an escape for him nor did it mean that he could avoid problems of state, of the colonies, or of work. He was not a divided man—a man who was pious and good with another side that made him a man of action. Because he had answered the call of Christianity, he did not feel he had to desert the city. Consequently, he maintained a constant tension between faith and the world, without permitting clerical tyranny. He did not mistake politics for religion.

Brother Charles had become a free man. He said what he thought, searching for the truth. He was neither totalitarian nor partisan, but a universal man, capable of listening to all, of being available to everyone.

Brother Charles never wanted two parts in his life, one sacred, the other profane. He did not wish to separate that which God had united: his life with Christ and his life with his fellow men. Brother Charles assumed the unhappiness, the loneliness, the poverty, the sufferings, and the lack of love of each. He knew what it was to be an orphan, and he knew how to welcome those whom he found abandoned.

A Saharan, Lehuraux, said of him much later:

We loved Father de Foucauld because of the paternal kindness he showed us when we realized all that we had left behind: family, religious work, friends from childhood, the charming and familiar places where we had spent our childhood—and all of that toward which our thoughts fly when we have hard times, during waterless marches under a torrid sun, heavy, hot dusty winds or violent sand tornadoes that put ones' nerves on edge. A simple word from the Father worked wonders and quickly dispersed the lapses that all Sahara travelers have known.

20.

A Protestant Doctor

Dr. Hérisson, a Protestant doctor sent to the Hoggar by Laperrine to care for the soldiers and the native population, gave a firsthand account of Brother Charles's existence at Tamanrasset.

On his arrival, in August, 1903, he called on Brother Charles.

"What do you advise me to do to help the Touaregs, Father?" I asked. "I have an order to follow your instructions."

"You must be simple, affable and kind," he answered. "In order to be loved, you must love them and make them feel that you love them. Don't be an adjutant or a doctor with them, and don't be offended by their familiarity or their easy manner. Be human, charitable, and *always cheerful*. You must always laugh, even in saying simple things. I, as you will see, laugh all the time, showing my bad teeth. Laughter creates good humor with them. It brings men closer together and helps them understand each other better. It cheers up a glum atmosphere, and that is a charity. When you are with Touaregs, always laugh.

"Give them medical care with patience, and make them well. Then they will have a respect for our knowledge and power and our goodness. If someone asks you to treat a goat, don't be upset. In my opinion it would be best if you stayed for a while near a Touareg encampment, not in the middle of it, but at the edge. Without interfering, you would be ready to receive them if they wish to come. Stay here for three weeks and that will give you time to know them and for them to know you. They don't know us. There are absurd legends about the French. It is said that we eat children, that at night we turn into animals, and so on.

"With the help of an interpreter, tell the ones who come to talk with you about our life, our families, morals, customs, the birth and religious education of our children, their godparents, marriage and laws of marriage, obligations of husband and wife toward each other and their children, the dead, the ceremonies, wills, those things which we honor and those we despise. . . ."

He told me to show the Touaregs photographs of the work in the fields of France, our flocks and herds, the life in the country, the rivers, farms, cattle, horses. . . . "Make them realize that the life of the French is made of peaceful honesty, work, traditions," he said. "Show them that the foundation of the life of our farmers is the same as their life, that we are like them, that we live as they live, but in a more beautiful country. You will no doubt have plenty of leisure because this country is very healthy, and the population is scattered. What do you expect to do?"

"The colonel," I said, "has asked me to gather samples of plants to be sent to Algiers to M. Trabut, Professor of Botany, who will classify them. I am going to try to start a kitchen garden at Tar-haouhaout."

"What would be interesting," Father de Foucauld said, "would be to know if some race other than the Touaregs had once inhabited the desert. There are tombs here, very old, which were probably tombs of pagans. They probably predate the Moslems. They are very likely the ancestors of the Touaregs, although the Touaregs don't wish to admit it. You might make some excavations. No one would mind if you were to exhume bones. You might be able to determine the relationship between the pagans and the Touaregs of today."

At his first meeting with the doctor at Fort Motylinski, Brother Charles had invited him to Mass. Hérisson replied that he was a Protestant.

"Do you follow your religion regularly?" asked Brother Charles.

"What do you mean by that?"

"Do you read the Bible?"

"No. I received religious instruction until my first communion at fifteen. We are religious in my family. My memory is good. Christian precepts are familiar to me. I don't need to read sacred books."

"You are wrong. One must read the Bible every day and carry out one's religious obligations. In my bookcases at Tamanrasset, I have a Bible, the Oswald edition, and I will send it to you."

"I thank you, Father. I will bring it back to you in two weeks. I want to meet the amenokal, Moussa Ag Amastane, as soon as I am a little rested."

"No, keep it until you leave Tidikelt. You must read it every day."

The Doctor described Brother Charles:

Short, graying, unkempt beard, missing teeth, hair cut by himself with scissors and no mirror, lively eyes, intelligent forehead. One senses in him a warmness, an intense mystic flame, an intense ardor in his faith. He has the look of a clairvoyant, a believer— he has a very definite personality, independent but entirely governed by his rule. . . . I sensed that Father de Foucauld is a gentleman of fine manners allied to Christian humility but that he would be intractable on certain questions, such as one's duty toward God, one's country, other men, and that, if you wanted to be respected by him, he would exact work without respite from you.

The day I saw Father de Foucauld really displeased was several months before I left the Hoggar when I told him that I had not done any anthropological research for seven or eight months. "I have seen," I told him, "that I would never achieve a result. I have learned nothing about the origins of these pagans. Were they ancestors of the Hoggars or were they another race altogether? From the start, my work was doomed to mediocrity."

Father de Foucauld reproached me for having no perseverance.

"The little you could have done," he said, "and left to your successors would have been work done. Others could take your results, even if they were negative, and continue to get on with the problem. In not following your research, you have set them back. As for the idea that your work would be mediocre, that is nothing but pride on your part. Your giving up could be very discouraging to those who follow you."

One must work. One day while I was there, a Negro came to beg. He was dying of hunger, he said. He was well built, but thin. He was about twenty-five. Father de Foucauld asked him why he didn't work at agricultural centers at Tit, Abalessa, and so on. He replied that he had no work. Father de Foucauld then showed him a small wooden box which was used to mold bricks and said, "Make twenty bricks for me and I will give you some wheat." It would have been hardly an hour of work; twenty small blocks like those children make at the beach would have been fine. But he refused. Father gave him nothing, except advice that he should work to live.

Father de Foucauld worked like a dog. He hated to lose time. "Watch out for the minutes," he said; "time is action." At his Hermitage at Tamanrasset, his time was alloted like clockwork. He had instruments on his wall, placed at his disposal by the Bouzarea Observatory of Algiers, that he would read three times a day and whose results he would note—maximum and minimum temperatures, barometric pressure, direction and velocity of the wind.

He received a great deal of mail from France, Algeria, and all over—twenty or thirty letters. He would read them and then slit the envelopes carefully and open them out, flat. He threaded them through one corner and hung them on his belt, and that was his writing pad. Next to them, he strung a pencil. He made instant notes on his observations. . . . When he wandered across Morocco disguised as a Jew, he kept a similar notebook hidden under his clothes. When he came across a variation of a verse of poetry from Touareg folklore, he copied it and put it where it belonged. Everything was kept in order and up to the minute.

After he read the letters, he addressed envelopes to the people who had written and stacked them like cards on his worktable. Each would be answered. The stack diminished with measured regularity. Father de Foucauld kept in contact with the outside world and he never put off until tomorrow his duty to be courteous and reply. For him, each letter was an occasion to revive the religious feelings of his correspondent. He kept his small folding worktable in perfect order. He is not a man to "watch and pray." His rule of conduct: "Work and pray, for you do not know the day nor the hour." Work.

He has the character of a Benedictine monk, which makes him like faculty scientists who amazed us in our youth. This character makes him the type of person, venerated by priests and laymen alike, who lights the way for the rest of mankind. His capacity for organized work makes me think highly of him. I am filled with admiration.

Colonel Laperrine invites neighboring Frenchmen to his table: Sometimes they are served first. No one is seated in any particular order. Father de Foucauld comes at noon with a bottle of white muscatel, his Mass wine. At the end of the meal, we each have a small glass. Each time we see the bottle, someone says: "Father, you are depleting your stock. It's too much. We shouldn't drink it!" But he laughs and insists, saying, "You can drink it. I have brought only what I am able to give." And, needless to say, we drink it with pleasure. We don't speak of serious things at the table. We tell stories, exchange pleasantries, or tease the colonel's cook. Father de Foucauld laughs. The colonel has a large repertory of stories that he swears are true. He is a good storyteller. Father de Foucauld laughs when everybody laughs. But if the story is a little off color, he doesn't listen. He becomes deaf, and he seems to think of other things. Then someone remarks that the conversation has taken "a playful tone" and that the ears of the father must be scandalized. If someone excuses himself, the father protests that he has heard nothing and nobody is embarrassed.

In these discussions, he prefers to squat on the ground next to the colonel, and serve as an interpreter for him. Usually there are Touaregs there who don't know much Arabic. Father not only knows their language, but he knows their character and habits, and he knows what has to be explained to them. In fact, the Touaregs say, "He knows our language better than we do."

Dr. Hérisson went on to say:
The natives respect him so much they have made him a judge. One morning I witnessed a very curious scene. He was in front of his door, dressed in white, his head slightly bowed. In front of him were two giant Touaregs, dressed in black, with black veils, standing very ceremoniously with a sword at their sides, daggers in their outstretched left arms, and lances in their right hands. Behind were four or five other Touaregs, squatting, probably witnesses. The disturbance was over the theft of camels and the beating given to the slave who guarded the herd. One was accusing, the other denying. Both had emphatic, theatrical attitudes typical of the Hoggar, imperial gestures, hammered out sentences. . . . Finally, the Koran was brought before them and the accused protested his innocence by swearing on it in front of Father de Foucauld.

Dr. Hérisson also reported that some of the Frenchmen took pretty young native girls as their wives

. . . in the manner of the country. . . . For them, it is simply a diversion. . . .

Brother Charles wished that they would set good examples for the Touaregs in showing them the solid virtue of marriage. He wished that the young officers would "have Christian weddings with young Hoggar ladies and that they would have children that would be raised in the Church." He wished a French couple who were teachers would move to Tamanrasset to teach the young Kel Rela.

Dr. Hérisson brought a cello with him to the Hoggar. He liked to play it at night under the calm, cool Sahara sky. One night he announced to Brother Charles, "I have vaccinated a dozen young Touareg noblewomen against smallpox. Dassine was the first."

Dassine was the remarkable woman who influenced Moussa toward a regard for the French. She was the woman who received Brother Charles so graciously, and they had many talks together, though he did not try to convert her.

"You love your God, I'll love mine," he told her. Nevertheless, he worked on her spirit at every opportunity. In January, 1908, when he had fallen sick, Dassine had gone to see him immediately and had had him treated, but not with the strange practices of the powerful sorcerers. Later, when he was bitten by a horned viper—which is almost always fatal—she asked Moussa to have a cow brought from Sudan, regardless of the cost, so that the milk could be given to him.

At the time of Dassine's vaccination, Brother Charles was surprised. He asked the doctor how he had managed, and why there were so many noble ladies in front of his door. . . .

"It's thanks to the cello," the doctor answered. "Dassine came with friends and she said, 'You have an *imzad*' [Touareg for "cello"]. 'Where is it?'"

The doctor said he would show them, and took the cello out of its case. There were cries and laughter.

"My, it is big. . . . It's the father of the imzad! . . ."

Dr. Hérisson played "the lowest chord and it sounded as powerful as an organ." He asked, "Would you like me to play something from my country, the songs of love?"

"Yes, please. Play. We'll listen!"

"I will," said the doctor, "on one condition: First you will be vaccinated for smallpox."

Dassine was the first to hold out her arm. "Vaccinate me," she said, and all the others followed suit.

"Now, while that dries," Dr. Hérisson said, "I will play you a pretty song about love. It is about a man who dies of unrequited love."

He played slow waltzes of Crémieux, *Je t'ai rencontrée simplement. . . . Je suis lâche avec toi. . . .*

Father de Foucauld was overjoyed. He had not expected that. . . . The doctor reported:

When I left him ten days later to go to Fort Motylinski to get supplies, books, and a change of air, he said to me, "Leave your cello here at the Hermitage. I will take good care of it. It is useless and dangerous for it to travel on the back of a camel. It pleases the Touareg women of Moussa's entourage, and when you come back, it will be here. It is a good way for us to spread our influence."

One day toward the end of the year 1909, horsemen arrived at Tamanrasset with a letter saying that a group of Ajjers Touaregs had been seen in the region. The lieutenant and his group of police were on duty far away, and Brother Charles was told to go quickly to the fort. According to Dr. Hérisson,

the fort was prepared to protect anybody who asked for protection. The assemblage was near Father de Foucauld's Hermitage. He came to see us. We asked him what he was going to do. We tried to get him to come with us to Fort Motylinski. He refused. He wanted to stay on there alone, without arms and guards, under the protection of God. Moussa Ag Amastane and his men were away. There was nobody at Tamanrasset to help him. I understood that he had resolved to be assassinated. That was the end which he foresaw, here, and that he wished.

The doctor continued:

At night, when he would walk up and down in front of his Hermitage at sunset, his arm resting on my shoulder, he would tell me that personal distinction was not due to the situations of birth or education. It is innate, and he had found among the simple people at the Trappist monasteries a remarkably high set of ideals. "We live side by side with people without knowing backgrounds or names, and each carries out his function according to himself. There was a peasant, with no education, who had aspirations and thoughts straight from his heart that were perfect in their beauty. He didn't even know it. It was wonderful to hear him. With no artifice and everything simple, he was eloquent."

"Father de Foucauld," said the doctor, "was a contradiction to what is said about famous men, for he grew in stature the more one saw of him."

At this time, caves in the Sahara with polychrome drawings were being discovered. Captain Cortier had first found some in 1909. It was the beginning of the putting together of the legend of Atlantis and Antinéa. The apocalyptical Sahara could keep the memory—or the illusion—of an ancient civilization of fishermen, hunters, farmers (the African countries bordering the desert have kept their dim memories of this past splendor).

"The minds of the people of the Aaghar," said Dr. Hérisson, "for a long time to come will be like the land in the Gospels that was filled with stone so that the seed that is sown cannot germinate. Father de Foucauld knows this, and in giving his life as an example, he has made a lasting impression on the minds of these primitive human beings. His way is not unlike the way of the primitive artists who engraved their impressions of the people of the desert on the polished rock of the Aaghar."

Dr. Hérisson gave this account of Christmas, 1909, at Tamanrasset:

We spent Christmas night in his Hermitage sitting on folding chairs facing each other, our elbows on his small worktable, which was lighted by a small paraffin candle, stuck on the table with no candlestick. There was nothing to drink: no tea or coffee. I remembered this from our conversation: "At a very early age, I became an orphan and I was brought up by my grandfather, Colonel de Morlet. We often walked in the Saverne Forest in Alsace. It is the solitude of places that I like. It helps me collect my thoughts. There was nothing to hear except the songs of birds and insects."

Father de Foucauld was back in his childhood . . . he was grave, dreaming out loud, having forgotten I was there. Suddenly he returned to the present and, seeing me, he said, sadly and apologetically, "You see, I have always been a savage."

21.

The Austerity of the Saharan Solitude

A great gap was left in Brother Charles's life by the deaths, in 1910, of three of his close friends.

On May 14th he learned that Monseigneur Guérin had died at the age of thirty-seven, exhausted by life in the Sahara. On May 16th, Whitmonday, Brother Charles wrote to his cousin:

That was very painful for me and has left a great emptiness. I could always count on him. The same day that I heard of his death, I also learned of the death of Commandant Lacroix, who had done so many things for me. He was at Algiers, Director of Native Affairs, and I could always count on him completely. All of this leaves me with a future full of difficulties of all sorts. But He who is Omnipotent is always there and He will never fail us.

Brother Charles had counted completely on Monseigneur Guérin for an association he wished to found. He had written to him in February, 1910,

Thank you for all you will do; I will do all that I can; and the Good Lord will do what pleases Him. Pray for me that He will use my life to do good. No matter what happens, if I am good my passage on this earth will be useful to mankind. If I am bad or mediocre, no good will come from me. As to this Brotherhood, there is nothing I can do until there is an answer, favorable or unfavorable, to the steps you are taking in Rome. I wait patiently. When the answer comes, we will see.

On May 16th he said to Father Voillard: "I never dreamed that he would not survive me, and I leaned on his friendship as if it would always be there. You know the void his departure has left. Only Jesus remains."

On June 29, 1910, he wrote to a White Father:

He suited the Sahara apostolate perfectly. Certainly, a priest is a monstrance who must disappear in order to show Jesus and he has no role other than to make Him be seen. This can be seen more easily in places where one reaches more souls, not by presenting the dogma, but by slowly bringing the goodness of Jesus to them and trying to make them say, "Because this man is so good, his religion must be good. . . ." He had hoped for the conversion of the Moslems of the Sahara, not in a set time, for nothing can make us see ahead in this time. He did not deceive himself about the difficulties.

Brother Charles had had a kind of presentiment. On February 2nd he had written:

The Good Lord has given me sweets during my nine years in the Sahara; my old friend Lacroix at Algiers and my old friend Laperrine in the Oasis; at Béni-Abbès, In Salah, and at intermediary posts, there were officers whose good graces never failed, and several of whom were good and true friends to me. In blessing Jesus who has sent me these favors, I realize that if they are to continue He will send others, for neither Lacroix nor Laperrine are eternal. I pray, Our Lord, help me profit from these present favors.

On August 15th he heard of the death of Abbé Huvelin, his spiritual guide for many years. "This is shattering for me," he wrote.

There was a fresh blow in November when Colonel Laperrine, who had been in command in the Oasis for nine years, asked to be sent back to France. On April 11th Brother Charles had written to Captain Regnault: "The Targui country has made progress under the direction of Colonel Laperrine in self-control, organization, commerce, agriculture. When I think of the way this country was six years ago and the way it is today, I thank God for what has been done and I pray that He will continue what has been started so well."

Brother Charles told Father Voillard in a letter of August 1, 1910, why Laperrine wanted to leave the Sahara:

> The reason for his departure is that he thinks, with good reason, that one should not hold on to his job forever. He has been in command of the Oases for nine years. He leaves them organized and grown throughout the Touareg country—in admirable condition. He left at the beginning of July and he will not return. I don't know his replacement. You will know before I do. For this, as for everything, I turn to Jesus.

Laperrine and Brother Charles never met again in the Sahara. But before he left, Laperrine arranged for Moussa Ag Amastane and several Touareg noblemen to visit France. They were very enthusiastic.

Dr. Hérisson wrote:

> Before they left, they asked whether we had many camels in our country and whether the pastures were good. They also thought that positions were hereditary as in their country. Here they had tribes of officers, others of secretaries, Marabouts, doctors, and gunsmiths.
>
> The French do the same thing, thinking that the Touaregs, Persians, Malgaches, Turks all live in their manner with the same tastes, hoping for universal suffrage, loving wine, tobacco, sausage, cards, and ball games. They think of the human race in the image of themselves.

In France the visit of Moussa Ag Amastane had tremendous repercussions. The press reported his trip, complete with photographs. Moussa crossed France with Captain Nieger, whom Laperrine and Brother Charles thought would be a good companion. He was taken to see everything. Nieger recounted:

> At Camp Mailly he saw a military review. He saw our red trousers, and the maneuvers of the orchestra were directed by a member of the Superior Council of War, General Durand. Nothing was overlooked. The demonstration concluded with a final bayonet assault, with the Tricolor flying, drums and bugles, and a firing of the famous 75's. That was something that wasn't often done for fear of accidents, but it made us very proud.
>
> As usual, people asked me what Moussa thought of it. He answered, "People who have such means of destruction at their disposal are crazy to make war on each other. . . ."

Moussa was taken to Madame de Blic's, Brother Charles's sister. Nieger said:

> Nothing has touched me more than seeing the emotion Moussa showed in the presence of the sister of his friend. For those who didn't know of it, the affection that man had for Foucauld was clear in every gesture, word, look and even in the gentle, modest way he said "Meryem," Madame de Blic's first name in Arabic. When he disembarked at Algiers, he wrote to his friend, "I saw your sister and stayed two days at her house. I also saw your brother-in-law. I visited their house and gardens while you, the neskin [poor, miserable man of nothing] are at Tamanrasset."

Moussa was deeply impressed by the violent contrast between Brother Charles's life as a Marabout and the life he could have followed. In his memoirs, Nieger explained:

> At Béni-Abbès he did not live a cloistered life in the strict sense of the word because he received French and natives who knocked at the door of his Hermitage, which he called his "brotherhood." He went nowhere that he wasn't called because of an emergency or to exercise his ministry. He was left free to measure out his solitude, to divide his time between prayer and work. That was exactly how he saw his apostolate at that time.

The trips he took during those nearly ten years lasted for months, one right after the other for hundreds and thousands of miles. They necessitated a life in common with officers, men, and meharists. One was always looking for contacts with the Touaregs, and itineraries were modified accordingly.

However difficult it was . . . this life seemed too easy for him. . . . His first steps into the Sahara life left him with considerable remorse; he was haunted by the thought of Béni-Abbès, which he had abandoned. But the attraction to the Sahara had been the stronger. . . .

There are deserts and deserts. Béni-Abbès, alive and with its palm trees and large population, was endowed with an important year-round military post. Tamanrasset, four miles south of the most advanced military post, without material resources of any kind, completely severed from Western civilization, offered the nearest possible thing to solitude and life among the most humble of humble. . . .

From any book on Foucauld, it seems to me that it is difficult to measure the austerity of his solitude in the Sahara. It is drowned in the evidence of those who saw him there and those who corresponded with him. The mass of documents obliterates the time factor. Foucauld stayed at Tamanrasset for eleven years. During those first years, months and months would go by without his seeing any of us. . . .

He didn't look for contact with us unless it would serve his cause. His goodness didn't hide his impatience. . . . He had a strict daily program, which he was loath to change. He wished it would be the same for those who had a role to play, a duty to fulfill. His rigorous self-discipline explains the use of this expression, "The Marabout is *ouar*," about him. It meant that Father de Foucauld is exacting, difficult to satisfy—but it was said in admiration.

When he was obliged to live with us, he took a gay part in our conversations. His favorite subject was the Touaregs, a subject he treated with variety, hoping to interest us in the vestiges of their old civilization. He found occasion to give us advice, taking care to avoid seeming out of his role.

AT THE HEART OF THE WORLD

Abdication of his precious isolation required from him an effort of renunciation and abnegation. I cannot forget that, strolling by his wretched *gourbi* one night, he said, "I have a horror of the world and its hypocrisy." Obviously, he was speaking of our world. I cannot believe that he attributed the Touaregs, whose vices and faults he knew perfectly well, with moral standards superior to our own. It is incontestable that he lived for them and that he appeared happy to be with them. . . .

His life with the Touaregs was so close to their own that it was the same, only sometimes more rugged. . . . He adopted as far as possible their spiritual and material conditions. He helped them with his advice, never fearing the smallest detail. He cared for their sick, if he was asked, and their dying.

Brother Charles was not ignorant of their faults. In June, 1910, he said: "I am not astonished that you are surprised at the morals of the Touaregs. Despite what anyone says, they are so far from us that we can't believe it. Basically, theirs is a society a little closer to the Apaches. The men steal, and the women applaud it and live freely."

On August 31, 1910, he wrote to Louis Massignon: "Waiting for the Divine Will, and after one knows It the duty is simple: love God and one's neighbor. Love your neighbor to arrive at the love of God. One love does not exist without the other. This existence of love and poverty, of solitude and goodness is a hard existence."

Nieger was right. The desert of Brother Charles was seen by men whose eyes were accustomed to cities or countryside. Undoubtedly the desert was a healthy place. Malaria was unknown in the Oases. Wounds badly taken care of, healed quickly. But the desert was a place to induce madness. The dryness, the electric air of the desert wore at the nerves of the most phlegmatic. In these immense spaces the solitude was not unlike the solitude in a prison cell, despite the differences in size, and was a frightening experience for any mind.

Brother Charles's life in the desert was by no means easy. The desert leaves a man alone. It supports no weaknesses. It crushes a man. Only if a man fights can he live and survive. Brother Charles had that kind of personal strength. . . . In the desert . . . where men fall dead of thirst a few hundred feet from the wells . . . in this desert where men's intelligence and hearts are turned to cinders . . . Brother Charles walked and worked, prayed and meditated, welcomed and listened. The desert is a place where a man had to be strong, as strong as the Touaregs. The desert was a place where, more than any other place, one needed friends or one was lost.

Brother Charles had within him a paradox that made this possible. He had a strong personality, and he loved solitude. He was a man alone who needed others and who wanted the friendship of others. In a way, this man of the desert was a little like the anonymous man who lives in the desert of the modern crowded cities.

In his desert, Brother Charles proclaimed that man needs solitude with the Beloved Being and friendship with all and that man can have the respect of God only by respecting others, for the love and the respect of the others is indissoluble.

22.

Advance Units

While Moussa was in France, Brother Charles continued his work. He wrote on February 2, 1910:

Since my arrival here in June, I have not left my (mental) cloister. I have gone out only to call on a desperately sick Frenchman, a day's walk from here, and to visit several camps in the neighboring mountains. Most of my time is spent working on the Touareg language. I intend to stay here until it is finished. I am in a hurry to finish so that I can devote more time to people and to prayer. It will be finished, hopefully, in a year.

[On May 16th] My time is almost entirely taken by the Touareg language. Relations with the natives also have their place, and I receive, as best I can, those who come. But I don't go out to see anyone, unless I am called to a sick person.

Brother Charles received letters from France that told him of Moussa's trip, a trip that was too official for his taste. However, he hoped that the amenokal would profit from it.

On December 9, 1910, he wrote to Monseigneur Livinhac:

Moussa Ag Amanstane, chief of the Aaghar, has taken a trip to France under the direction of Colonel Laperrine and Captain Nieger, Chief of the Arab Bureau of In Salah. He is expected back any moment. I hope he will return with the wish to see his compatriots bring up and educate their children, instead of leaving them as free and ignorant as the gazelles of their mountains. The question of instruction and education is tied up with the nomad life. As intelligent as he is, one wonders whether he will react against the errant tastes of his race and try to do something to settle his people. If only this country is well administered, time itself will take care of this problem, for this is more a country for tilling than for pastures. There are soil and water for cultivation, while animals, on the other hand, often suffer from the drought. The greatest obstacle to agricultural development is the laziness and the vanity of the inhabitants who, by an unhappy prejudice, look down on people who till the soil. . . .

Brother Charles prepared for Moussa's return and wrote down three things that he wanted him to understand if he were to work for the salvation of his people:

1. Arrange for the education of the children and young people who remain as abandoned as animals.

2. Arrange for their instruction according to a certain plan.

3. Work to make the people stationary. Of the nomads, certain ones should be left as shepherds.

The first two are conditional on the third. Education and instruction seem incompatible with nomadic life.

For the "Kel Ahaggar," or for the majority of them, the passage from the nomadic to the stationary life would be easy. The strong tribes are almost all sedentary. The camels, with their shepherds, go great distances for grazing. But the tents, with the families and the goats, are nearly stationary, moving within a twenty-five mile radius. Furthermore, peace—due to three years of French occupation—has already brought results in the sense of settling people. When I arrived, there was only one house at Tamanrasset. The rest were huts. Now there are fifteen or twenty houses, and more are constantly being built. The huts are disappearing. It is the same, I am told, in other villages. . . . Cultivated fields have multiplied. Every well-to-do Touareg owns fields. Unfortunately, they do not cultivate them themselves. They use the *haratins* of Tidikelt. They watch the harvest, the Touaregs, but they won't pick up a hoe. Monks in this country who cultivated the soil with their own hands would be a great help.

More than ever, Brother Charles wished that he would be joined by other evangelical workers. To be a missionary worker means to take courage from the Gospel and to live by it, wherever one is. Brother Charles wished that someone would understand the way of the pioneer and would follow that life in the Sahara.

On May 16, 1910, he wrote to Father Voillard:

Contact has been made with the natives, confidence established, acquaintances made. This grows daily, and as soon as my work on the language is finished I will devote more time to the Touaregs. After almost six continuous years here, I know the people and the language. I ask Jesus for a pious and devoted priest who could learn the work and who would continue it better than I have. . . .

On May 13, 1911, he replied to a Trappist of Our Lady of the Snows who had hoped to join him:

You have asked me what my life, the life of a missionary monk, is like; it is founded on these principles:
    Imitation of the hidden life of Jesus of Nazareth;
    Adoration of the Holy Sacrament;

Establishment of oneself among the most forgotten heathen people, doing all possible for their conversion.

A life as austere as life among the Trappists, but harder because the poverty is greater; harder because the climate is difficult and tiring; harder because the food is completely different from that in Europe, but one must not introduce costly European food, and one must live as they live in this country—on grain, dates, and milk products. For clothing and housing you will find nothing more poor and rustic—nothing resembles France, but it does resemble that of Jesus of Nazareth. Your life would be completely different from that in the Trappists, where there were strict rules to obey. . . . Here there is a family life, completely simple. . . . Here there is no chanted Mass, no vocal prayers other than the breviary, but there will be much adoration, prayer, and silent words at the foot of the Holy Sacrament. I have been alone for ten years. Having been given this vast country of infidels to convert, if the Good Lord gives me brothers, it would be better for the salvation of the people if they went off in groups of three or four than to form one heavily manned monastery. These posts of three or four would be advance units which would prepare the way . . . for other religious groups to follow. . . .

Moussa returned to Tamanrasset for Christmas, and told of his trip. Dr. Hérisson said:

Moussa and his followers did not envy the French in Paris. In fact, they didn't want to stay too long in France. They saw that it was rich, populated, and fortunate. They told me: "France is one big garden. Peace reigns among the men. One is not attacked or robbed by people you meet in the streets, busy, agitated. One could go and come among the strangers without having to carry a sword or dagger for protection. God must love the French to have given them such riches. But we were homesick for our own country, our families, our people, our servants, our goats and camels. . . ."

They thought that God had given them a poor country and left them not knowing how to use the forces of nature but that He had given them a true religion, wisdom, a calm life, and the assurance of Paradise in the future. No one wanted to return to

Paris for a second time, but France was "marvelous and a source of wonder."

Brother Charles left for France to stay from January to March, 1911. He left Tamanrasset on January 2nd. There were two reasons for his trip, as he wrote to Father Voillard on January 26: "To try to find a companion—a priest who is called by God to share my life —and to try to interest a few priests whom I know in the project for my Brotherhood."

In Paris he saw Marie de Bondy, and he celebrated Mass in the Church of St. Augustine, where he was converted. His friend Louis Massignon was often there. In Lyon he mostly saw Abbé Crozier, from whom he hoped to have help for his association.

On the return trip, he stopped for a visit with the White Fathers at Maison Carrée, and he chose Father Voillard as his spiritual father to replace Abbé Huvelin. Father Voillard told him that he must take a trip to France for a few weeks every two years, advice that Brother Charles welcomed.

On the way back to Tamanrasset, he passed the post at Aoulef. One officer remembered the days Brother Charles spent there: "His affability and gentleness were matched by the extreme humility toward everyone, big and small alike. His humility made us uncomfortable because we knew of his brilliant past and we also knew that had he wished, he could have been our commander."

The officer had prepared a copious lunch with an omelet and with fried meatballs and chicken, but Brother Charles ate very little. Eventually the officer realized that it was Good Friday, and he apologized to Brother Charles, who laughed and said, "The Good Lord knows very well that the Saharans aren't aware of the date and that they fast all year long."

Brother Charles went to In Salah, and Captain Charlet, who was in command of the Saharan company of Tidikelt, wrote of his visit:

> He is truly interesting and friendly. He was at our table, and we were charmed by him. He knows all there is to know about Arab, Moroccan, and Touareg matters. But he is also familiar with worldly matters. One can say anything in front of him, and he says everything himself, lowering his eyes and his voice enough so that no one is shocked.

Easter Sunday we went to Mass, which he celebrated in a tiny room in a tiny mud hut. The altar was a camp table, Pernod bottles served as cruets, a sardine can was the dish for ablutions, and everything was attractive, extremely clean, and well arranged. The Stations of the Cross were drawn by him on small pieces of pine, two by three inches. Alone, the chalice looked pretty. His chasuble was made of a fine white linen with a small silk cross embroidered in the center.

On May 3rd Brother Charles was back at Tamanrasset: "I have had a big welcome from all the people. Progress is being made. The land is being cultivated, and houses are replacing huts. The cost of provisions is lower and, happily for everyone, the nomads are beginning to settle."

He fervently hoped that plans for a railroad would materialize. It could mean much progress for the Hoggar. On May 6, 1911, he wrote to Captain Voinot: "I hope they will really build it, this Trans-Saharan. Things sometimes go quickly after a period of lengthy negotiations."

He planned, in a month, to go to what he called "my country house at Asekrem."

23.

The Most Central Point

The preceding May, Brother Charles had started to build a new Hermitage, his "country house at Asekrem." For some time he had noticed that the Touaregs spent the summers in the mountains, where they took their flocks to graze.

"The Hermitage," wrote Brother Charles, "is about thirty-five miles from here, in the heart of the Aaghar at the most central point of the mountain chain, which is the citadel of the country. . . . It is on the plateau called Asekrem, more than 7,800 feet high. It has a room and a chapel."

To go from Tamanrasset, one followed a vague trail that wound across immense canyons, rocky gorges, and steep cliffs. It was a landscape of great masses of fallen rocks and summits that were like skyscrapers. It is understandable that the Touaregs called this part of the country their *Koudia,* or fortress.

Before going to Asekrem, Brother Charles waited for the return of Moussa and the man he called his "professor." They finally arrived, and on July 4th, accompanied by Ba-Hamou, who was a great student of the Touareg language, Brother Charles started off.

On June 7th he had explained to one of his childhood friends, Gabriel Tourdes, the role of his two Hermitages:

I have two Hermitages in the Aaghar. The one at Tamanrasset is a thousand feet from the village and its hundred inhabitants. It is surrounded by mountains and nearby encampments of Nomads; the other is at Asekrem, thirty-five miles from Tamanrasset, at an altitude of 7,800 feet at the top of a mountain with encampments in the neighboring valleys. The first Hermitage has more of the town about it. The mail is delivered every two weeks by a man on a camel who comes from In Salah, nearly four hundred miles away. There is a main road between Algeria and Aïr, between In Salah and Zinder. Caravans come from Damergou, Aïr, Nigeria. Water as fresh as that from our Vosges Mountains is in good supply. There are chickens, eggs, and vegetables as well as grain and butter. There are men who, for a few sous, will carry wood, bring bread, and help with chores. The view is beautiful and the sunsets are magnificent. The Hermitage at Asekrem is more severe. I am absolutely alone high on the mountain that dominates the countryside. The view is marvelous. You can see the entire Aaghar range, which goes north and south to the immense desert plains. The peaks, piles of rocks, and tall needle-shaped formations make wonderful shapes to see. It is a wonderful solitude, and I love that. Nearby there are many ravines, and when it rains the ground is covered with sweet-scented grass, and the

Touaregs come quickly and pitch their tents to get the good of the fresh mountain water. . . .

At the beginning of July, he wrote:

> . . . One cannot see the view at Asekrem without thinking of God. I have to force myself to stop looking. . . . The view and the feeling of Infinity seem so close to the Creator. . . . The solitude and the savage aspect show how much one is with Him and how little one is in the world He has created. . . . As I arrived, there were rain, thunder, and lightning. Thunder is beautiful in the mountains. The temperature here is like the end of October in France. It is 16 degrees [centigrade] at noon. It is difficult to imagine that it is July, and even more difficult to realize that I am in the Sahara. . . .

However much he liked contemplating the view, Brother Charles and Ba-Hamou had to get on with their language studies, and Brother Charles had to be ready to receive the Touaregs who would visit him.

"There are plenty of people around when there is pasture but at the moment everything is dried up and the land is empty for twenty-five miles. The solitude suits me, for it gives me time to work. . . ."

Eventually people began to arrive. "I am satisfied with my stay here. Even though it is dry, people come to see me every four or five days. As they must travel a day or two to get here, they spend the night . . . we have a couple of meals together and a good visit. That helps relations more than an hour's visit which we usually have at Tamanrasset. So the work that is done here is satisfactory. . . . My presence here has brought several officers, and that is also good. . . ."

Even in the solitude of the mountains, Brother Charles did not want to cut himself off from the world. At Asekrem more people came to see him and their visits were more satisfactory.

On August 14th he received an assortment of packages, and among them was the altar that had belonged to Abbé Huvelin, his spiritual father who had urged him to establish the hermitage at Asekrem.

The altar, which had served in the heart of Paris, arrived on the back of a camel at the high place of Asekrem, the place that was for Brother Charles what Alverne had been for St. Francis of Assisi. The next day, Brother Charles celebrated Mass for Abbé Huvelin at Asekrem.

On September 1st, a Touareg, Mohammed Ag Akroud, visited Brother Charles, bringing with him his mother, brothers, and sisters. On November 24th Brother Charles wrote: "There are no gracious manners, delicate attentions, or marks of friendship that they have not shown me since then. Not a day passes without my seeing him or one of his family. Don't worry about my having enough water or wood; he keeps me supplied. Everybody works; it is a happy family. They are the best and most interesting neighbors in the world."

Brother Charles was happy leading the life of a brotherly neighbor. On November 24, 1911, he wrote to Nieger's wife:

I am in my château of the mountains, completely happy in every way. It has the most beautiful view in the world. Its immensity and beauty raises one's spirit toward the Creator. The sunsets are marvelous and make one think of the end of life and of the eternal peace. At the same time, this solitude is good for relations with the Touaregs. . . . One sees fewer people here but those one sees, one knows better.

On December 7, 1911, he wrote to Monseigneur Levinhac:

There is a plague in the Aaghar that only the establishment of some of your sisters can help. The number of infanticides is staggering. One-quarter or perhaps one-third of the children die at birth. Morals traditionally are very loose. But the same tradition does not permit the birth of children out of wedlock. When that happens, the honor is saved only if the child disappears. It seems that the remedy, while waiting for the grand remedy, conversion, would be to bring in several nuns who would be prepared to take in newborn babies. That way mothers would have a way to hide their mistakes. Then severe laws for the country should be laid down by the French officers who are in command. I have already asked for severe laws and I have been told that I am right . . . but that it is all very difficult . . . to put women in prison and have them guarded by Arab soldiers! I have been told, "Establish the nuns . . . and we will immediately establish the law."

There are, in the lives of certain saints, some extraordinary phenomena. Among others, a saint is often found in several places at the same time. In a way it could be said that Brother Charles was all over the Hoggar at the same time. He knew everything that was happening; he was occupied with everything; he was on the alert for everything.

On November 24, 1911, in the solitude of Asekrem, he heard of some serious events that made him indignant:

> While Moussa was in the Aaghar at the end of August or the beginning of September, there were several regrettable incidents in the encampments. The brigadier had come to dig wells very nearby; a young girl, closely related to Moussa, was raped by a soldier; then, somehow, the public water, from Moussa's community, was so badly rationed that the well-digging project had to be abandoned and the troops had to flee, leaving their baggage; and two of Moussa's best camels died of thirst. . . . It is sad to see subalterns undo in one day all the good that officers of all grades have done with such devotion.

It became cold and windy at the lofty Asekrem: "My Touareg co-worker has groaned so much since coming here that I promised to send him back to Tamanrasset for Christmas. When I promised, I hoped that the dictionary would be finished before Christmas. But it is not and I have at least three more months of work, so I must follow him there. I would so have loved to stay here for Christmas."

But his stay at Asekrem had made Brother Charles very tired, and he had another collapse. "Perhaps it will not be bad for me to go to Tamanrasset not only for the good people I will see, but for myself. I seem to have run out of strength, not having had fresh food. I am all right. The spell I had day before yesterday is nothing, but my strength is lacking. At Tamanrasset I will find eggs and vegetables that will help me. I am getting old. . . ."

He arrived back in Tamanrasset on December 15th. That Christmas of 1911 seemed much like Christmas, 1907. "The drought has lasted over twenty months; there hasn't been any milk, butter, meat —the principal riches of the country—during that time. In 1911 the two harvests were failures. There is nothing to eat. And nobody has clothes since clothing is bought only when there are products to sell."

On December 10th, from Asekrem, Brother Charles had written to Henry de Castries:

Will the generations that follow us be given the sight of people from North Africa speaking together, "Our Father who art in Heaven, hallow'd be thy name. Thy kingdom come. Thy will be done on earth as it is in heaven," addressing God as the Father of all human beings who are brothers through Him? I don't know. That is the secret of God. But we must work toward it with all our strength. That is putting the second commandment, "Love thy neighbor as thyself," equal to the first, "Thou shalt have no other gods before me."

Down from his mountain for Christmas, Brother Charles wrote:

Since my return here, my life is filled with praying and receiving my neighbors. I must see all my poor neighbors. They are becoming my old friends, for I am in my seventh year at Tamanrasset. The sweetness of solitude—I have known it most of my life. Even before I became a Christian, I loved solitude with nature and books, where the world is invisible and sweet. In solitude one is never alone. The spirit was not made for noise, but for taking things in. Life is a preparation for Heaven, not only through deserving work, but by the peace and communion with God. But mankind throws itself into infinite discussions. The little good he finds in noise should prove how far he has strayed from his vocation.

The year 1912 was unlike any Brother Charles had known. He had never been so absorbed with the life of the Sahara, the daily existence of the Touaregs and the Sahara officers. His six months at Asekrem had not taken him away from the problems of the moment. He found new vigor, in fact, to become more a part of the world and to work harder in his service to his fellow men.

24.

Civilization

First of all, people were talking again about the Trans-Saharan railroad. Things were becoming more precise. On February 1, 1912, Brother Charles wrote: "Nieger writes me that the government is considering it very seriously. One would have to be blind not to see that it is necessary. I am extremely happy, for a railroad in this region would bring more civilization and more civilization would mean more Christianity. Savages cannot be Christians. . . ."

On February 16th he expected "Captain Nieger and several members of a mission to study the railroad problem."

He wrote to his cousin: "The Trans-Saharan is a profound joy for me not only for the good it will bring the people . . . but also because it will bring us nearer. Traveling will be much cheaper; one can make the trip in a few days, and there will be a telegraph."

Brother Charles made great plans: "Once the railroad is in, the Aaghar may become a popular health spot. The air is dry and healthy, and there is good weather all the time. With an altitude that varies from 2,000 feet to 9,000 feet, one can choose one's own temperature."

On March 31st he wrote to his cousin:

Thank you for your article on the crossing of the Sahara by plane. It is bound to come. It is even easier than the author thinks. People who don't know the country are haunted by visions of sand and sandstorms that do exist in certain regions, but they can be avoided by going from Oran to the Aaghar and from the Aaghar to the Niger or Chad. . . . But will someone do this in our lifetimes? At my age, I think it is more likely that I will see the railroad, because that will be less expensive and ready sooner.

He spoke again of aviation in a letter of April 16: "That may become an excellent means of transportation, but there is still progress to be made in it. Meanwhile I hope that Jean [his young cousin] does not get involved in it."

The Trans-Saharan was never built, and one of the most informed men of the Sahara, François Vergniaud, wrote in 1960: "The governments were too preoccupied with politics of the moment to carry out a coherent program: the history of the Trans-Saharan illustrates the triumph of little minds over those then dismissed—so quickly and so definitively—as visionaries. . . ."

Brother Charles was well ahead of his time. What he had wanted for the good of all was ruined by men who were shortsighted and looked only at their own interests.

He realized that the Trans-Saharan could have helped prevent a famine such as the one he saw around him in the Hoggar. And that famine brought about serious consequences. On February 16th Brother Charles warned Captain Charlet of the situation at Tamanrasset. Captain Charlet was astonished to learn that Moussa had not delivered the necessary butter and grain to the meharists of Tidikelt as promised. Without having seen Moussa, Brother Charles defended him to the captain: ". . . as for the grain, he is to blame but not wholly to blame. . . . He should have sent a serious man to each village at the moment of the harvest to collect what was due. . . . Instead Moussa was drinking milk and sleeping in the Adrar. With all his good qualities, he is lazy. He is, as M. Gautier said, like a wild animal that sleeps for long periods and then awakens ferocious.

"However, the harvest was bad. In eight years I have not seen a worse one."

Brother Charles explained in his letter that Moussa had not promised to deliver anything that the Hoggar was not able to produce. Owing to the drought, there was not much butter produced and, said Brother Charles, "he had not promised to bring butter from the Niger or Sudan or anywhere else."

Brother Charles continued:

It is well that you did not lend the three thousand francs to Moussa. In fact, I hope you will never lend him a cent and that you will warn others at In Salah, such as shopkeepers and Ahl Azzi, that you do not want them to lend him money or to sell to him on credit. If they do it, it will be at their own risk. On this question, Moussa must be treated as a prodigal and he must be protected from himself. He is a combination of an intelligent man and a savage. In the memory of mankind, an Aaghar noble has never paid his debts. It appears monstrous and exorbitant to him that we should expect him to. . . . I think, on the other hand, that it would be only fair if we paid him for the services he has rendered and compensate him for the considerable expenses he has had continuously in rendering services to the State. He has never asked for payment, and I think we should give him decent sums for that from time to time. What are these expenses? We are constantly asking him for convoys to go to various places. . . . Never once has he mentioned what the State has cost him. He is as dignified about that as he is "noble" about not paying his creditors.

At the same time, Brother Charles wrote to Nieger, telling him the situation and defending Moussa.

On May 16th he wrote to Captain Charlet:

Don't trust Moussa in money matters involving his people. His needs and his debts make him very grasping. When he was rich, he gave with both hands. Now that he has nothing, he tries to take anything in sight, and he is constantly sniffing around to see where he can borrow or who will give him a handout. He is on the decline. "Poverty makes people misunderstood" and "Hunger drives the wolf from the forest." Everyday he becomes a greater liar, and that is regrettable. . . .

In effect, Brother Charles asked the French not to demand more of Moussa than he could give. He also felt that Moussa should be paid what was due him and no more and that he should not be given money to distribute among his people himself.

He wrote to Charlet:

One of the worst faults of the native chiefs is that they keep their people away from us. They obstruct their contact with us and they take for themselves whatever we give them instead of sharing it with their people. . . . I wish that every last Touareg, Haratin, and so on, would be paid by us directly and that nothing would be handled by native intermediaries.

On February 18th Moussa called on Abd Isa, the "servant of Jesus," who was for him "a friend, counselor, and disciplinarian." Brother Charles took that opportunity to try to make him understand how to better himself. On Easter Sunday, 1912, he made a list of recommendations for Moussa:

1. Surround yourself with good men, discarding good-for-nothings.

2. Guard against foreign Arabs who come only to eat off the country and off of you.

3. Try to be stable and settled.

4. Reduce your expenses. Be humble. Only God is great. Anyone who thinks he is great or who tries to be great doesn't know God.

5. The first duty is to love God with all your heart and above all else. The second is to love all men as yourself. From this love of your neighbor follows the triple law of Brotherhood, Equality, and Liberty. "When Adam delved and Eve span . . ." where was the noble, the Imrad, the slave? If someone wants to know what the prophets think, say, and do, they can come to me and I will read the Gospel to them.

6. Do not ask for or accept gifts. In asking for gifts, you put a burden on your friends. In accepting them, you become the slave.

7. Pay your debts and don't make new ones. Don't borrow from friends—it is not dignified and it is a burden for them. Borrowing from strangers makes you a slave. God, in His Holy Scriptures, often advises His chiefs never to accept gifts; it is difficult to refuse to do something that is unjust from someone who has given you a gift, and if they do something bad, it is difficult for you to punish them. There is always a danger that good or better people would not be treated as well as someone who has given a gift.

8. Do not give gifts and do not unnecessarily offer hospitality or you will always have money problems and debts and you will

always be surrounded by scoundrels, for they are the ones who are attracted by hospitality and you will have to ask for presents and money from your most devoted Imrads in order to continue. They will hate you, finally, because of your demands for money, because of your wastefulness, and because of your entourage.

9. Eliminate the slaves and scoundrels who do nothing but eat, make fun of you, and are good for nothing.

10. Whenever it is possible, go frequently to see an officer but see him *alone*. Things are better accomplished face to face. Talk without an interpreter, frankly and sincerely, and the officer will become a true friend. Don't ever tell a shade of a lie.

11. Never lie to anyone. Lies are contrary to God, for God is Truth.

12. Provide good men as guides because all the Touaregs may be judged by them.

13. Don't praise anyone to his face. When one loves and respects someone, that shows in his confidence and acts. Flattery is base, good only for the Arab *thaleb*.

14. Don't be slow and lazy. Know how to manage your time. . . .

25.
"In Fifty Years"

Brother Charles was not simply concerned with Moussa's problems with his own people. He talked with him about the questions of politics and the presence of France. He spoke of liberty, equality, and fraternity for the nobles and the slaves of the Hoggar. But how did he see relations between the French and the Touaregs?

This, for example, was included in his advice to Moussa:

Make your people learn French so that they can become natural-
ized French citizens, our equals and not our subjects, always on
the same footing with us, never bothered by anyone anywhere.
That will come sooner or later. Anyone who can see ahead will
take that step. . . . Probably before too long all of the military
and all of the employees of the Aaghar will be of the race of its
people.

About this same time, Brother Charles wrote to a French captain
named Pariel:

What a beautiful empire: Algeria—Tunisia—Morocco—Sudan—
Sahara! What a beautiful empire—providing the French make it
French and civilized and do not simply hold it and exploit it. If
we try to civilize it and to raise its people—who now number
thirty million and who will, if there is peace, number sixty million
in fifty years—to our level, then this African empire will, in half
a century, be an admirable continuation of France. If we forget
to love our neighbor as God, our common Father, has asked and
if we forget the word "fraternity," which is written on all our
walls, and if we treat these people not as our children but as something material to exploit, then this union with us which we have
given will turn against us and we will be thrown into the sea at
the first European difficulty.

Brother Charles also expressed these long-range views to his sister
on January 30th, to Commandant Brissaud on August 15th, and to
his cousin on September 21st. All these letters were written in 1912.
   Of fraternity, equality, and liberty, Brother Charles always put
fraternity first. Throughout his life in the Sahara, he cried out
against segregation. He lived with the Touaregs. With fraternity, he
wanted equality. He wanted the Touaregs to have the same rights
and the same privileges as the French. He wanted the people of
Moussa to learn French. He wanted the country's military and its
governors to be "of the race of its people." He looked forward to
the time when the Europeans would be replaced by the Touaregs
and when the Touaregs would be ready to take over these functions.
He wanted the Touaregs to reach a point where they would have
both administrative and economic freedom.

Again in a letter to his sister, Brother Charles spoke of "unity." All his life, "unity" was uppermost in his mind. In 1900 when he hoped to become a priest and when he took *"Jesus Caritas"* as his motto, he wrote: "The *blessed* charity that I have combined with the name of Jesus . . . *The Charity* . . . but charity reigns less and less among the clergy and among the priests of the Holy Land. All my life will be spent in furthering charity with everyone and among all. 'That they be one as we are one.' . . . 'It is in this that you will be recognized as my disciples.' "

The wish for "unity" among all was the fundamental preoccupation of his priesthood, something he never stopped hoping for. He thought that the greatest good France could bring to the African people was unity. In 1881, when he had visited Morocco, and when he was a nonbeliever, he reported a shocking state of division between men of different races. His feelings were reinforced when he realized that the various races crossed the country simply to tear each other apart. France, he thought, had brought about a great step forward: the gradual cessation of the *razzias* was a defeat for this barbarism. And another advance in human respect was the constructive peace work the French officers tried to carry out.

But there was no possibility of true unity unless the respect was reciprocal and the exchange continual. Brother Charles wanted people to keep their individuality but to profit from the riches and knowledge of other people. He hoped that the modern world, with its railroads, airplanes, and telegraphs, would be a world of peace, progress, and unity.

He worked for liberty, equality, and fraternity. He passed many of his days in the Sahara working to preserve the language of the Touaregs and to establish it as a known language by relating it to French. François Vergnaud, in his book on the Sahara, says: "He did an enormous scientific work. Is it generally known that our essential knowledge of the language, literature, and customs of the Touaregs is due to him?"

Brother Charles's work kept this language, which was the bond for thousands of people, from falling into obscurity. Scholars today, whether believers or not, see with horror how the techniques of modern civilization destroy the customs of primitive people and doom them to eternal loss.

Brother Charles respected the richness of this little-known language. He was not a man who reduced men to pure spirits. It was his belief that Christ had wanted to save every human being, body and soul, and that every human being was entitled to respect as a person in order to further the good of all mankind. That was what Christ had wished and had shown by His own example. As had Jesus, his friend, Brother Charles believed in friendship.

Friendship, for him, was not one way; he looked for reciprocity. He was happy, he wrote to his cousin on March 16, 1912, to see the "true and serious relations of friendship established." Brother Charles was the opposite of a man who arrives in a conquered land and thinks that he is superior and that it is he who has brought everything to the conquered people. Brother Charles went to the Hoggar as a pauper and he welcomed with joy all that the Touaregs who received him gave to him. Pauper though he was, Brother Charles found himself richer from the culture and the centuries-old experience of the Touaregs.

He wrote on February 16, 1912:

In countries where everything is unknown, each thing one learns leads to a host of other things we don't know; the more one knows, the more one sees that there are other things that one doesn't know. That is the story of every day I have spent in this country. That is why every day the work I have worked on for such a long time grows longer.

When Brother Charles came down from Asekrem, he found something more than famine and misery at Tamanrasset; the whole region was in a state of unrest: holy war was being preached throughout the Sahara.

On Christmas, 1912, Brother Charles wrote to his cousin: "The Turks are doing their best to preach a holy war among the Arab tribes in Tripoli, but that doesn't bother us. The Touaregs, very tepid Moslems, hold the holy war, the Turks, and the Italians in equal indifference. . . . But don't wory about a holy war in the Sahara. The Sahara is big."

But, in fact, the situation was serious. In Tripoli the Turks had redoubled their efforts. War between Italy and Turkey had been declared on November 3, 1911. The entire region was in a volcanic state. Two groups of Touareg chiefs, in September, 1910, had gone to Tripoli to protect their claims. The Agger, which was between Tamanrasset and Tripoli, was particularly troubled. A report from Lieutenant Gardel in 1911 stressed the consequences of the Turkish infiltrations on this war: certain tribes were taking advantage of it to carry out raids. This report also indicated that at El Barka the "undeniable rights" of Moussa Ag Amastane, which all of the inhabitants claimed, should be protected. When war was declared between Turkey and Italy, Captain Charlet was ordered to occupy Djanet to prevent uprisings in that region.

Brother Charles had described the Touaregs as being tepid Moslems. In this affair the political and religious situations were intertwined. The Turks preached a holy war to gain their end, and Brother Charles thought that because the Touaregs were not strong Moslems, there would be no trouble. In that vein he wrote to the Duke of Fitz-James:

My thought is that if little by little the Moslems of our colonial empire in Africa are not converted, there may be a nationalist movement not unlike the one in Turkey. An intellectual elite will form in the large towns, taught by the French. This elite will have lost all Moslem faith but will keep the label of it, and by it will influence the masses. On the other hand, the masses of the nomads and country people, removed from us, will stay ignorant, will be firm Moslems, and will continue to hate the French and hold them in contempt because of their Moslem religion, their Marabouts and because of the contacts which they have made with the French (authorities, settlers, and merchants) which have not always been of the type that would endear the French to them. The national sentiment or the barbaric will show forth in the educated elite the first chance it gets. For example, this group will use the Moslem religion to reach the ignorant masses the moment France has internal or external problems, and the plan will be to create an independent African Moslem empire. The northwest African empire of Algeria, Morocco, Tunisia, and French East Africa has thirty million people. If peace continues, that number will be doubled in fifty years. The country will have made great material progress; it will be rich; it will have railroads; and the inhabitants will be well trained in the use of our weapons, the elite having been taught in our schools. If we have not turned this people into French citizens, they will chase us out. The only way to make them French is to make them Christians.

To understand that letter, one should read a letter he wrote to Father Voillard on December 22, 1912:

Our mediocre, so as not to say bad, administration provides too few officers, and there are miscellaneous evils, and the result is that we are kept too far away from the population which is ready to meet with us. This doesn't keep me away personally, for to me they confide their troubles, but the French in general are kept away, and for them the French and Christians are one.

That should not be read out of the context of the times. At the end of 1911 and in 1912, Brother Charles was faced with a dramatic situation. He saw that in Turkey men who were Moslems in name only were using the religion as a "lever" to "influence the masses" and to "stir up hatred."

These men that Brother Charles opposed were not sincere believers. They were using their religion to create violence and dissension. Reading the future well, Brother Charles wanted peace and prosperity to reign in Africa so that the people would turn away from the false holy war and would establish their bonds of friendship in France. Brother Charles wished that the Touaregs, who were tepid Moslems, would abandon their religion, which they cared little about, and become Christians; he hoped they would disengage themselves from the passions created by what was called a holy war, and live in unity with France and thereby enjoy a long period of peace.

Brother Charles did not want to employ violence to get the Touaregs to comply with his wishes. In a letter dated December 11, 1912, to the Duke of Fitz-James, Brother Charles outlined France's two responsibilities in Africa. First was "administration and civilization" for countries, "creating unity for the first time." In considering the inhabitants of the country, he saw "the Berbers, capable of rapid progress. The others, the Arabs, are slower. . . . The Negroes are completely different from all others. . . . But all are capable of progress." Brother Charles saw the progress of all the people as a responsibility.

The second responsibility was evangelization:

There must be enough good priests (not to preach, because they would be received the same way as a Brittany village would receive Turks coming to teach Mohammedanism, only more barbarically), but to make contacts, become liked and respected and to establish confidence and friendship. Next we would need good Christians, lay people of both sexes, to do the same thing and also to go places such as to the houses of Moslems where a priest could not go. They would give a picture of the Christian life, the Christian virtues, the Christian family, the Christian spirit. Good nuns would be needed to take care of the sick and to raise the children. They should mix in with the population, scattered in two's or three's wherever there are a priest and Christians. . . . This will result in conversions in twenty-five, fifty, or a hundred years. They will follow, just as fruit ripens, in the measure that enlightenment is spread. . . .

And Brother Charles said:

If these unhappy Moslems never see a priest but see only so-called Christians who are exploiters, unjust and tyrannical, giving vice as an example, how will they ever be converted? Why would they not hate our holy religion? Why would they not become more and more our enemies?

He continued in the same letter:

It is first necessary to know the population. We know very little of them. That is partly due to Moslem customs, but it is an obstacle we can overcome. The deplorable condition is that, to a horrifying degree, we are ignorant of the natives of our Africa. For the past thirty-two years I have rarely left North Africa (except for ten years between 1890 and 1900 when I was in Turkey,

Armenia, and the Holy Land). I have yet to see anyone—not an officer, missionary, colonist, or any other who knows enough of the natives. As for myself, I know my little Touareg corner passably, but the rest very superficially. There is a vice that must be remedied: the administrators, officers, missionaries should be in much *closer contact* with the people. They should remain in the same posts for *longer times*.

This was written in 1912. Brother Charles was exactly fifty years old.

26.

"Life Is a Battle"

In December, 1911, Captain Charlet was ordered to take Djanet, capital of the Ajjers. Maneuvering quickly, he succeeded in meeting Attici. Attici was the chief of the Ajjers who, thirty years earlier in 1881, had lain in ambush for Colonel Flatters and succeeded in massacring his mission. Attici fled, and Captain Charlet brought back to the Hoggar the dissident Touaregs whom the assassin of Flatters had taken with him in his flight thirty years earlier. Attici took advantage of the chaos to make many raids.

When the news of the new flight of Attici reached Brother Charles, he said:

As you say, Attici's flight will bother no one but him. It is better for us that it happened on one condition: that neither he nor Sisi Ag Khatkhat is ever accorded *aman,* and that they will be deported from this French territory forever with the order to shoot without further process if either ever sets foot back here again.

. . . Deportation is the best thing and it is they who have made this possible for us. Their presence anywhere in our territory would have had inconveniences. To kill them would be odious. Permanent deportation on pain of death solves everything. I sincerely hope that Ahmoud [another Touareg chief who took the side of the dissidents and who was with Attici in Tripoli] will be another one who will never set foot on our territory. He will never be anything but a problem. In general, the fewer nobles there are, the better off we will be. I wish the Imrad would all return, although those in the tow of the nobles are not the best of the lot; and I hope the nobles don't return. France is not so short of men after all, and when the men are Apaches, it's best that they should be deported for ever.

Attici and his comrades were plunderers pure and simple. And it was his friends, the Touaregs, that Brother Charles was protecting when he gave information against these plunderers and when he hoped that they would be thrown out of the country.

In April, 1913, an event took place that turned out to be a turning point in the history of the Hoggar. Ahmoud had formed a commando group at Rat, and he planned a raid on Djanct. On April 8th Lieutenant Gardel, head of forty spahis, was attacked at Esseyen, twenty-one miles south of Rat, by 350 Touareg dissidents: Gardel reported:

Our adversaries used the terrain very cleverly. They move in small groups across the open spaces, practically on their hands and knees and hiding behind small shelters. Their tactics are obvious. They are well informed about our forces. They will try to surround us. One might think they are troops trained for a European war. . . . I would not be surprised to learn that the Turks of Rat or of someplace had directed their clever maneuvers.

The fighting lasted three days. Insults were hurled: " 'Moslems, abandon the infidels! Come with us. We wish to fight only the Christians. Leave them. . . .' A Saharan, Aflane Ag Salem, a noble from the Ahaggar, replied: 'The French are our brothers. We have had only good from them. We will stay with them until death.' "

Gardel remained master of the territory.

The press reported this event which gave peace for a while to that corner of the Sahara. But it was not only a French victory. Moussa claimed it as a victory for the Hoggar. Ben Messis wrote a poem to the glory of Gardel, "Blessed Be His Mother!"

On August 24, 1913, Brother Charles wrote to Gardel:

Like you, I hope that Ahmoud and Inguedazzen stay permanently with the Italians. It is just punishment for those who have made fools of us. Also, it will be difficult for us to prevent them from collecting debts from their former Imrad, and that should be avoided. And as people put themselves under the protection of France, they have a right to a system of justice, to social equality, to the suppression of castes, to the abolition of abuse, and to the protection from unjust violence and exaction.

He wrote again, on December 28th, to Gardel, who was then thinking of retiring from Native Affairs:

It is true that the institution of Native Affairs has faults. It is true that certain vile characters are permitted to emerge, develop, and steep themselves in cynicism. But rest assured that you will never be confused with those people. Permit me to quote a principle that is a directive for life. It is from the great African, St. Augustine: "Know that you will have progressed on the road to perfection the more you have sought general interest rather than your own personal benefit." The "general interest" is that our natives should be governed with dignity and that men of honor and valor are consecrated to this work. Things are not always what they should be, but a good officer can diminish the bad and do good. He advances in rank, and the higher he goes, the more good he can do against evil. Life is a battle. For the good, for the progress of the natives, for the reign of justice and humanity and for the honor of France, officers worthy of the name should not be discouraged in front of the bad and abandon their share of the work. They must stay and fight against it and strive to make good prevail.

It should be said that Gardel had fallen victim to "low maneuvers." Brother Charles, in a letter of August 19th, gave him strong encouragement:

"The palm of the hand cannot cover the Sun," says a Touareg proverb. Truth will out. . . . I am not at all surprised by the jealousy and low maneuvers of which you are the object. But don't worry. . . . Keeping on a straight line, continually looking for the public good and forgetting one's personal interests gives one an interior peace and a feeling of having accomplished something. That, in this life on earth, is the greatest happiness. . . . Ambition, base acts, ugly doings, and all the things that attract greedy souls are pitiful to those who can keep above the mire and who, in the spirit of Light, look only to do good now and to await Infinite Goodness in Eternity.

As he had often asked of Moussa, Brother Charles asked the French officers to devote their lives to general interest.

Moussa often came to him for help, and he often gave warnings to the French. On March 31, 1912, Brother Charles wrote to Captain Charlet:

A representative of Moussa came here on March 17th to tell me that a *hartani* named Ben Beidari, originating, he thought, from Tidikelt, who had come to spend some time in the Adrar—and had recently spent several months at Tarhaouhaout trading, having crossed Tamanrasset and having spent the night of the 16th to 17th of March there in the hut of a *hartani* who gave him hospitality—passed along the following: "Letters from French authorities arrived at Tarhaouhaout specifying that a certain number of young Touareg girls should by force be put at the disposition of the soldiers. They also specified that a certain number of children should be forced to learn 'the reading of the *roumis*'." The Targui word which is used to explain this reading has a double or triple meaning. It means "reading" and more often "religious reading" and sometimes "religion." . . . The representative from Moussa, the uncle of our brigadier Ouenné, is a good man and he tells the Touaregs that there is no injustice or tyrannical act to fear from us. I have promised to ask you in seize Ben Beidari, who is on his way to In Salah, and to punish him severely to keep him from doing this again and to make him an example of what would happen to others.

Probably influenced by this, Brother Charles added it to his material for a long note on "the reorganization of the annex of In Salah" that he wrote to Laperrine in May.

There had been many changes since his arrival in the Sahara, but the administration of the territory had not changed accordingly. The annex at In Salah had one lieutenant and two hundred meharists to police and administer the area. Until his death, he continued to ask that the functions of the annex of the Tidikelt be divided among three annexes so that the Tidikelt, the Ahaggar, and the Ajjers each possessed an annex with a garrison.

That was the object of the note to Laperrine. But it was useless. The note stayed in the government archives.

On December 1, 1915, he wrote to Captain Duclos, "After three and one-half years I see nothing to modify in that which I have written. The changes seem to be even more desirable and necessary than ever." A year later, on the same day, Brother Charles was assassinated at Tamanrasset.

On April 10, 1916, he launched a new appeal to Commandant Meynier:

Plead with God that it will be remedied before it is too late.

Today the period of administration has come. The lieutenant knows the country; he sees the injustices and abuses and offenses that should be stopped. He sees where progress should be made. The people turn to him for justice; but he is submerged. He cannot be with the tribes and at the headquarters with his men at the same time. Another thing makes it impossible to govern the country by one officer: if this officer is replaced, everything he has learned is lost. Knowledge cannot be transmitted from one man to another in a few days.

The second part of the note makes a moving plea:

May I draw your attention to the interesting problem that the Touaregs present. There are two classes. One was the vassal of the other. They have been equal since this occupation. The plebeians who were vassals until 1908 are of a pure Berber race that has long been established in this country. They are hard workers, economical, peaceful, attached to their soil, gentle, intelligent, nearly settled even though they live in tents, raising goats and growing gardens. They form the biggest part of the population and they own nearly all the country's riches. Then there are the nobles who were the lords until 1908. They are also Berbers but of a race that came to the country by a conquest of a relatively recent period. They are lazy, wasters, quarrelsome, violent, intelligent, and daring. They are nomads who travel far with their herds of camels and, before the French conquest, lived mostly from looting. Today they are a weak, impoverished minority. They must either blend with the plebeians or disappear. With a little direction, the plebeians are capable of making rapid progress in civilization.

In the third part of his note, Brother Charles outlined ways that would help the Touaregs to progress. One condition was that there be officers who understood and respected the life and customs of the Touaregs. He proposed that the officers be promoted on the spot and that officers for annexes would be men who had previously held inferior positions in the same country:

The officers must be known to have characters worthy of respect and confidence. Their actions must be known to be for the public good and not for their own interests. It must be known that they will not be unjust and that they will repress abuse, that they will tell their superiors the truth in all matters, that their goal is to do good through serious work, and that they understand the wisdom and work necessary to aid progress. One bad act undoes the good of many good acts.

The manner in which Brother Charles concluded his note was a terrifying warning for the expiration of the "fifty years":

If we do not know how to attach these people to us, they will throw us out. Not only will we lose this empire entirely, but the unity which we have given them and which they have for the first time since the world exists will turn against us.

27.

"Bursts of Indignation"

On February 2, 1910, Brother Charles had said to Father Voillard: "By the Grace of God, the first officers who came into this country under Colonel Laperrine were all good and admirably gentle with the Touaregs. Wherever an officer passed, the people changed from being defiant and suspicious and became friendly."

Dr. Hérisson also described Laperrine:

With great frankness and humor, he poked fun at the anticlerical politicians whom he found shortsighted and uncultured. But he himself is sometimes breezy and irreverent in what he says. He judges men by their actions. Appearances do not impress him. As with all true colonizers, he has a broad view and a mind that is tolerant and understanding. The object of his life is to bring peace to the Sahara, to unite Algeria with the Sudan, to know the country and its people, and to make the people know France and to help the people improve their lot.

When the situation in the Sahara became serious, Laperrine had returned to France. In 1912 he had fallen sick, and it was probably during his convalescence that he wrote an article for the *Revue de Cavalerie* about Brother Charles. It is interesting to read what this impetuous man had to say. It is also interesting to see something of Laperrine about whom Charles André Julien had this to say, "The perpetual renewal of the spirit that refuses no task, the surge of a visionary without which one does not control reality, the gift of oneself, faith in the work to be done, the sense of duty, the taste for struggle, the willingness to be a leader, the love of a new country and its people—no bit can hold back these thoroughbreds."

Here are a few passages of Laperrine's account: "On his arrival in the Sahara, out of humility, he wished to remain unrecognized, and took the name of Brother Charles of Jesus. But he was too well known along the Algerian-Moroccan frontier for that to be a success."

Laperrine described the hermitage at Tamanrasset:

Less than 6 feet wide by 24 feet long and an average height of less than 6 feet. I say average because he was obliged to use branches of tamarisk as beams, and they were variously curved so that the ceiling was full of unexpected holes and bumps. Modern architects might do well to see it as an idea for contemporary design.

The length of the house is divided into three rooms of almost equal size: the room to the west is for living, then the bedroom-workroom, and then the chapel.

The door is worth describing. The threshold is up almost 3 feet, requiring a bit of gymnastics to hop up. It appears that this is a deterrent to scorpions and horned vipers, neither of which is fond of acrobatics. Then there are windows, about 1½ feet wide, which have window frames covered with imitation linen.

The Palace of Asekrem is larger, with four rooms 6 feet by 12 feet. With ceilings 6 feet high, it is luxurious.

As for Brother Charles's life, Laperrine says:

He does not show his asceticism. When he eats at the table with officers . . . he takes something of everything, eats as everybody else except that he does not eat meat on Fridays. One almost has to spy on him to realize the severe regime he imposes on his miserable body, which he doubtless does to atone for the delicious dinners he ate at Saumur. We heard of his illness of 1908 only through letters from Moussa Ag Amastane, who was worried by his frequent fainting spells.

There is nothing complaining about Father de Foucauld's piety. He is gay, a charming talker who shares his erudition in an amusing way. He is convinced that the misunderstandings between the French and the natives stem from the French not being sufficiently informed about the native religion and customs. He considers it a duty to initiate the officers and men in the Sahara into the Arab and Touareg mentality, which he knows very well.

Along with gaiety, he has a goodness, tact, and a broad-mindedness that conquer everyone's heart. He has made a conquest of every European in the Sahara who has met him. Most of them keep up a correspondence with him, telling him of their troubles and their joys, and often asking his advice. Among the ones who have asked his advice, there are a Jew, several Protestants and a former secretary of the Young Revolutionists of the Midi of France!

He has the same success with natives. You can't count the number of Chambas and Touaregs who have a real veneration for him, doubled by a solid friendship.

In long conversations with them he tries to learn as much as he can about their customs, traditions, history, and language, and at the same time he tries to teach them about France, the officers in charge, and the advantages they can derive from our civilization without breaking with their religion.

His personal influence is strong. The chief of the Hoggar Touaregs, Moussa Ag Amastane, never makes a decision without consulting him.

Laperrine, who was called "the children's general" because his nice smile attracted children, tells of Brother Charles's relationship with the young:

The Touareg adolescents and children show complete confidence in him. Their veneration is mixed with familiarity. They consider him a big brother who understands them and with whom they can joke and have fun. Their jokes are harmless. Because of his missing teeth, they named a craggy rock with a large gap, which legend had attributed to the stroke of a giant's saber, "the jaw of the Marabout."

Certain young people confide in him to a point where it resembles confession. If he does not give absolution to penitent Moslems, after having scolded them severely, very often he works on their behalf to get pardons for them from the authorities, their parents, their good friends—depending on the nature of their error. In some cases the drama ends in vaudeville: a marriage.

Illustrating the confidence children had in Brother Charles, Laperrine told of something that happened at Asekrem:

A serious accident happened to the head of a family living several meters from his "château." Everyone lost his head, except for a little thirteen-year-old girl. In the midst of the confusion, in the middle of the night she went to Father de Foucauld for help. He got right up, taking medicines and bandages he thought would be needed, and followed her. The little girl, having been brought up among rocks like a young goat, had had no difficulty climbing up to Asekrem, but it was another thing to descend with a man who was by no means so nimble. At dawn, camel riders on their way to hunt wild sheep saw a curious spectacle that would have made a beautiful picture: the little girl in the middle of the huge stones leading the Marabout by the hand and showing him with a stick where he could step without falling.

Laperrine wrote of Brother Charles at work:

He began studying the language, the customs, and the history of the Touaregs the minute he arrived in the Hoggar. Just as methodically, he seized every opportunity to pass along to the officers everything he learned; furthermore, the minute he found an answer to a question, he wrote it in a report or in a book so that others could know what he had learned.

Thus he has already compiled a dictionary of Touareg-French and another of French-Touareg, and a dictionary of proper names. He has collected and translated over three thousand poems and he has translated and analyzed quantities of texts from intelligent Touaregs that give the customs and history of the Kel Ahaggar. At the moment he is working on an enormous translation into French of the language, and for every word and expression he will give a bit of local tradition, custom, or historical fact. It will be a sort of encyclopedia.

Through some peculiar humility, he has decided that he does not want to have his work published under his name. Since an anonymous work is worthless, he has found the following solution. In 1906 he asked an old comrade from the army in Africa, a military interpreter named Motylinski, to join him and to study the language. Motylinski was old; he overestimated his strength, and died soon after his return to Constantine. Foucauld took it upon himself to put his notes in order, and he took that occasion to incorporate his own work on the Touaregs, their customs and their language, under the pretext that it was Motylinski who, in collecting the first texts, had set down the methods of work that should be adopted. So the poor Motylinski is supposed to have done in four months work that it took his friend seven years to do.

For his task, Foucauld needed a man who knew both Arabic and the language of the Touaregs. There was only one man who could do it. He was Ba Hamou, son of the governor of Rat, who had, after many adventures, become secretary to Moussa Ag Amastane. This Ba Hamou, fat as a monk out of Balzac, intelligent but lazy as a rattlesnake and as gluttonous as he was lazy, was an amusing contrast to Father de Foucauld. However, Father de Foucauld turned his faults into qualities, and by dispersing generous quantities of sugar and tea, he extracted a remarkable amount of work from him.

I have often been asked what De Foucauld did to kill time at Tamanrasset and Asekrem. In reality, he didn't have a minute to himself. To the long hours of work with Ba Hamou were added talks with the many visiting Touaregs, caring for their sick, acts of charity, and so on. In order to have time to say Mass and to read his breviary, he works into the night. He has seven or eight volumes on theology (St. Thomas Aquinas, I think) in cases under his bed, but he hasn't read a page. . . .

Certain visits of the Touaregs give a bit of local color. It is a windfall for Father de Foucauld when he gets his hand on certain of the very old ladies of the noblesse because they are the ones who know the most about traditions, legends, genealogy, poetry, and so on. Nothing is funnier than the sight of Brother Charles holding court, pencil in hand, in the middle of a circle of old dowagers who are sitting on the ground talking, sipping tea, and smoking pipes.

Laperrine tells what use Brother Charles made of a stereoscope:

Views of the Sahara where the Touaregs can spot known people are the most popular, along with shots of a Paris steeplechase. The person who was looking would tell the others what he was seeing, accompanied by grand gestures. This was very useful to De Foucauld for his linguistic studies. He knew what they were seeing, and he listened to the words and turn of phrases they would use to describe it.

People have also asked if Father de Foucauld makes many conversions. No. He has not made one, and what is more, he is not looking for any to make. He says that it will be some years before Moslems can be converted. He preaches Christian morality simply by the righteousness of his character, his goodness, his justice, and his selflessness.

[In concluding, Laperrine wrote:] Until now I have mentioned only the goodness and indulgence of Father de Foucauld. I would give a false idea of his character if I did not mention that his indulgence is not without limit. When he finds that he is dealing with people who are dishonest or who misuse their strength to oppress the weak or who are slackers, his indulgence runs out. Then he has great bursts of indignation.

28.

Ouksem, His Child

As 1912 drew to an end, Brother Charles was alone in the heart of the Sahara; but he was happy:

The holy days of Advent, always so touching, are particularly touching here. Tamanrasset with its forty lights of the poor farmers could well be Nazareth and Bethlehem in the days of Our Lord. . . . I am always working on the language . . . there is so much to do. . . . I haven't seen anyone from the French Army since August.

In the year 1912, an old project of his began to take shape: a trip to France with a young Touareg boy. On May 16, 1912, he wrote to his cousin:

It is a unique way to dispel a mass of errors, to bring them closer to us, to let them know a little about France. And that is a way of getting them closer to Jesus, of bringing them to Him.

There is a young Touareg boy whom I have known ever since I came here who is remarkably good. Confidence and affection are well established with him and his family. He is so fine that we can hope for great progress from him.

On October 19th he wrote to Father Voillard:

I have always wanted to bring a Touareg to France to let him see our life to open his eyes to new ideas. Abbé Huvelin encouraged me to do that. This year the idea seems possible. The Touareg who is the best one I know . . . would like nothing better than to accompany me.

On July 12th he wrote again to Father Voillard:

We will not visit museums or curiosities, but show him the affectionate family life of Christians, show him the Christian life and how religion is a part of life. The young Touareg whom I will bring is twenty-one. He was seven when I first met him, and I know him and all his family well. . . . He is serious, intelligent, well mannered, and of the best plebeian family of the country. This is a country of castes. There are plebeians and patricians, and the plebeians are morally superior and are the hope for the country.

On April 27, 1913, Brother Charles and Ouksem left Tamanrasset. It was a happy voyage. For one thing, Brother Charles was to see his family. On April 9th he had written a friend, "In twenty-three years, I have spent fourteen days with my only sister, ten days with my cousins—my closest family."

On June 11, 1913, aboard the *Timgad,* he wrote to Monseigneur

Livinhac: "The first two stages of our crossing have gone well. The sea has been so beautiful that even Ouksem had no seasickness. He says he likes a boat better than an automobile. I'm glad we are traveling first class because Ouksem finds it so agreeable."

They arrived at Marseille on June 12th. Brother Charles did not want his young friend to be received as Moussa had been. He did want his friend to be a guest of his family as he himself had been a guest of the Touaregs, and he wanted him to be received as a member of the family and not as a native of the Sahara.

Wherever they went, there was simplicity. When Charles was with his family, Ouksem was a member of the family.

"I remember," wrote a friend, "that sympathetic child's great admiration for the Father. I saw the two of them down on their hands and knees, using a carving knife to cut out trousers that the young Touareg was to sew during his leisure." The Touareg also learned how to knit so that he could later teach the women of his tribe. He became quite adroit, but Charles had difficulty and dropped stitches. Ouksem also learned to ride a bicycle.

Charles lived a completely family life. He ate whatever was served. At night, when Ouksem slept, he took care of his prayers and correspondence.

On July 3rd he wrote to Father Voillard: "Thanks to God, Ouksem has not been sick a minute, nor does he seem to be homesick. Everything he has seen has been good for him. He has visited schools, hospitals, convents. . . ."

Brother Charles presented Ouksem with a beautiful gift: a magnificent Lebel gun. It was the best money could buy. Ouksem wanted to shoot it at once on the property of Marie de Blic, Charles's sister.

Just before leaving for Africa, Charles wrote his thanks to his sister. "I see that his joy at the prospect of seeing his family is tempered by his sadness at leaving those of you who have received him so well in France. The apostolate of kindness is the best of all."

Charles's family and friends found him on this voyage—the longest he had ever made, and his last—to be a complete realist who, with disarming simplicity, saw through everything.

Brother Charles and Ouksem rejoined the Touaregs on November 22nd. On November 25th he wrote to Father Voillard:

> I am happy to be back in my life of solitude and regulation. The Touaregs come to me more often than ever. It is obvious that Ouksem's trip has increased their confidence in me. If I wished it, conversations would go on from morning to night. I must limit them, though, and continue my work on the language.

On February 10th, he wrote to Father Marchal: "Ouksem's trip is bearing fruit. Before, I saw his father often, but now I see him every day. All my friends here are coming more often. But the hour to talk of Jesus has not yet arrived. . . ."

29.
"As They Really Are"

The trip to France in 1913 gave Brother Charles an opportunity to think over the entire situation in the Sahara.

He wrote about slavery, noting that a French law of 1905 prohibited the buying and selling of slaves throughout the Ahaggar. While he said that the laws were respected, he added, "There are about six thousand Kel Ahaggar who hold about three thousand slaves, all black." He said, in general, the slaves were well treated; but morally, "the slave population is the worst thing in the country." He concluded:

> Most of the Kel Ahaggars know that in principle France does not permit slavery and that it is simply to avoid disorder from sudden change that slavery is tolerated and that this tolerance is

temporary and that an end will be put to it. But they cannot really accept the fact that the end will come. They can't imagine who will care for the animals. . . .

It is difficult to get them to admit the injustice of slavery. After all, they are Moslems, and their faith embraces slavery and even defines the rights of the masters. The more attached the Kel Ahaggars are to slavery, the more the French authorities should work against it, taking every opportunity to force progress, accepting no setback until slavery is finally abolished in the Ahaggar.

Brother Charles also worked to interest the French in settling at Tamanrasset. For this, he met M. Bourdarie, director of the *Revue indigène* and discussed three projects with him:

1. A young student who wished to devote his career to the study of the Ahaggar—history, language, archaeology, and so on.

2. The establishment of a charity hospital for illegitimate Touareg children (help from the antislavery society had been promised).

3. The acceptance of one or two couples to go to establish a Franco-Touareg school.

Brother Charles wanted his idea of brotherhood and unity to become fact. He wanted to do all possible to get the French to settle in the Hoggar and to know the country and the people better. He promised M. Bourdarie material for articles for his magazine.

But he did not confuse issues, as can be seen in a letter to a young Saharan lieutenant on December 28, 1913:

I am of the same feeling as the *Revue indigène* in that I want the same result in the end, which is that our subjects will one day be our brothers. But there are four *sine qua non* conditions:

1. Careful choice of administrators (civil or military);

2. More administrators who will be in direct contact with the public;

3. Longer tour of duty for administrators (requiring a certain amount of on-the-spot promotions);

4. Progressive and rapid suppression of the native chiefs.

The *Revue indigène* carries some articles written by ambitious people who simply want to get talked about and who want personal gain. It's too bad for the journalists and editors that modest people stay away and that the ambitious come forth. I told that to M. Bourdarie, in whom I have confidence, and this is what he told me, "Try to find some good correspondents for me. That is all I ask."

Naturally you would find it difficult to do a serious, critical article, but I think a short piece on some Algerian subject would be very interesting to the readers of that magazine. For example, an extract from a Chamba or Touareg story could give a picture of your over-all work. Anything that shows the friends of the natives as they really are is a good work. . . ."

He wrote to his family of his plans, and on April 26, 1914, he wrote back to one of his nieces in answer to questions about how a Frenchwoman could do good for the Touaregs:

1. One must be willing to spend a long time with them to learn their language (which isn't difficult) and to be known by them. Good can be accomplished only when you know them and they know you.

2. One must have patience and gentleness. The Touaregs go quickly from extreme savagery to excessive familiarity.

3. One must know something of medicine, particularly of illnesses of young women and babies, and how to take care of the sick with no doctors and no pharmacies.

4. One must know how to give vaccinations;

5. Be capable of bringing up a child abandoned by its mother at birth;

6. Be able to teach elementary hygiene;

7. Know how to wash, iron, and cook well enough to teach a little to the natives;

8. Be able to tell how to plant a garden, build a chicken coop and a shed for goats.

It would be good, but not mandatory, to know how and when to shear lambs and goats, how to spin. . . . It would be good to know how to crochet and knit in order to teach the women. The women know how to sew very well and they can cure hides and make beautiful works of leather. They think that spinning, weaving, knitting, and so on, is undignified. They don't like to try anything new.

. . . One of the most important things to teach the Touareg women is personal care. They never wash themselves or their clothes and they put butter on their hair. They don't have fleas because fleas don't exist here, but they are covered with other parasites. They say washing makes them sick, which has a grain of truth, since they wash in the open air and don't dry. . . . It would be a good idea for a Frenchwoman in this country to have a good supply of soap and ordinary towels to hand out to these women. Furthermore, there are many women who ask for something to make their hair black when it begins to turn white. A few bottles of black dye . . . would make many friends.

30.

Lay Missionaries

Brother Charles had had the idea to found an Association for some time. He wrote statutes for it at Eastertime in 1908. His idea was to put good Christians with the Moslems, to teach the Moslems and bring civilization to them so that finally they would become Christians.

His first trip to France in 1909 was a start, and Abbé Huvelin had given him encouragement.

This Association, wrote Brother Charles, "would produce a return to the Gospel . . . love for the Holy Eucharist . . . a surge toward the evangelization of infidels." Farmers, settlers, merchants, artisans, landowners—Christians of all walks of life—would help the missionaries and would be missionaries.

Brother Charles wrote about his "lay missionaries":

They will do all for all to save them. In hating evil they will love mankind. . . . They will remember that all men are children of the Heavenly Father who wishes to see unity in the great family of mankind as a father wishes to see it among his sons.

. . . If we are poor, we should not look for ways to gain that which we want to give as alms, for that would be contrary to the example of Jesus. Let us follow His example in all things. In Nazareth, He was poor and could give little. But the little He could give He gave willingly. He gave His heart, His tenderness, His compassion, His kind words, His care, His service. The houses of the brothers and sisters must be made known to the unhappy —they must be made known to neighbors as houses of charity.

. . . One does good not by what one says or does but by what one is, in the measure of grace that accompanies these acts, in the degree to which they are acts of Jesus manifesting themselves through us. By the examples they set, the brothers and sisters will be living sermons. Each must be a model of evangelical life. When one sees them, one will see the Christian life, the Christian religion, that which is the Gospel and that which is Jesus. The difference between their lives and non-Christian lives will make it apparent where the truth lies. . . .

To save us, God came to us and lived closely with us from the Annunciation to the Ascension. To save our souls, He continues to come to us and to live with us each day and each hour in the Holy Eucharist. And so must we—to save souls—go to them, mix with them, live closely with them.

. . . As the Christians of the early Church, the priests and the laymen form one heart and one spirit. "Love one another—it is by this that you will be recognized as my disciples." "May they all be as one, as we are as one." "I am in them and you are in me, so that the world should know that you have sent for me." It is with accord, union, brotherly love that Jesus says his disciples will be recognized. He wishes them to be at one as He is at one with His father. He shows them the cause and principle of their union and of His love which is present in each of them. . . . Those who let Him live in them and act in them are of necessity one. He announces that this union and brotherly love will convert souls and lead them to faith.

Brother Charles talks further of the union among brothers and sisters: "They must be gentle with each other, and anger, rudeness, bitterness, obstinacy, coldness, and impatience must be as far from their hearts and lips as they were from the heart and lips of Jesus. They must be united; they must be of 'but one heart and one spirit.'"

Brother Charles asked that the Christians of the world unite to consecrate themselves to the non-Christians. "These people are like orphans. Spiritually, they are abandoned children. It is an obligation to take in and raise these orphans and foundlings."

The principles he wrote in his statutes were the principles by which he lived at Tamanrasset. Beginning in 1909, he wrote many letters to young French boys and girls, trying to interest them in following his vocation. It was his belief that lay people had an important role in evangelization: "The ecclesiastical world and the lay world don't realize what they can give to each other. Laymen are needed side by side with priests, seeing what priests don't see, going where priests can't go. . . ."

This was his answer as to why there were so many non-Christians:

The fundamental virtues—Charity, Humility, Gentleness—are missing or they are too weak. . . . Charity is the foundation of our religion. It asks each Christian to love his neighbor as if he were himself. Consequently, the salvation of one's neighbor is as important as the salvation of one's self. *Every Christian must be an apostle.* That is not advice; it is a command—the command of charity. . . .

All force must be abandoned; we must banish militant ideas from ourselves. Jesus taught us to go "like sheep in the midst of wolves," not to speak with bitterness and unkindness, not with arms. . . .

We must read and reread the Gospel without stopping, so that we will have the spirit, deeds, words, and thoughts of Jesus before us so that we may one day think, talk, and act as He did.

The application of this is difficult because it touches on funda-
mentals of the inner spirit and because the need for it is universal.
But the difficulties mustn't stop us. The bigger they are, the more
important it is for us to work quickly, with all our might. God
helps those who work for Him. God has never forgotten man.
It is man who often forgets God.

The Association became a preoccupation for him. In February,
1910, he had no luck in finding a priest in France who was willing
to take charge of the Association. He sent the statutes to Rome, but
he had heard nothing since 1911. "The silence does not surprise me,
for I lived for a time in Rome fifteen years ago. I do not give up
hope, nor will I ever."

During his trip of 1913, Brother Charles had seen the Archbishop
of Paris about his project. And he spent the day—September 25,
1913—in Viviers with his bishop, Monseigneur Bonnet, who was
very interested.

Brother Charles did not, however, limit his project to the French
colonies. He was thinking of the entire world. On November 5, 1913,
he wrote to Father Marchal, "Would you be good enough to send
me the title, publisher, and price of the *Atlas of Missions* that you
told me about, or any other documentation about missions established throughout the world?"

In July, 1914, he spoke further, about the lack of faith of the
young of his time and about the painful struggle between men of
different classes:

We must react by simplicity and moderation in our own lives
in hope that we will be an example for those around us. By
Christian fraternity we must fill the chasm that is created by the
differences in conditions. . . . I don't think we should talk much
or write much, but we must reform ourselves . . . we must try to
reform those whom we influence . . . try to spread reform. We
must work continuously, without becoming discouraged, against
ourselves, the world, and the Devil until the end of time. Act,
pray, and suffer—these are our methods.

On August 24, 1914, he wrote to his cousin that he thought he would leave Tamanrasset the following February to stay in France until October: "It is for my little Brotherhood that I plan such a long stay in France."

31.
"For All Mankind"

Abbé Crozier worked for the Association. He arranged to have published, in Lyon, a small, thirty-two-page pamphlet entitled *Union apostolique universelle* (Universal Apostolic Union). The author's name was not mentioned, but Christ with a heart and a cross was on the cover.

The first part of ten pages was called, "Un apôtre au Sahara" (An Apostle of the Sahara), and it was the first biography of Brother Charles of Jesus. The name De Foucauld was not mentioned:

> Brother Charles of Jesus—that is the name he bears before God —has an apostolate of Charity in the Touareg country. He cares for their sick and infirm; he is often their counselor. . . . Brother Charles of Jesus gives to each all that he can. He talks to them of God and of His Justice, His goodness, His love, and of the moral law we carry in our consciences and in our hearts. He has not made a conversion, for, as he says, "As a seed of the Gospel, I must decay in the soil of the Sahara to prepare for future harvests. That is my vocation."

Abbé Crozier emphasized that Brother Charles looked beyond the world of Moslems: "The conversion of Moslems does not satisfy his zeal. He thinks of all souls that are separated from the truth of the Catholic Life, and especially of all infidels."

Brother Charles began by consecrating himself to the Moslems, and then he looked toward non-Christians the world over.

A few years after it was published, the pamphlet, with Brother Charles's call for help, was read by hundreds of thousands of people.

As did Jesus Christ, he calls workers of good will to respond to the wishes of the Master of the Harvest. . . . Recently, he was accompanied by one of his Touaregs to visit France and his family. He visited devoted friends to whom he confided his hopes and his sorrows, and he asked them again that auxiliaries be sent to the mission in the Sahara which fills his soul and heart. . . .

If Catholics wish to conserve and enrich their faith, they should all become apostles that hand their faith on to other people.

In the nineteenth century in Lyon, a humble girl, Pauline Jaricot, had founded a work called The Propagation of the Faith, which had tremendous reverberations. Its aim was to interest Catholics in the non-Christians of the entire world. Abbé Crozier saw Brother Charles's Association as a new form for the twentieth century of that earlier mission. If nineteenth-century missionaries had given non-Christian nations evidence of martyrdom, the twentieth century should rouse itself with missionaries who should spend their lives bringing evidence of friendship and love to the masses of non-Christians.

The first words of the second part of Abbé Crozier's pamphlet were very significant: "Jesus Christ was the first apostle, the apostle of His father: 'As my Father has sent me, so I send you.'"

Every Christian is sent by the Father to preach Jesus Christ to all people on earth. The Association did not impose obligations on its members:

"The Universal Apostolic Union asks no new responsibilities. It directs all men toward the meaning of the Incarnation, the Redemption, and the Church, which exist and work only to enlighten, save, and vivify all men, leading them to Jesus Christ."

That is simple, and the proposed methods are also simple:

To practice this universal apostolate, one must pray, act, suffer. To pray, act, and suffer are the Christian life. I can and I wish, simple Christian that I am, in order to make my life better understood and better lived, to have *an apostolic life, perpetual and universal.*

An apostolic prayer is the simple offering to Jesus: "O Father, I offer unto You Your Son Jesus Christ."

Abbé Crozier discussed the second way, *to act,* and he asked for lay apostles, wishing that all Christians would comprehend their vocation and work to preach the love of Christ: "Such has been the practice of the Church down through the centuries. Aquila and his wife Priscilla rendered great service to St. Paul at Corinth, Asia, and Rome. He calls them his coadjutors. He expresses not only his gratitude to them but the gratitude of every Church founded among pagans."

For the third method—*to suffer*—Abbé Crozier, having looked at the works of apostolic men throughout the ages, wrote, "Christians, who work and suffer, cease to work and suffer without guidance, merit, and goal."

These three methods were Brother Charles's goal throughout his life. He never stopped praying for the Touaregs, for all mankind, and for the non-Christians of the world. He never stopped suffering and working for them. Above all else he hoped that all men could love one another as brothers, could live in union and harmony together.

Inspired by him, Abbé Crozier ended his treatise with a prayer of Jesus on the eve of His death: "May all be one."

In a letter written during Pentecost, 1916, to Father Voillard, Brother Charles said that Abbé Huvelin, in 1909, had told him to turn the project of his Association over to Monseigneur Bonnet:

. . . I presented it to Monseigneur Bonnet, who told me to work at top speed for its realization. He also told me to extract brief statutes from the project, high-light the goals, to stay in the Sahara myself and not to change my life but to find one person who could take the necessary steps to bring life to the work and to try to establish the headquarters in some large city such as Paris, Lyon, or Marseille. Paris was his preference, and I was to present it to the bishop and even go to Rome, if necessary, to obtain Papal benediction. . . .

Since then, nothing has progressed. Monseigneur Bonnet is always encouraging. Although it remains a project, it has several brothers and sisters, some of whom are very fervent. Outside of the White Fathers at the Trappist, I know only four or five ecclesiastics. I have asked two of them to take my place and establish the brotherhood. Their piety, zeal, and authority make them suitable for this work. One of them, Canon Caron of Versailles, refused because of too much other work. The other, Abbé Crozier, refused because of his age and infirmities. A third, Abbé Laurain (Saint-Sulpice, Paris), tried; but he had to refuse, finally, because of the weight of his other work. A lay brother, very fervent, is capable of assuring publication of the Bulletin and, if God lets him live (he is at the front), he can render great service. But I have not yet seen an ecclesiastic who will take the work to his heart and devote himself to its realization. I am less capable than almost any other priest to do what has to be done. Having learned only to pray in solitude, hold my tongue, live among books, and talk with the poor—all of which I do badly—I am nothing but ignorant, timid, and incapable.

On July 18, 1916, he learned of the death of Abbé Crozier, the principal recruiter of the Association. To Joseph Hours, from whom he received the news, Brother Charles replied: "More than ever I think of our brotherhood. . . . I think I will go to France soon after the Armistice and make every effort to establish it and put it into operation. I would like not to leave France until that is done."

And if Brother Charles had lived, we would probably have found him, after the war, working to establish his Association.

On October 1, 1916, two months before his death, he wrote, "I look upon the long months that the war keeps me in the Sahara as a time for retreat during which I pray, reflect, and ask Jesus to let me know the form our Union, our brotherhood, should take."

32.

"Peace to All Men of Good Will"

The situation in the Hoggar was so difficult that by December 13, 1913, Brother Charles had put his affairs in order and drawn up his will. He wanted the little he had to be used to serve evangelization. He gave most of his papers and possessions to the White Fathers, for they had done the most to help evangelize the Sahara. He concluded:

> I wish to be buried on the spot where I die and rest there until the Resurrection. I forbid that my body be moved or that it be raised from the spot where the Good Lord will have made me finish my pilgrimage. Burial will be simple, without a coffin, and the grave will have no monument except a wooden cross.

But his heart lived in peace. "One must pray and hope always. Love hopes for all. When one is praying to the Heart of Jesus, how can one not hope?" he wrote on November 27th. And on February 10, 1914:

> God is the Good God. He knows of what He created us. He sees our desire, our will to do what He wishes, and He sees our misery. He loves us more than a mother, more than a husband. . . . Our love, the union of our will with His, the acquiescence to all He wishes from us is all He wishes from his poor creatures. Peace to all men of good will.
>
> [On February 17:] My life is the same. I am well. It is cold and dry; not a drop of water. I have just finished my first dictionary. I estimate that it will take me five years of work to finish what I have started. Will the Good Lord give it to me? May His good will make it possible!
>
> [On March 17:] Don't worry. I don't have the strength to kill myself with work. When I have gone a little too long, I see it

quickly and I slow down. I give all I can, but it is far from what I was once able to do. Also, I am so often interrupted by visitors that I have many unexpected times of recreation.

Pages of his notebooks listing visitors have been found for February, 1914. The pages are full of the names of his Touareg friends.

An officer, Meynier, passed several days of the winter of 1913–1914 at Tamanrasset, and he recounted what he saw:

The program of the second day was planned by the Father. It was his opinion that in tribes who have a certain culture, a feminine element was necessary. No one can ignore the important social role women played in the middle of patriarchal traditions (it is sometimes said matriarchal traditions). He proposed that we invite all the ladies of the Touareg aristocracy . . . to our big tent to offer them a "cup of tea."

In the afternoon, we received the "ladies" from nearby. They arrived beautifully draped in motley blankets and accompanied by young servants or young friends.

Among them was the famous Dassine, whose beauty, poetic talent, and the platonic love that her cousin, Moussa Ag Amastane, had for her made her a celebrity throughout the Hoggar. The ladies sat on the rug of the tent and we—the doctor, the journalist, my secretary, and myself—sat facing their half-circle. Father de Foucauld sat apart on a modest stool. He served as interpreter and broke the ice. Several noble warriors (including my dear Ouenni, my flag-bearer) came quietly into the room, lowered their *lithams* over their foreheads in respect for the "noble ladies," and seated themselves behind the women. The conversation started with polite questions about the health and news of absent friends. Dassine, who was absolutely hidden, except for one eye, answered our questions with a pleasant, but muted, voice.

"Why are you covered up when everyone in the desert knows the reputation of Dassine, the great poet, the joy of the Imzad?"

"It's because I no longer merit the reputation. I am an old woman, and it is more fitting for the younger ones to shine in their turn."

The young ones, on the other hand, had lifted their veils and had put their heavy blankets near them, showing with pleasure their young faces which were, as is the custom, too heavily made up. . . .

I showed the ladies photographs of my wife and children. "Can it be possible," they exclaimed, "that wives of the *Nassare* put such strange and cumbersome structures on their heads?"

Questions went back and forth. We asked to hear some Touareg music. Dassine, deciding to uncover her face, which is still beautiful, took her violin, her *imzad,* and played a melody for us— muted and played with one chord, using a primitive bow—in which the women of nomad warriors wish to express the different emotions in their existence. Romance, songs of the honor of warriors, joy of their return, plaints for the lost.

The doctor whom Meynier mentioned was Vermale, who had decided to study in the Hoggar. "I couldn't be happier than to see that you want to study here," said Brother Charles. "Ethnology, anthropology, anthropometry, mores, and customs—it goes without saying, with all my heart, I will do all possible to be useful to you. I will tell you the little I know, and I have books on these subjects that are at your disposal."

The doctor wrote in his diary: "His hermitage is a poem—imagine a room forty-five feet long. . . . Inside, there are great quantities of things . . . books in homemade bookcases. But all is in perfect order. I cannot understand how it can hold so many things and still leave room for someone to live."

He found Tamanrasset different from other *ksours* of the Hoggar because there were few huts left. They had disappeared, and houses were in their place:

These constructions make Tamanrasset look like a little farming village. It is thanks to the Reverend Father de Foucauld that Tamanrasset is in a relatively flourishing situation. His counsel and example have led numerous Touaregs to work the rich ground for their living. Among them, the Dag Rali and their chief, Ouksem, are particularly interested in agriculture, and their perseverance is bearing fruit today.

It was true. There had been such change in Tamanrasset and the Hoggar that on July 21, 1914, Brother Charles could write this to an officer:

The Ahaggar, so long a haven for bandits, has become a country of great peace and calm. The nobles, who were the bandits, are now impoverished, almost annihilated, and the few that are left are diminishing in number. They have begun to enlist, which is the best thing they can do. The Imrad, the plebeians, are, in general, good people, peaceful and hard-working. They have improved their agriculture and are becoming settled. It is the beginning of civilization. When you saw Tamanrasset, there were two houses and the rest huts. Now there are two huts and the rest are houses.

Brother Charles wrote on July 23, 1914:

The drought continues, and the consequences are paradoxical. It has been four years and eight months since it rained. This drought has reduced to nearly nothing the goats and sheep that we saw were so numerous. . . . Meanwhile the country is not dying of hunger. . . . The continued drought has pushed the people toward agriculture. Fields and houses are multiplying. There are no more *zéribas*. All have been replaced by houses.

"My neighboring Touaregs continue to be very affectionate," he wrote. But, he was having trouble with Moussa, who

continuously adds new debts without paying old ones. . . . The situation, it appears, is very strained between Moussa and the Kel Rela. . . . I don't yet know the whole truth and it is not easy to know it. The Taïtoq and their Imrad—poor and plundering—are said to have stolen a number of camels that were in pastures belonging to the Kel Ahaggar. Moussa protested . . . and it looks as if war would have followed if the French authorities had not been there.

33.
A Man of Prayer

With all of Brother Charles's various occupations, one is inclined to forget that first and foremost he was a man of prayer. At the core of his life there were long moments in the heart of each day of solitary contemplation of God.

Here is a timetable that was compiled by him on December 21, 1911; he followed it as scrupulously as possible:

3:30 A.M.– 6:00 A.M.:	PRAYERS	3:30–4:00	Angelus: Veni Creator Matins, Laudes
		4:00–5:00	Preparation for Mass. Mass, acts of Grace.
		5:00–6:00	housework and *frustulum* (breakfast) prime, terce, sext, none Holy Gospels and written meditation. Elevation. Imitation.
6:00 A.M.–11:30 A.M.:	WORK		
11:30 A.M.–12:30 P.M.:	PRAYERS (and lunch)		Angelus. Veni Creator Examination.
12:30 P.M.– 6:00 P.M.:	WORK		

| 6:00 P.M.– 8:00 P.M.: | PRAYERS and collation | 6:00–7:00 7:00–8:00 | Vespers and Rosary collation and house-work Compline, Consecration |

Angelus, Veni Creator
Examination.

That, then, was his day: seven and a half hours of sleep, eleven hours of work, well distributed in two parts of five and a half hours each, one in the morning, the other in the afternoon. (The work was intellectual work, it should be noted.) The rest of the time was for prayers, household chores, and meals, and the meals must have been eaten quickly, as only thirty minutes was allowed for three meals. Nearly five hours were devoted to prayer during the important hours of the morning and again in the evening. These hours were filled first with Mass and the Breviary, which took close to three hours. He has not noted the hour for the Adoration of the Holy Sacrament. If his hours of prayer took place in his small chapel before the tabernacle, he does not seem to have given a definite time for Adoration of the Eucharist. Circumstances forced changes between Nazareth and Béni-Abbès.

At the bottom of his timetable, Brother Charles indicated reading to be done during free moments (no doubt on Sunday):

> Free moments—The life of Our Saviour (Fouard)
> 2 pages of the Rules
> 2 pages of the Union
> reading on Missions

During the last five years of his life, Brother Charles rarely mentioned the state of his soul as he had between 1890 and 1900 when Abbé Huvelin was his spiritual father. With Father Voillard, who succeeded Abbé Huvelin as his spiritual father, Brother Charles spoke more of the experience he had had and of his projects for evangelization. If he hoped, after years of work, to be able to put prayer above all else, events did not let him have his wish. He wrote to Father Voillard on May 14, 1911: ". . . my soul is in great need of solitude, prayer, meditation. I can spare for that only half the time I should for my own and other souls, for I must finish the linguistic works."

On December 6, 1911, he wrote, "I do not give enough time to prayer, meditation, religious reading, but I think it is better to continue as I am, for I do not want to take away time devoted to the Touaregs."

However, if Brother Charles had been able to finish his linguistic work before his death, it is doubtful whether he would have devoted more time to prayer. "The works I have started will be finished, I think, in three years, if the Good Lord grants me life," he wrote on October 19, 1912. "It gives me joy to think that I will then have more time to give to souls—make more visits, hold longer conversations, have more intimate contact." On December 7, 1915, a year before his death, he said, "If nothing interrupts my work, it will doubtless be finished in a year . . . then I will have time for the Brotherhood which I want to establish. It will also give me more time for the souls here. . . ."

During his last retreat, Pentecost, 1916, he wrote about his Association: ". . . during these days which I have spent in semi-retreat, I have prayed particularly to God to make me know His Will on the subject. . . . I feel that God has helped me. I have rewritten the statutes to make them brief and extremely simplified."

One thing should be underlined in the spiritual life of Brother Charles during these last years, and that is the active aspect of his contemplation.

His prayers had become *active*. He asked for the difficulties and sufferings that came his way, for they were, as he said to his friend Louis Massignon, "the chance to state and prove our Love of Him."

On July 31, 1909: "By the struggles and sufferings undergone for Him, we declare our daily love. It is more than a declaration . . . it is a declaration with proof."

On August 31, 1910, he wrote, "The periods of anguish, waiting, uncertainty are times of grace for the spirit, for when it suffers, it prays."

On May 29, 1914, "May each misery give birth to a double act of humility and love, confidence, hope." On July 15, 1916:

We must tell ourselves of the graces that God has personally given us since our birth and that of our infidelities, and then we will find —we above all who have lived far from God for so long—proofs of His love for us that are more sure and more touching than the many proofs we have of our misery. Thus we can lose ourselves in His love with limitless confidence.

For Brother Charles prayer was an occasion to declare to God that one wished to love Him and to lose oneself in Him.

That is what he wished to express to his cousin as he recalled words Abbé Huvelin had given him twenty years earlier, words of St. John of the Cross: "Work, suffer and remain silent," he wrote on February 10, 1914. ". . . I understand one's insensibility to prayer and the incapacity to pray with this sorrow on top of all others. It is the effect of too much unhappiness and preoccupation. The spirit is numbed. It seems that one feels nothing and is before God without the power to follow a single thought."

On August 24th:

One suffers usefully when one suffers in the love of God, that is, in having the will to love Him, the will to do as He wishes, in wishing that all He wishes, and not what we wish, will be done. . . . To love God means to wish what He wishes, to wish that His will will be done. It is not to feel that when one loves Him gratuitously, gently, independent of ourselves, that that has no merit. . . . When one suffers knowing what one loves, one suffers less, one produces perhaps less fruit. The grain of the wheat must die. . . .

34.
Officers' Briefing

At 5:00 A.M. on September 3, 1914, a fast courier arrived from Fort Motylinski to tell Brother Charles that war had been declared between France and Germany and that the whole of Europe was going up in flames. As Brother Charles considered this explosive news in the peace of the Hoggar, he thought about Strasbourg, where he had been born, and he thought of his former army friends who were then at the front.

On September 15th, his fifty-sixth birthday, he wrote to his cousin: "Evidently my duty is to stay here to help keep the people calm. I will not leave Tamanrasset until the war is over." On the same day, he wrote to his sister: "The Touaregs have never even heard of Germany. They will certainly remain in their habitual calm, occupied with their material interests, without suspecting that there is a storm raging in our country at home, unless there is violence from Algeria, Sudan, or Tripoli."

Madame de Bondy had sent him a subscription to *l'Echo de Paris*, and Brother Charles kept up with the news. For him the meaning of the war was simple: "It is a struggle for Europe's liberty, which has been seriously threatened."

He read the casualty lists that were published in *l'Echo de Paris*. On November 24th:

In the lists of killed in action I have so far counted ten friends, mostly from Africa, several of whom I loved dearly.

. . . I wrote Laperrine who is at the front. He sees things clearly and he is wise and gives good advice. I asked him, if Algeria and the Ahaggar remain perfectly calm, whether I should not go to France to try to serve until peace, as a chaplain or a stretcher-bearer.

Laperrine replied, "Stay there!"

More than ever, Brother Charles enjoyed the confidence of the Touaregs. "The confidence of the Touaregs never ceases to grow," he wrote on December 7th. "The slow work in preparing for the Gospel proceeds."

For two months, at that time, a pernicious fever spread in the area, and Brother Charles asked for the services of a doctor. Around Christmas Charles came down with it and ran high temperatures almost daily, suffered severe headaches, and had difficulty breathing. He was finally forced to call Dr. Vermale at Fort Motylinski. The doctor wrote in his diary:

> The Marabout suffering from scurvy was not in very good condition. I have seen this coming for some time, for he leads the most unhygienic life imaginable: incessant work, no relaxation or exercise, unbelievable diet. I got here in the nick of time. Thanks to strength-giving medicine and to a complete change of diet that I imposed, the sickness is checked.

Calm in the Hoggar did not last long. In Tripoli the Italians progressed from Rhadamès to Rat, but they had to retreat:

> The Italians advanced too fast without having adequate strength. They organized in the south of Tripoli in the spring and summer of 1914. Then in the last months of 1914, they sent a big part of their troops back from Tripoli to Italy. Those two unwise actions resulted in the revolt in South Tripoli, very close to our border and only about ten days' march from here. We need not fear that the revolt will win . . . but we can not be sure that the Tripolitanian revolutionaries won't cross the border. We have reinforced our border patrols.

The big Association of Senoussistes, whose principal center was in the Koufra oasis, poured forth intense propaganda during 1914. In the Northwest, Moroccan plunderers took advantage of the situation to step up their raids. In October, 1914, raiders carried off some of Moussa's troops, and Moussa himself barely escaped into the night: "Then Moussa got some men together and went after the raiders, forcing them to retreat, taking with them their spoils and several soldiers; our soldiers joined in the chase, and now every-body is after the common enemy."

Moussa had but eighty warriors and the camel riders of Tidikelt, who were not numerous. Everyone was caught up in the excitement. Brother Charles increased his advice and encouragement in an effort to save the common good. He tried to help Moussa, kept the French officers advised of the situation as he saw it, and gave very precise military advice.

Moussa may have been trying to profit from the situation:

It seems incredible that he has not received letters from Ahmoud and communications, direct or indirect, from the Senoussistes. I think, with his usual prudence, he is holding back. He behaves correctly. But it is evident that he is watching events, trying to be up to date and well informed. His secretary's sudden arrival here is, I think, an effort to keep him well informed about what is happening in Europe, Ajjer, and Tripoli.

In the same letter, March 12, 1915, Brother Charles wrote to Meynier of his regret about the reverses the Italians had had in Tripoli and about their imprudence: "Engaging, without discern-ment, natives as soldiers, arming men whom it would have been wiser to disarm, negotiating where it would have been better to fight. One cannot negotiate with men who are liars and who believe that we lie too. 'Negotiating with the Senoussistes is to play the flute to fish.' "

Meynier asked him whether Ben Messis was reliable. To this Brother Charles replied: "To improve his financial situation is not only useful but, in my opinion, just. Also, in my opinion, he de-serves and merits an honorary position, which will make him serve better. But to give him an administrative position is dangerous."

On another point, he wrote: "As you say, Moussa's victorious pur-suit will make him the *bête noire* of the Moroccans, and he must expect attacks against him. I have urged him to stay in the Adrar, to protect the country."

Brother Charles agreed that severe measures should be taken about the nobles:

Like you, I find that strong measures and severe sanction are indispensable to discipline the turbulent element of the noble tribes of the Ahaggar and the Taïtoq. The Imrads enjoy our peace and enter into the hard-working and peaceful life we show them. The nobles wish to live only by begging and plundering. They refuse all work and look only for the chance to return to their old life of plundering. By happy coincidence, the punishments given the nobles for their acts of war against tribes under the protection of the Afrique-Occidentale française will keep the most important of them in prison during the war in Europe.

. . . I can understand that you need time to think about the successor to Saint-Léger. It is as important as it is difficult to find a good chief for an annex so vast and so special; and how much the war has reduced the choice of officers. . . . You can imagine with what joy I see the broadcasting system at In Salah, and with what joy I have learned of the roads for automobiles around Ouargla.

Captain Paul Duclos was named to the Annex, and Brother Charles wrote to Duclos on April 16th, "You can sense my joy . . . joy for the good of the public which comes before everything. . . ."

He asked that the nobles live in the Adrar and not go to the Ahaggar. "It is better that the nobles do not come here and hinder the progress of others. When this progress is greater and when the Imrads are at a point where they are not influenced by the nobles, then the nobles can come here."

He asked that the village of Abaliba be protected, "where there are one hundred *haratins,* fine prey for Moroccan looters."

He warned the officer not to have "too much confidence in Moussa. . . . Moussa is intelligent, energetic, and courageous . . . and he is a liar and a cunning trickster. . . . I think Moussa is loyal to France because he understands, since his trip to France, that it is necessary."

But Brother Charles's essential work was not to give advice. "The Algerians, the Touaregs . . . we must do more for them than we have done in the past," he wrote on February 21, 1915, to Monseigneur Livinhac. "Their education, good civil administration, their direct contact with honest French people, and, above all, settling them and improving their material well-being."

He had much hope that the peace would bring, "in Europe, justice, liberty, and a long period of tranquillity."

And in a letter of May 4, 1915, to Captain Duclos, he wrote, "May God give us the grace to profit by this peace and use it to improve ourselves and to make progress in all our colonies and to educate them as a good Mother Country should her children."

Earlier he had written, "It is our duty to raise our colonies to our level, to make them like us as parents do their children, to be fathers to them, fulfilling our duties, and not to be exploiters."

This is the opposite of contemptuous paternalism that keeps children in an infantile condition that prevents them from attaining their majority. With all his heart Brother Charles wanted to help the Touaregs become adults. We have read about his vigorous work to help the Imrads become adults ahead of the nobles. At the same time, he worked to have the Imrads become equal to the French. He used realistic methods, and not abstract ones that would be difficult and ineffective in working with the natives.

On July 15th he wrote to Laperrine: "Despite the drought and the locusts, there are more gardens in Tamanrasset. There is not a single *zériba* left. There are only houses, and many of them have fireplaces. Several *huratins* have begun to learn a little French; nearly every night they come to ask me how to say this or that in French."

On November 24, 1915, he wrote to Duclos about work in the Hoggar:

Instead of sending dates or grain during the planting season, I urge you to use the funds you have left to establish a workshop to make bricks at Motylinski. . . . The Baïliq could buy the bricks at a decent price, but at a price that would permit the workers to live. (One hundred bricks might bring a half-liter of wheat, barley, or dates.) The Baïliq would accept all the well-made bricks brought to them and would give a shovel and a mold to anyone asking for work. This workshop would give work to anyone who needs work and who isn't lazy. And it would furnish the Baïliq with a stock of bricks that could always be used and that were bought at a good price. The cost would not be too great. Alas, it is often sufficient to mention the word "work" to a beggar to send him quickly on his way, and you will never see him again. If I were you, that is the way I would use the funds.

He also tried to break Moussa of the habit of begging: "One must hold the purse strings and not entrust them to him. . . ."

At the same time, Brother Charles thought that one's word should be kept:

I have received a letter from Moussa, and he asks that I write you in his name. . . . The delay in his salary is inconceivable. It was not necessary to put him on salary, and I did not advise it. I preferred irregular gifts so that we would hold the purse strings. But since he has been given the salary, it must be paid regularly.

In the same letter of December 1st to Duclos, Brother Charles asked for strong measures to be taken against burglars, who were often freed slaves:

Some of the Touaregs who owned slaves have become impoverished and have been obliged to free ones they couldn't feed and couldn't sell. . . . The number of those freed has multiplied —they are bad workers who don't know how to work the land and who have many vices, do not seem to be trustworthy, find work with difficulty, and are habitually lazy. In 1915, around Tamanrasset, there have been seven grain thefts committed by freed slaves. This area has about thirty houses. All the thieves were taken to prison at Motylinski. But for some of them the term will be too short. I think that there should be a severe repression . . . not just to stop the present wave, but to prevent it from being worse in the future. . . .

To put a stop to these thefts, he proposed again the brick workshop at Motylinski and also another workshop:

A workshop that would use the convicts for three or four years after they have served their prison term to build roads, under the direction of a French officer and some men, between Ahaggar and

In Salah, between Ahaggar and Ajjer, between Ahaggar and Adrar, and so on. They would be fed (a pound of grain a day), clothed (ten yards of cotton every four months), and paid two sous per day. They would be considered prisoners and they would be warned that they would be shot if they tried to escape. This sort of workshop for public works would make people think twice about stealing. It will give the punished a chance to get in the habit of working. It will help provide badly needed roads. It will give the jobless thieves an honest living for a good period of time, and it may lead some of them to a life of work. There is nothing frightening about the number of freed slaves. They will not amount to much, but their children will be better and their granchildren will be like the *haratins* who here, at least, are a good people.

In everything, Brother Charles wanted a long-term policy. He wanted everything that was done to be well considered beforehand. "I beg you to recommend instantly to whoever takes command of the Ahaggar that they *study carefully every problem for a long time before taking any action* that concerns the Administration," he wrote to Duclos on January 9th.

As an example of long-term policy, Brother Charles wished that the nobles would disappear from the Sahara and that there would be a true democracy, but in the transition he thought that all power should be placed in officers' hands.

Speaking of Moussa, who was a noble, he wrote on November 24, 1915:

It would be most regrettable to give him command of the Kel-Ajjer or the Taïtoqs. Either might cause dissidence in a short time. In error, the Kel In Tounine (who were originally dependent on the Taïtoqs) were put under Moussa in 1904. Immediately there was dissent. If the Taïtoqs were placed under Moussa, some of them would probably join Abidine. It would not be wise to put a man as ambitious as Moussa, who was an old friend of Ahmoud, in the proximity of Rat, Ahmoud, and the Senoussistes. The truly best method is to put all tribes of the Ajjer under an officer and without the use of an intermediary (an intermediary serves only to separate the officer from the people so that he can trample over the people). The same should be done for the Taïtoqs, for the Kel Ahnet, and so on. Moussa's command should be kept as it is, neither enlarged nor diminished, until his death. At his death all the Ahaggar tribes should be put under an officer, without an intermediary. . . . Then, it will be necessary to divide the Tidikelt country into three annexes and three companies: Tidikelt, Ahaggar, Ajjer. That is indispensable.

More than ever, Brother Charles saw the need for good officers. On All-Saints' Day, 1915, he wrote to Gardel: "There will be no shortage of work after the peace. Our colonies of Africa—Algeria, Morocco, Tunis—need officers like you to make justice and goodness reign and to bring progress to the natives."

On November 13th he wrote to Captain Duclos:

I know no one in the Algiers Direction of Native Affairs, not even by name; . . . they surely know you, however, and they must have confidence in you. Couldn't you tell them officially:

1. The officers of the Tidikelt are extremely independent; therefore, only superior men should be sent there.

2. There must be a rule that no officer who has ever served in the Tidikelt as an enlisted man be sent back to the Tidikelt. (I am sure that when peace comes, there will be many enlisted men who have become officers because of the war that will ask to be sent to Tidikelt, and the most undesirable will be first on the list.)

He wrote further to Duclos on October 11, 1915:

Concerning the men in the company, I must tell you something that Saint-Léger has perhaps not said enough about. There are two men who must never again set foot in the Ahaggar: Sergeant X . . . , who is known to all the natives as a thief, and Brigadier Y . . . , who allowed a woman from Moussa's encampment to be raped by one of his soldiers, which caused as much of an uproar as you would imagine. I regret that these two men are still in the company. . . .

In a letter of November 4th to Duclos, Brother Charles requested that the tax exemption that had been granted the Kel Ahaggar in

1914 because of crop failures be extended to 1915. And he asked Duclos to act on an important measure:

There is great economic good to be done in the Ahaggar by your recommending to your soldiers that they not requisition the camels sent by the Kel Ahaggar to Tidikelt to get dates. The return of these camels is awaited, and when they don't return when they are expected, people feel desperate. They are discouraged about sending them to the Tidikelt, and one fears for the future.

In January, 1916, Moussa was attacked once again by Moroccan raiders, and the French post in the neighborhood sent him no help. The officer in charge was antagonistic toward Moussa. Brother Charles immediately asked Commandant Meynier to relieve the officer of his post:

I fear that he will do irreparable damage. Far be it from me to justify Moussa. He is tricky and an inveterate liar, along with many other faults, including begging. Far be it from me to trust his entourage of nobles. All the nobles are our bad-spirited enemies who must be led with a firm hand. On the other hand, you know M——— and you have spoken of him in frankness. You know his irresistible tendency to think and do the opposite of the thoughts and actions of his superiors and predecessors. I don't think it is bad will or disobedience on his part, but it is very bad will and very bad character secretly to think the opposite of what he has been told, and to wish for the opposite of what he has been advised and ordered.

To my way of thinking, the reason he dislikes Moussa, though he may not realize it himself, is because Moussa was well treated by his superiors and predecessors. Things having gone this far, it seems very unwise to me to leave M——— at the head of the Ahaggar.

Upon hearing that the officer in question had spoken of imprisoning Moussa, Brother Charles wrote to Meynier, "In my opinion, he should be recalled immediately."

At the same time he wrote to the officer: "I agree with you about the bad will of the nobles and Moussa's shortcomings. However, I believe you should be patient and that you should take no rigorous measure against Moussa unless you have the specific authorization to do so. If you act otherwise, I think that you will be disavowed, and that would be unfortunate."

Meanwhile, tension was growing between the Ahaggars and the Taïtoqs. Brother Charles wrote to Duclos:

. . . there has always been rivalry between the Kel Ahaggars and the Taïtoqs. It's an old story of arguments that goes back fifty years. . . . The Kel Ahaggars are much stronger than the Taïtoqs, who would probably have been annihilated if we had not intervened. Because they know we will hold the Kel Ahaggars in check, the Taïtoqs are insolent to them and they are constantly stealing from them. The Kel Ahaggars have been complaining to Captain Charlet, M. Depommier, and Commandant Meynier for three years, but, because of the number of things to be done and the few officers to do them, the Kel Ahaggars have never been given any satisfaction. . . .

There were other problems between the tribes for which Brother Charles asked that a law be set down:

There are certain things to be settled that are not under the Moslem law, or any other. The only two laws known before our arrival were for the individual: *pleasure,* and in case of controversy, the *law of the strongest.* People whose parents are from different tribes should not be able to choose the tribe they want to belong to. The law should state that, without exception, children must belong to their mothers' tribes (conforming with the custom of the Ahaggars and Taïtoqs). Another law should state that each person's fortune is his own, regardless of its origin, and belongs solely in his tribe, and that no one from another tribe has the right to requisition it or to set a tax on it with the pretext that part of the fortune originally came from a different tribe.

A third law should declare that when a woman marries a man from another tribe, the fortune of the woman is to be managed by the husband and is under the protection of his tribe *as long as the marriage lasts.*

A serious and active officer of the Ahaggar finds that more than one law is needed to avoid quarrels and attain peace.

35.

Political Views

In a letter to Duclos on March 4, 1916, Brother Charles set down the historic conflicts of the Sahara, and pursued the problem of the native chieftains.

> . . . I think it is necessary to suppress them . . . and to substitute for them a French administration that would deal directly with the people. . . . The chiefs take every benefit for themselves while putting all responsibilities on the shoulders of their people whom they feed upon. They continue old abuses and they obstruct contact between the people and us for fear of losing their influence. They commit many injustices under the cover of the French, and they oppose any form of progress because ignorance and barbarism are more favorable to their regime of injustice. We wish the opposite. Therefore, they must be suppressed, not by a single written order, but each at an opportune moment. For the Ahaggar, the right moment will be at Moussa's death. His past service and present attitude (despite his faults) require that he keep his position until then, unless there is some new development. For the Taïtoqs, the moment is now. For the Ajjer, luckily, this solution was adopted at the beginning.

Brother Charles did not wish the country to be ruled jointly by the natives and the French because that would sanction the chieftains and thereby hold back over-all progress of the people. He did not think assimilation was the answer because it would be utopian and dangerous to promote a mixture of the races. He had, at one point, thought that might be a possibility as he had watched with happiness the marriage of a French soldier to a native girl. But he had finally concluded that it would be a long and difficult time before the two bloods could mix harmoniously.

". . . Over-all progress will be very irregular," he wrote to Duclos on March 15th. "Different means will often have to be used in our various colonies. But we must keep in mind that progress is our goal."

Progress, he maintained, was threefold: "intellectual, moral, and material." He thought education for the natives came first, followed by the science of morals and then material well-being. All three should be advanced at the same time. He urged the French not to lose sight of the goal, and to follow it "during the centuries that the colonies belong to us."

Not only did Brother Charles not expect France to have a permanent guardianship; he did not expect the guardianship, for however long it lasted, to be secular.

He did expect France to serve the natives as long as was needed to bring progress to them, whatever the cost, until progress was flourishing in their country.

Brother Charles saw the French administration as the only possible answer to bring the principles of liberty, equality, and fraternity to the natives. The natives could never administer their own country until they understood these principles. "Progress . . . can be accomplished only by a French, purely French, administration into which natives will be admitted only when they have not only acquired French citizenship and French education but also a French mentality."

Whether this progress was reached with or without France, for Brother Charles, was a secondary question. He wanted them to be better off, to grow, and to have more liberty. The real question, for him, was human and spiritual growth for his friends the Touaregs.

As material progress appeared, Brother Charles was very excited: "I am delighted that a telegraph system has been started in the

Sahara and that the road from In Salah to Ouargla is being built and that one from In Salah to Motylinski will soon follow."

On January 9, 1916, he wrote to Duclos:

> Dr. Vermale has written that they are going to build an infirmary for the natives at Fort Motylinski. I am delighted. It would be good if it would be an almshouse at the same time. The old, freed slaves—of both sexes—often have no family and are miserable and no longer able to work. A rustic construction would be just fine. Sadly, the money from Baïliq is often badly spent. Expensive buildings are built here and there where simple, inexpensive ones would do . . . less good is done than could be done. . . . If there are extra funds, perhaps the road from Motylinski could be slowly begun.

Brother Charles was always looking for projects that would offer work to the Touaregs.

36.
"We Do Not Administer Justice to Them"

Suddenly events took a catastrophic turn, as can be seen by Brother Charles's letter of April 28th to Dinaux:

> After an eighteen-day siege, Djanet was captured by the Senoussistes on March 24th. . . . From the first hour of the siege, the entire population of Djanet went over to the enemy. The people in Tamanrasset are very excited. The news spread quickly because

the courier was questioned by the natives and he told all he knew. ... What will the enemy do next? Will Djanet be enough? Will they attack Polignac, Fort Flatters, Motylinski? ... One must be prepared for the worst. ... Captain Duclos ordered Motylinski to be put in a state of defense. But Motylinski is indefensible against cannons and even an enemy that doesn't have cannons, if their troops are numerous. Defense is almost impossible because of water. Goatskins and barrels can hold only a certain amount of water.

Brother Charles proposed that the garrison at Motylinski look for a new place, "in the mountains, a place that is impenetrable, that has water, and that cannot be taken by a cannon."

He wrote to Constant, who was responsible for Fort Motylinski, and told him to surround himself with soldiers and to ask the civilian population to take refuge in the mountains. The safest place in the Sahara at that moment was not the fort, which would be attacked first and which could not be defended, but the mountains. Twenty years earlier Brother Charles had seen the Armenians massacred by the Turks. He did not want the Touareg women and children to suffer the same fate.

In the same letter, Brother Charles, for the last time, asked that the French administration see that justice was done for the Touaregs:

We do not administer justice to them and we do not make them administer it. For over two years they have complained to our officers about thefts they have suffered from people of French West Africa, including one assassination, and they have received no reparations. It has been nearly two years since they reported the theft of over fifty camels. Nothing has been done about that. Other matters between the people of the Tidikelt and even among themselves have had the same result. No solution is ever reached. The complaints are noted. They are told they will receive word and to wait for that. Then nothing happens.

France failed in her first duty: to render justice.

The French themselves lacked justice. They misused their power to requisition camels:

> They are often used for things that have nothing to do with the public interest, officers' wives, and so on. The price paid for the camels is often ridiculously low. The camels are not taken care of and they are killed by fast marches that they haven't been trained for, and damages are not paid to the owners for their loss, and so on, and so forth.

On April 30th he had another serious complaint. Fort Motylinski had run out of cash and there had been any number of convoys that could have brought money. It was impossible "to buy food for the men who were working on the roads." "It's lamentable."

Because of the state of war, Brother Charles permitted severe punishments and even capital punishment for what he considered real crimes: "Two *haratins,* very bad types, tried to escape to Djanet to go over to the enemy. Caught and convicted of having tried to join the enemy, Constant had them shot. This punishment was unanimously approved by the natives and had a good effect."

While Brother Charles categorically opposed all unjust repression, he was in complete agreement with the Touaregs who thought that justice should be strictly enforced.

On May 31, he wrote to Duclos:

> Ahmoud has tried to get Moussa to join the revolt. I have no proof of this, but I don't doubt it. Moussa has turned down the offers and has remained loyal and we can't ask more of him than that. . . . He has a good position with us, and he realizes that if Ahmoud and his partisans should prevail that he would lose out. The intelligent chiefs . . . wish for peace and security above all. We give them that, and while our regime isn't perfect, it is acceptable. They would rather not change it. They know perfectly well that if Ahmoud invades and raids the Ahaggar, the country will be ruined. They, like Moussa, prefer to remain loyal. . . . The Kel Ahaggar likes neither us nor the Senoussistes. We are all foreigners to them. But they know us and they find our regime bearable—the intelligent element and friends of peace, represented

by Moussa and most of the plebeians of note, prefer our regime. They make up the *young* of the Ahaggar. The old Ahaggars— nobles, women, and people with nothing—are secretly on the side of Ahmoud.

By June the news was better. Djanet had been retaken. Moussa had come out against the Senoussistes.

On June 4, 1916, Brother Charles wrote to Duclos:

There is another man to single out because of his fine attitude. That is Ouksem (the father-in-law of the young man who was a companion on a trip to France), a very intelligent young man who is the chief of the Dag-Rali, the most important plebeian tribe in the Ahaggar. . . . In Salah has sent us a brigadier who seems perfect to me—a good farmer from between Auch and Pau, a Frenchman of good old stock. I am delighted.

Brother Charles never ceased to remind his friends that France had a responsibility for the human development and evangelization of these people. On June 13th he wrote to a priest, "What dreadful punishment will be hers if, by frivolity, indifference, or selfishness, she does not do well by the duty that she has been entrusted with."

On July 7th Brother Charles wrote to René Bazin, whose article about his life and work he had just read in *l'Echo de Paris:*

Isolated missionaries such as I are extremely rare. Their role is to prepare the way so that those who replace them will find friendly and trusting people who will be a little bit prepared for Christianity and, possibly, a few Christians. . . . We must make ourselves accepted as reliable friends by the Moslems so that we are the ones they appeal to when they are in doubt or sorrow and upon whose affection, wisdom, and justice they can always count. It is only when that has been accomplished that we can begin to do some good for their souls.

My life is to have the closest possible relation with those around me and to do all for them that I can. When some intimacy is established, I talk face to face with them of God, telling each person as much as I think he can comprehend: turning away from sin, perfect love, penitence, the two main commandments of the love of God and of one's neighbor, conscience, meditation, duty to think of God . . . telling each of these slowly, with caution.

There are very few missionaries clearing the way in this capacity. I wish there were more. All the priests of Algeria, Morocco, Tunis, every army chaplain, all pious laymen could be missionaries. The government forbids the secular clergy to engage in anti-Moslem propaganda. But that is directed at open propaganda. Friendly relations with many Moslems would lead them slowly, gently, and quietly toward Christianity, and that would not be forbidden to anyone. All the priests in our colonies could try to turn their parishioners into Priscillas and Aquilas. That would be propaganda in a tender and discreet way toward the infidels, propaganda of love and prudence that was for goodness above all. It would be as if we wanted to bring back to God a relative who had lost his faith. . . .

37.

"As Long as You Did It to One of These My Least Brethren, You Did It to Me"

It would be wrong to think that life was easy for Brother Charles. But he always had hope. On September 7, 1915, he had written to Madame de Bondy: "Tomorrow will mark ten years that I have said mass at Tamanrasset, and I have not made a single conversion. One must pray, work, and be patient." He had done much for the Touaregs, but there was so much to be done.

On May 5th, to his cousin:

I understand how hard it is for you to not do all you would like to do; but God is a better judge than we. We put visible and tangible work first, while God puts Love first. . . . He loves us. He has blessed us. . . . He is a Good Shepherd always watching out for his sheep. . . . For myself, I need to be faced with these truths so that I will be consoled for having done so little and for being so miserable. . . .

At the beginning of 1916, Brother Charles wrote a series of short meditations. The most dominant theme was his passion to devote his life to being a savior, as was Christ, and to make mankind understand that God loved them and to show people how to live together, loving one another.

On January 1st he wrote:

Jesus wished that his name "Saviour" would signify his life's work. The work of our lives must be in imitation—the salvation of souls.

May the name of Jesus be always in our hearts and on our lips in this life, and may He be our consolation and our hope at the hour of death.

Other passages from his meditations are:

Jesus entered into the world and announced Peace.

Shed everything of yourself and put yourself in the last place.

Books show the way, but God, by His grace, makes us understand and gives us the strength to continue.

Our Lord, in His manger, taught us *gentleness,* accessibility, and familiarity to the humble.

The world promises few things, transitory things, and yet it is served with ardor; God promises immense and eternal good and yet the hearts of men remain cold.

Spend your life in the love of God and your neighbor.

In His manger, Our Lord taught us to go even unto those who repudiate and ignore us and to remain in their midst with patience and perseverance.

Lord, teach me to do Thy Will; teach me to lead a life that is humble and worthy of the Kingdom of Heaven and of Jesus.

Fear only one thing: that you do not love Jesus enough.

Work as best you can for the salvation of souls and the glory of God.

Nothing is more perfect or better than love, because love is born of God and depends only upon Him.

Love can do everything. It can accomplish many things that tire or exhaust those who do not love.

Love is prompt, sincere, pious, gentle, prudent, strong, patient, faithful, constant, magnanimous, and need not be sought after.

All things being equal, abjection is preferable to honor, abandonment to being surrounded, penury to richness in order to be more like Jesus.

As soon as one begins to think of oneself, one ceases to love.

He who is not ready to suffer and to give himself entirely to the will of his Beloved does not know what love is.

Think less of the gift of he who loves than the love of he who gives. Be more touched by the affection than by the gift.

"Lord what wouldst Thou have me do?"—may this cry of St. Paul be that of all our lives.

You have shown me Your love in this way: I was not, and You created me: I wandered far from You; You brought me back to follow You and commanded me to love You.

After reading a history of the martyred saints of Japan, he wrote, on February 5th, "Pray for the conversion of Japan and work for it with all strength."

And this testament:

Be kind and compassionate, and do not be insensitive to any misery. See Jesus in all people. Do unto others as you would have others do unto you.

In light of the love and the virtue of the saints, we must humiliate ourselves and convert ourselves: what they have done we can do. God has never forsaken man.

At every opportunity, enlighten your neighbor and bring good to him.

Be firm but gentle, and keep severity for yourself.

Be prepared to sacrifice all to help your neighbor: "What ye do unto one of these children, ye have done unto Me."

. . . One does good in haste, for charity is urgent. . . .

Respect our most humble brothers, for they merit it. Treat them as favorites of Jesus, for they are the most simple and pure, and they are without vanity. Let us mix with them as God wishes, being one with them and doing good for their bodies and souls.

On June 20th, this meditation:

He descended with them; He went to Nazareth and He was submissive.

When you are invited to a feast, seat yourself at the last place.

That is what He did from the moment He entered into the feast of life until His death. He went to Nazareth, the place of His hidden life, the ordinary life, the family life, the life of prayer, work, obscurity, silent virtues—practiced with no witness other than God and His neighbors . . . setting an example for thirty years . . . of obedience, humility. . . .

The older He grew, the more wisdom and divine Grace emanated from Him and showed in outward acts. . . . May it be the same with us: may the grace received at our christening and that received from the Holy Sacraments and that which God gives in abundance to faithful souls all bear fruit in our work. May every day of our lives grow richer in wisdom and grace.

These were notes Brother Charles made during the last year of his life. He was full of love for Jesus and of love for all mankind.

On August 1, 1916, he wrote to a member of the Association:

Think of others and pray for them. Devote yourself to the salvation of others by the means in your power: by praying, being good, and setting an example. . . . When you give alms to the poor, it is to the Creator that you have given. When one puts goodness into the heart of a sinner, it is Purity that one has created. God wished it so, thus making charity to one's neighbor a second duty, "alike unto the first" duty, which is the love of God. . . . There is nothing from the Gospel that has impressed me more or had a bigger effect on my life than this: "As long as you did it to one of these my least brethren, you did it to me." When one remembers that those words came from the mouth of the One Who said, "This is My Body, this is My Blood, . . ." one is sent with great force to seek Jesus and to love Him in "these children," these "sinners," these "beggers," and to use all spiritual means to convert souls and all material means to relieve human misery.

All mankind, Christians and non-Christians, should devote their lives to serving "these children." At the beginning of the twentieth century, Brother Charles asked that everyone work toward the organization of a city or fraternity that would be extended around the world.

If Brother Charles foresaw the end of the French empire in Africa, his vision was even more prophetic; he foresaw the immense structural transformation of the universe and he hoped for brotherly unity in this great city that would finally be the entire world. He wanted every man to be a brother to every other man, and every man to be a "universal brother."

In his own existence, Brother Charles showed that God is the Father, that all men are brothers free and equal, and that God is the Spirit that unites.

Love had asked him for his life, and he had said "yes." He gave his life to each hour of the day, one by one without stopping. He lived, minute by minute, the litany of events. He wished to pattern himself after Jesus. He spoke of the Gospel in simple terms that could be easily understood and with words that were full of hope. He used not only words, but action and silence.

In his daily life, the words of the Gospel became alive. He lived it in a pure and new way that was compact and true. He cried out with truths in the face of human dramas, problems—in the face of slavery. He believed that there was a bond between men. He said that each time justice was slighted, Jesus was assaulted. He turned faith and Gospel toward the interests of mankind. As a man and as a Christian, he felt degraded—as did another Christ—when he saw the oppressed and the persecuted.

All his life he walked in the last place, toward the most destitute. He looked for the prodigals, those who had no past, no heritage, those who had no voice, those who were unable to comprehend the world, those who were incapable of thinking and transforming, those who had no future, no hope.

He went to live among them and he became one of them. He refused to be part of a society of master and slave. He welcomed everyone, he listened to everyone and he made friends with everyone without distinctions.

Brother Charles was a witness on the side of unity. He was on the side of the weak, poor, little people. He was against no one. Evil was the only thing he condemned. He opposed segregation and hate. He opposed prejudice of race and class, and he fought against such prejudices.

Brother Charles was a friend and a neighbor of the Touaregs. Their problems, moral or material, were his problems. He loved to talk to them and to listen to them. He learned their language well enough so that he could think as a Touareg. There were no barriers between them. This contact with others gave him a very real life. He had confidence in others. Not only was he full of welcome for others, but as an example of true goodness, he felt that these people were good for him.

His friend Louis Massignon wrote:

He never asked for anything, and he never claimed anything. He lived, waiting the hour of grace, seeing that no soul was wounded or troubled. The more humble the service, the more grace is shown. I recall the affectionate and discreet way with which he quickly lifted from the hands of an embarrassed young Moslem a holy picture that a kind priest, without thinking, had handed him.

Brother Charles of Jesus was host to the most humble. He lived among them in the last place. He understood that Jesus is among them.

38.

Refuge for the Poor

On September 15, 1916, his fifty-eighth birthday, he wrote to his cousin:

> The news is bad from the Tripolitanian border. Without having been stopped, our troops have turned back in front of the Senous-sistes; they are no longer on the border, but well on this side. After having recaptured Djanet, they evacuated it. . . . This retreat in front of several hundred rifles is lamentable. It is clear that the Senoussistes will advance without having fought. If nothing is done, they will soon be here. I am sorry to worry you. . . . My life continues in its customary outward calm.

However, there was a change in Brother Charles's life. He no longer lived in his Hermitage. The officers were worried about his being isolated at Tamanrasset. Constant offered him hospitality at Fort Motylinski; but, preferring to live with the *haratins,* Brother Charles refused. However, thinking of the *haratins* who were defenseless, Brother Charles agreed to have a small fort built at Tamanrasset.

In the same September 15th letter to his cousin, he wrote:

Recently, I have added a new kind of work. I have built an enclosure forty-two feet square with a well which can serve as a refuge for the population here in case of attack. . . . It is stocked with supplies, tools, and medicines. I have moved my Hermitage to it. The new installation is half a mile from the old one, and closer to the village, which is an advantage. . . .

He wrote to a friend who was an officer:

I have transformed my Hermitage into a small fort; there is nothing new under the sun. In seeing it now, I think of the convents and churches that were fortified in the tenth century. How old things return and how things we thought were gone for ever suddenly reappear! They have given me six cases of ammunition and thirty rifles, which takes me back to my youth.

But the fort and the arms were to defend the poor people around him, and they understood that. They were at one with Brother Charles. An alert on September 20th demonstrated the loyalty the natives felt for him:

They formed a group circling the officer in command of the neighboring fort and they circled around me, ready to defend the fort and the Hermitage. Their loyalty was very touching, and I am extremely grateful to these poor people who could have taken refuge in the mountains and had nothing to fear but who chose, instead, to stay in the neighboring fort and in my Hermitage even though they know full well that the enemy has cannons and that bombardment was certain.

Again, on October 30th, he wrote to his cousin: "I thank God that my Hermitage had been transformed into a refuge that could be defended. It was of great help during the false alert we had forty days ago."

On November 28th Brother Charles finished work on copying the Touareg poetry, and he wrote to Susbielle of his other joys:

The telegraph has been installed at Ouargla, In Salah, Fort Flatters. . . . In three or four months, it will be in at Fort Motylinski; . . . a road for automobiles going from Laghouat to Mzab, to Ouargla, to In Salah and to Tamanrasset was opened several months ago. The first automobile reached In Salah in August.

But together with this work and this progress, there was material and spiritual misery, and Brother Charles's heart was heavy. On October 30th he wrote his cousin:

> I am afraid there will be a terrible famine this winter, and that which you have sent makes it possible for me to provide the necessities for the people here and nearby. No one will be *dying* (literally and not figuratively) of hunger. There are two harvests here a year, one of wheat, one of millet. The first is in the spring, the second in the fall. The first was poor and the second was nonexistent. This follows four harvests that were nearly failures and eleven years of drought. The country cannot take much more of it.

Brother Charles thought of his friends, the poor, and he provided them with reserves of grain. They would have bread, and he could die peacefully.

But there was also another kind of nourishment that was lacking, and Brother Charles never stopped seeing it and thinking of it. "The state of the people around me makes you weep," he wrote to Madame de Bondy on October 15th. "They are completely surrounded by evil and wrongdoing! It is so difficult for them to lead lives that are good!"

IV

FRIDAY, DECEMBER 1, 1916

O<small>N THIS DAY</small>, the first day of December, Brother Charles wrote to his cousin:

> Our annihilation is the most powerful means we have to unite ourselves to Jesus and to save souls; that is what St. John of the Cross repeated in nearly every line. When one wishes to suffer and to love, one can. One does the most of what one tries the most to do. One feels that one suffers but one doesn't always feel that one loves, and that is added suffering. But one knows that one wishes to love, and wishing to love is to love. One finds that one doesn't love enough. That's true. One will never love enough. But Almighty God who knows of what He has molded us and who loves us more than a mother loves her child has told us—and He does not lie—that He will not cast out those who come to Him.

He wrote to his friend Louis Massignon who was at the front:

> One should never hesitate to ask for a post where danger and sacrifice are the greatest, where the most devotion is required. Honors—let us leave them for those who want them. But danger and hardship let us always claim. As Christians, we must set an example of sacrifice and devotion. That is a principle we must

follow all our lives, simply, without questioning whether vanity has entered into such conduct. It is our duty. Let us do it and ask God to help us do it in all humility and in complete love of Him and of our fellow men.

Friday, December 1, 1916. Night began to fall. Brother Charles was alone. Some forty men approached his Hermitage. They were the Senoussistes and the Touareg dissidents. Among the Touaregs was a *haratin* named El Madani to whom Brother Charles had given hospitality. Night was falling; Judas went to the door of the Hermitage. He called, announcing the mail. Recognizing his voice, Brother Charles opened the door and held out his hand.

He was seized and dragged outside the door of his small fort. He fell to his knees and was ordered to put his arms behind his back, and they were tied to his ankles. They questioned him, but he was silent. He prayed. A boy of fifteen was left, a rifle in hand, to stand guard over him while the others pillaged the Hermitage. Suddenly there was a cry: two camel riders were arriving. There were gunshots. Panicking the boy fired the gun at Brother Charles. The bullet entered behind the right ear and came out through the left eye. Brother Charles fell without a cry. The drama had lasted a scant twenty minutes.

Brother Charles had arms inside, but he had not used them. He died without fighting, a victim of violence. He did not die a martyr; he was assassinated. And his death could not be a seed of discord between the French and the Touaregs or between the Christians and the Moslems.

Brother Charles had settled close to Tamanrasset, near his friends, near the poor. It was because of the betrayal of one from their midst that he fell. The "universal brother" died alone. His death, the last act, was the silent burial of the seed that falls in the earth.

Three weeks after his death, his tiny monstrance, still containing the Host, was found in the sand. Like the Host, like Christ, poor and hidden, it had sunk into the ground of man. It was buried there, like a grain of wheat, to ripen and become, with Jesus Christ, the daily bread of men, his brothers.

Epilogue

The death of Charles of Jesus went almost unnoticed. The Union that he founded numbered, in 1916, only forty-nine members. Nevertheless, from this small, faithful group there sprang an astonishing posterity. They had received from Charles, as a testament, a Directive, or Rule.

A member of the Union, Louis Massignon (who died in 1962), compiled the material for an informative biography, which was written by René Bazin and in which was shown, in the style and in the light of the time, the spiritual aspect of Brother Charles. This book is the source of numerous other biographies, of unequal value.

Cheap sentimentalism and the cinema wanted to make of Father de Foucauld a monk-cavalier of heroic proportions. But a quiet influence was exerted at a deeper level, its underground current appearing some thirty years after the death of Charles of Jesus. This was the work of a number of members of the Union, who gathered together regularly and prayed in its spirit.

The desire to follow Father Charles's example rose in many hearts: some responding to his strictly solitary calling, others ministering to the material needs of abandoned peoples, the poor, and the sick.

In 1933, as a result of these writings and projects, there sprang up simultaneously two congregations.

A male congregation of five young priests was established, in September, 1933, at El-Abiodh-Sidi-Cheikh, in South Oranais, taking the name of Brothers of Solitude. The life of the desert, and then the contact, during the war, with the living conditions of the masses brought about the formation of the Little Brothers of Jesus—who in 1963 consisted of a brotherhood of 250 members scattered throughout the world—to realize a living application of the designs of Father de Foucauld. (The process of canonization has not formally granted to Brother Charles the title of founder of the order.)

A feminine congregation, the Little Sisters of the Sacred Heart of

Jesus, was founded in August, 1933, at Montpellier, and faithfully followed the Rule of May, 1902. It is established in France, in Morocco, in Tunisia, at Tamanrasset, and in India.

In 1939 there arose the Little Sisters of Jesus. The war and post-war period led them through the same evolution as that of the Little Brothers. There are nearly eight hundred members working in many ways among abandoned peoples throughout the non-Christian world.

At the end of 1950, the lay posterity of Father Charles increased tremendously. Drawn from secular societies of priests and of lay-men, the Secular Brotherhood of Charles of Jesus established a holy union, another association that has continued the Union or Rule.

There have also been a number of persons of great initiative, for example, Jean-Marie Peyriguère, who died in 1959, and who was undoubtedly the greatest figure among the disciples of Charles de Foucauld.